D1572519

DUTY BEFORE SELF

John T. Mitzel

DEDICATION

This book is respectfully dedicated to the men of the 781st Tank Battalion. They answered their county's call, emerged from the cities and farms of 1940s America, and made a terrific contribution toward winning WWII. They then quietly returned to civilian life, picked up where they left off, and led the rest of their lives as quiet heroes. Greatest among these equals was my father, Francis A. Mitzel. I always regarded him as a hero, but it wasn't until I wrote this book that I realized how much a hero he truly was.
JTM

DUTY BEFORE SELF

The Story of the
781st Tank Battalion in
World War II

John T. Mitzel

4880 Lower Valley Road • Atglen, PA 19310

Library of Congress Control Number: 2013951932

Printed in China
ISBN: 978-0-7643-4340-7

We are interested in hearing from authors
with book ideas on related topics.

Published by Schiffer Publishing Ltd.
4880 Lower Valley Road
Atglen, PA 19310
Phone: (610) 593-1777
FAX: (610) 593-2002
E-mail: Info@schifferbooks.com.

Visit our web site at:
www.schifferbooks.com
Please write for a free catalog.
This book may be purchased
from the publisher.
Try your bookstore first.

CONTENTS

ACKNOWLEDGMENTS

Thanks to my dad, Francis Mitzel, for piquing my interest in the 781ˢᵗ. I'm sorry I waited so long to ask the questions that started the whole ball rolling. I would have liked your input.

Thanks to Jonathan Gawne, author of *Finding Your Father's War*. We've never met, but his wonderful book got me pointed in the right direction, and my questions soon became a ton of cold, dry facts. The facts cried out to be known, and a story was set to paper.

Thanks also to Cindy Livingston; she helped me to connect with many of the vets, and the story became human, readable, and engaging.

Thanks don't go far enough for Joe Graham, who was so fantastic at giving me support, encouragement, facts, and along the line he became a friend. He answered questions, gave me leads to other vets, and even edited the first draft! Without Joe's help and encouragement I couldn't have done it. (One day Joe voted me an "Honorary Member of the 781ˢᵗ." It was one of my proudest moments.)

Thanks to Homer Turner, Joe De Gorter, Vince Sutphin, Arnie Simpson, Ronald O' Donnell, Gerald Mercier, Erksel Rhodes, and Joe Trombetta for the stories. Heroes all.

Thanks also to my wife, Kim, who helped collect the stories and the pictures, and spent days helping me at the National Archives instead of being at the beach. Her occasional prodding and nudging was appreciated.

Thanks to Dave Fink, for answering too many questions about organization and the Army, Steve Meuse for editing help, the great folks at NARA, the Eisenhower Museum, the Patton Museum, and the rest for their help in finding and digging through their Archives.

1. TANKS, BUT NO TANKS

The advent of new weapons during WWI really upset the status quo in the various combatants' armies, and the U.S. Army was no exception. At the war's start, the Army was neatly broken into two camps: Infantry (with the Artillery branch neatly subservient to it) and Cavalry. The two camps had agreed upon a line of demarcation in the "sandbox" of responsibilities, and each did not usurp the other's territory. Cavalry scouted, and made breakthroughs at weak spots in enemy lines, while the Infantry exploited those breakthroughs and slugged it out with opposing forces. But by the end of WWI, there were new, powerful – and to some, very frightening – land-based weapons that had appeared, including the airplane, machine gun, and the tank. And while the power of these new weapons was not fully realized, they were frightening to some people, not so much for their potential destructive capability on the battlefield, but because these weapons erased that neatly drawn "sandbox" line. Set aside the fear of change that organizations routinely embrace – even more terrifying, some factions foresaw *extinction* as a possible outcome. Defining the roles *and the ownership* of these weapons was the real problem of the change. The French, English, and U.S. Armies were all dealing with these same problems in the postwar years, and some integrated the new weapons into their systems better than others. The postwar Germans, who were shrugging off the bonds of the Treaty of Versailles, were also dealing with these questions behind the scenes, and they arrived at the best, different solution.

In the time period between the "War to End All Wars" and the next World War (the 1920s and 30s), a desperate struggle took place *within* the U.S. Army, as they struggled with assimilating the new creatures called "Armored Fighting Vehicles." This entailed not just figuring out if the weapon was viable, but who administered it, who developed the weapon, who decided on how it was to be used, and a host of similar issues. Each of the branches in the Army – the Infantry, Artillery, the new Armored aficionados, and the Cavalry – had their own ideas. Like four blind men describing an elephant, each naturally based their ideas for utilizing this new weapon on what they knew best. Coupled with impoverishment as the U.S. government slashed defense budgets during the Depression, proponents of the new weapons had to fight for a slice of the meager funding, as well.

The Infantry branch needed to counter the new terror of the trenches – the machine gun nest – and they wanted tanks to be salted through their organizations to be used as "portable machine-gun nest destroyers." Their vision of the tank was a moveable bunker, bristling with machine guns and small bore weapons that waddled up to a machine gun nest, neutralized it, and waddled off to wait for the next summons. This "vision" came to be known generically as an "infantry tank."

The Artillery branch saw tanks as self-propelled guns, and so wanted them to be attached to the artillery groups, able to provide portable indirect fire support to the Infantry. Having had some luck killing tanks with artillery pieces in an anti-tank role in the Great War, the Artillery officers saw the anti-tank role as being *their* province via towed anti-tank guns (in other words, *not* a job for tanks).

The Armored visionaries saw troops of scouting tanks ranging far and wide, with large numbers of heavy tanks sweeping over battlefields and engaging each other. They actually envisioned tank warfare as something like a giant naval battle, with "battleship" tanks and "cruiser" tanks wheeling in majestic formations as they fought amid oceanic waves of grain. Their vision of a tank even came to be known as a "cruiser" tank. Because of the fluidity and motion of such a battleground, this vision would mean that trench warfare was obsolete. They further postulated that, once the enemy armored forces were vanquished beneath the amber waves, the Infantry could walk in, clean up, and consolidate the position. The true Armored disciple envisioned a completely separate and equal branch of the service, having its own command structure and free from interference, on a par with the Infantry/ Artillery/ Air Corps/Cavalry.

The Cavalry would, in hindsight, seem to be the natural fit for these new armored creatures. By trading hooves for tracks, they could simply get on with their pre-established mission. But the Cavalry saw its scouting role threatened by first the airplane, and now the armored vehicle. Knowing their cavalry charges had been rendered downright suicidal by the machine gun, the Cavalry hugged their horses, dug in their collective heels and hooves, and categorically stated that nothing would ever replace the horse. One young Cavalry officer even went to great pains, writing and publishing a long dissertation that detailed why the horse was totally irreplaceable in the U.S. Army. His name? George S. Patton.

Each of these disciplines and their radical ideas (to the others) upset and downright terrified the traditionalists, who were reacting to this fundamental change with the fight/flight/freeze reaction. Nobody understood the others' viewpoint, and so each branch tried to wrest control, and threw roadblocks where possible to impede the others. Except for the Cavalry, who looked this mechanical gift horse in its motorized mouth and wished it would just go away. There was some exchange of ideas between the former allies, but at any given time, the likelihood that any two countries agreed was remote. Overall, the U.S. did tend towards the French model, with Infantry and Cavalry in control, and the tanks hanging back "on call" behind the foot soldiers. Following lessons learned in the Civil War and WWI, the U.S. Army structured its ground forces to inflict and withstand battles over large fronts – a hammer or anvil, so to speak.

Enter the Germans, who had secretly, and not so secretly, arrived at a completely different conclusion. Each of the former Allies watched in horror as the Panzers steam-rolled Poland in September 1939, demonstrating a power, flexibility, coordination, and maneuverability of their armored force that was eye-opening. This wasn't the broad-front hammer blows the U.S. Army had envisioned: this was a rapier-like thrust of massed armor over a concentrated front that tore through the spread-out defending resources with ease. Moreover, the German tanks were *out front*, leading the troops and sweeping opposition.

When the Panzers repeated the performance and blew through the Low Countries, sweeping the French and English off the playing field in the Spring of 1940, the U.S. Army realized that all their tanks might now be obsolete, and finally took action. The U.S. Army had held large-scale maneuvers in 1939, 1940, and 1941 over much of the states of Georgia and Louisiana, and tested the performance of U.S. armored forces. Overall, the results were grim, and the exercises pointed out several flaws in the development of the Armored Force, the armored vehicles, and their mode of employment. The U.S. Army suffered a domestic "Dunkirk," if you will. The U.S. War Department, seeing the "real-world" drubbing of the French model (which closely resembled the U.S. model), and having it sadly reinforced by the poor results at home, made immediate changes to strengthen the armored capability of the U.S. Army.

On July 10, 1940, the Armored Ground Force (AGF) was created, based at Fort Knox, KY, with Brigadier General Adna Chaffee in charge. Chaffee was one of the armored disciples, and had been preaching the doctrine of "mechanized warfare" since the early 1930s. He was a great choice to get the U.S. Armored program on a good footing, but he did make the traditionalists nervous. Since there was no Congressional authorization for a separate Armored branch of the Army, the AGF was technically established "for purposes of service test." Starting out with about ten thousand men, the AGF was responsible for outfitting, training, and quickly releasing properly-trained and equipped armored troops into the main body of the Army. As a secondary task, the AGF was assigned the job of testing and evaluating new vehicles and new or revised systems, and they created the Armored Force Board (AFB) to do the testing. The AFB did the testing and passed their results to the AGF, who then made recommendations to the War Department on which equipment to buy and which to avoid. The AGF made policy decisions on tank tactics, vehicle designs, and the type of tank the Army needed. Because Chaffee was "Pro-Armor," the ball was sent rolling in the right direction.

The AFB kept a couple of tank battalions at the Fort Knox site as sort of "house bands," whose job it was to do the testing. On vehicles, they tested the *overall* combat system: how well it shot, how well it moved, its maintenance needs, and the logistical needs – the works. But they also tested other items, such as clothing and snow-suits, as well as serving as a data gathering unit for other design teams – they once measured the height of *all* the personnel at Fort Knox to plot an accurate bell curve of the height of the average soldier, so others knew how much headroom to design into a new item.

Unfortunately, expediency took the place of directed growth or logic, in many cases. The Army, in uneasy anticipation of the coming fight, anxiously wanted to expand enormously, and the Armored Ground Force (AGF) needed lots of equipment to outfit the new units. But they were a couple of years behind the eight ball, and couldn't wait for the "new and improved" anything to be tested and developed. They needed stuff now, and so the existing, and in some cases faulty designs, were pushed into large scale production.

A good example of such expediency in action dealt with the M4 Sherman tank. A tank's turret holds the main gun and rotates on the hull via a large bearing called a "turret ring." The overall diameter of that turret ring is a tank design fundamental. The larger the ring is made, the larger the turret that can fit on the hull, and therefore the larger the gun that can be fitted inside the turret. This was a basic Sherman design flaw – because the Sherman chassis was carried over from the M3 and the tanks prior to that, the maximum diameter ring was too small to facilitate further gun growth. A 75/76mm gun was about all that could be reasonably accommodated in the size ring allotted. Increasing the size of the gun meant increasing the size of the turret, which couldn't be done without increasing the turret ring size, which in turn couldn't be done without making the hull wider between the tracks, which basically meant a whole new vehicle. And they couldn't wait for the new vehicle, so design flaws were part of the baggage.

The AFB testing of vehicles was therefore always pressed for time, and the testing had to be completed as fast as humanly possible, since lives were sometimes literally riding on it. This situation didn't start to ease until early 1943, but until then, the U.S. Army placed itself in a situation where it had plenty of tanks, but didn't have any really *good* tanks.

Unfortunately, General Chaffee died of cancer in August 1941, and Major General Jacob Devers was appointed to take his place. Devers was from the artillery branch, but seemed to be fair, data-driven, and without extreme prejudice pro- or con-tanks. In March 1943, Devers got a new boss, Lt. General Leslie McNair – another artilleryman, but this time one with several firmly-entrenched preconceived notions. In General McNair's world, tanks didn't fight other tanks. Tanks were to be used as a thrusting, breakthrough-creating tool to pierce the enemy's lines at weak spots, and then to run amok behind their lines, severing communications and destroying support infrastructure. Tanks were specifically *not* intended to attack strong points. Later in the war, this became well-known to the German adversaries, who knew the Americans could be counted on to try to flank strong points.

If enemy tanks *were* encountered, General McNair wanted "Tank Destroyers" to handle them. As first envisioned, TDs were small, towed, flat-trajectory, artillery pieces. Hopefully the AT resources were already situated and the enemy attack was expected. If caught by surprise, the guns and crews were expected to rush forward, unlimber, and set up the gun before they could then take on the advancing enemy tanks. Expecting this to be accomplished while under fire, and in sufficient time to do more to the enemy tanks than wave "goodbye" to them, seems overly optimistic.

General McNair even went so far as to establish a separate Tank Destroyer Board and testing facility in Texas, which created a lot of squabbling and turf battles within the armored ranks.

At first, the AGF tended to construct large Armored Divisions for delivery to the Army. But soon the sneaking suspicion crept in that tanks might need infantry support to survive, and recognition that infantry had a genuine need for local armored support was conceded, so the genesis of the "tank-infantry team" concept was born. This was a truly symbiotic relationship, and both the armor and the infantry came out way ahead, but the concept needed to go through some painful experiences before it was truly perfected. But this posed another problem – the armored divisions didn't have enough foot soldiers to allow the armored division to generate these "tank-infantry teams" by themselves. The GIs had to come from Infantry. But this might cause the mighty armored divisions to be sundered and doled out to infantry divisions. What to do? Compromise!

The AGF then created separate smaller Tank Battalions, which were intended to be attached to Infantry Divisions as needed to form these tank-infantry teams. That way, the large Armored Divisions could remain intact and the AGF could still retain some level of influence over the Tank Battalions. When it was born in 1940, the AGF had one Tank Battalion, the 70th, and it quickly created four more (the 191st through 194th). Not long after, the 192nd and 194th left Ft. Knox, bound for the Pacific theatre, where they were overwhelmed and destroyed by the Japanese advance in the Philippines soon after Pearl Harbor. This left the 191st and 193rd at Knox. Many of the volunteers and early draftees who were earmarked for armored service were in this core group, and on January 2, 1943, the Army used this core experience, breaking up the two older units and "seeding" other new Tank Battalions. One of the "seedlings" was the 781st Tank Battalion, which, upon inception, was at first attached to the AFB at Fort Knox.

In all, over time, 65 separate Tank Battalions were created. And except for an all-too-brief period of time, they were armed with weapons that could not compete toe-to-toe with their European adversaries. They had tanks, but no *tanks*.

2. YOU'RE IN THE ARMY NOW - ROOTS OF THE 781ST TANK BATTALION

On January 2, 1943, Lt. Colonel Harry L. Kinne, Jr. was detailed to take command of and populate the 781st Light Tank Battalion, stationed at Fort Knox, Kentucky. At the same time, overseas, the Russians were victorious at Stalingrad, the Allied forces were just starting to gain momentum in North Africa, and the Japanese were slowly being pried from Guadalcanal.

Lt. Colonel Harry L. Kinne, Jr. (b. 6/6/06) was a career Army Officer, 36 years old and fresh out of Army Command and General Staff School. The Enlisted Men were a mix of experienced troops transferred from the 191st Tank Battalion and raw recruits from the Armored Force Replacement Training Center. Some of the officers came from the 191st, 741st, or 742nd Tank Battalions, and the rest were fresh out of Officer Candidate School. Lt. Col. Kinne personally interviewed and screened each of the prospective second lieutenants who were graduating from Officer Candidate School at Knox and hand-picked his junior officers. The transferees from the 741st and 742nd tended, for the most part, to be discards. Once formed, the 781st lived in two adjacent buildings near the corner of Gold Vault Road and Ninth Street in the Fort Knox facility. Their vehicles were parked across Seventh Avenue from the barracks.

New soldiers were first exposed to Army life at "Reception Centers," which were located near large U.S. cities. Here, the new men learned some basic Army tasks and got their numerous shots. They also were given an initial aptitude test, so "round pegs" could be placed in "round holes" and the men could be assigned to compatible tasks. But if the needs of the service dictated, a round peg would be force-fit into a square hole, if that's all they had. From the Reception Center, the new soldiers were sent to the recruit training center of whatever branch of the service for which they were deemed to be best suited. Armored candidates were sent to the Armored Force Replacement Training Center at Knox. The background of the men in the 781st shows a delightful slice of the loaf that was America in the early 1940s.

Sgt. Frederick Williams was one of those experienced troops transferred from the 191st. He was a "Weekend Warrior" in the West Virginia National Guard when the war erupted. When that happened, the 191st was "nationalized" by FDR and all members became Army Regulars overnight. Since Fred was married with three kids, he would have been exempt from being drafted had he not been in the 191st, but he was in the wrong place at the wrong time and found himself in the Army for the duration.

Homer Turner was 20 years old, just one year out of high school in Texas and attending Allen Military Academy, having gotten a football scholarship when his college football aspirations were cut short by an invitation from the local draft board. The trip to Abilene, Texas, for his induction was notable, as he had "only been out of the county maybe two or three times!" After induction, he was identified as a potential Armored Force member, so he was sent to Fort Knox for tank training. He was initially assigned to the 191st and was one of the founding members of the 781st.

Joe Graham had volunteered for early draft status in June 1941, with the aim of getting his one year's service out of the way quickly so he could go back to his career in insurance underwriting. This was another outstanding example of bad timing. The Japanese attack at Pearl Harbor caused Joe's hoped-for twelve to eighteen-month-long hitch to become a forty-nine month stint, because after December 7, 1941, all draftees and volunteers were "in for the duration." Joe, at 24, was selected for the Officer Candidate School, and upon graduation he was one of the candidates that was personally interviewed by Lt. Col Kinne and selected for the 781st. Joe was not very mechanically inclined, and had never driven a car, so he was amazed and chagrined to wind up in the mechanized force.

Vince Sutphin was an electric meter reader outside Richmond, VA, and was drafted in late 1942. He, too, was detailed to Fort Knox, and after Basic Training was assigned as a clerk in the battalion Post Office and Message Center when the 781st was formed. Vince was not happy with that assignment, and kept earning marksman and weapons proficiency badges while hoping he could transfer to one of the "line" companies.

Originally a "Light" Tank battalion of about 700 men, the 781st, as originally configured, had three Tank Companies: "A," "B," and "C." These were the muscle of the organization, having the Grant/Sherman medium and Stuart M5 light tanks mixed together. There was also Headquarters Company, which had the command, reconnaissance, communication structure, and the battalion's artillery and mortar resources; and the Service Company, which provided administrative services, supplies, and maintenance sections that kept the tanks running. The 781st had three Tank Companies; each Company had three Platoons. Each Platoon had five tanks in it, broken into two "Sections." So, if we ignore the HQ Companies: 2 Sections = 1 Platoon; 3 platoons = 1 Company; and 3 Companies = 1 Battalion.

Independent tank Battalions, like the 781st, were designed to be "portable," and could be attached to Infantry Divisions on a temporary basis, providing a heavy-hitting armored punch when required. The structure of the independent tank Battalions – having three Companies – was done on purpose to align with the three Regiments that formed the Infantry Division. That way, each Infantry Regiment in a Division could have a Tank Company assigned to it, and the "leftovers" of the tank Battalion – HQ and Service Companies – could be attached to their counterparts in the Division, and provided additional trained resources, so as not to overtax the Infantry Division's resources. And when the task was done, the tank battalion could be moved to the next infantry division and repeat their role. As shall be seen, while the concept worked well, it also resulted in overworked independent tank battalions that got bounced from division to division without a break.

By January 1943, the Armored Ground Force School was a two-shift operation, trying to crank out as many trained troops for the Armored Divisions and Battalions as possible. To their credit, the training program was getting feedback from the field, and tried to include lessons learned. For example, Building 1538 at Fort Knox was built in the shape of an LST (Landing Ship, Tank), and was used to teach troops the proper techniques for loading, unloading, and maintenance of vehicles while at sea. This was to get soldiers familiar with techniques later used in Africa, Normandy, and Marseilles. This building still stands today, and was being used to house historic armored vehicles for the Patton Museum. In 1943, Fort Knox covered over one hundred thousand acres and had over 3,500 buildings. Over the Mess Hall doors was a sign that stated: "Through these Doors the Best Soldiers Walk." This wasn't bravado – the troops believed it. Homer Turner recalled that "we were like para-troopers – nobody messed with us!"

The efficiency of the training got better, and the demand for trained troops skyrocketed after December 7, 1941, so the duration of the training got shorter. As more and more Divisions and Battalions were quickly trained and then released for duty, the number of troops under direct Armored Ground Force control at Fort Knox actually grew smaller. The previously secondary task of testing new vehicles by the AFB took on a greater importance, as inadequacies of current designs were painfully driven home by the same feedback from the field.

3. THE "MILLION DOLLAR TANK TEST"

The Army had a long-standing problem with its tank engines that it needed to resolve, and the very first assignment given to the 781st was to test tanks for the Armored Force Board to help resolve that problem. Being newly assigned to the AFB, the 781st was sort of a "house band," and was used to perform testing on the AFB's behalf for anything that came along – vehicles, equipment, whatever.

During the 1920s and 1930s, tanks were still a new vehicle type whose future appeared sometimes in doubt, and whose specification was in constant flux. The typical engine supplier at the time didn't want to develop a specialized engine for a vehicle that was so new, might not be around long enough to amortize the development expense, and might also have no commercial application. The first tanks used bus, truck, or farm implement engines, but as tanks evolved, those engines became hard-pressed to motivate the increasing tonnage of the tanks. In desperation, the Army looked around and found two candidate engines that already existed, both recently used in aircraft. The candidates were the Liberty V-12 water-cooled gasoline engine and a gasoline-powered air-cooled radial engine. After looking them both over, the Army selected the radial engine taken from an aircraft. Neither engine was a paragon of reliability, but at least the air-cooled aircraft engine did not require the cooling plumbing and radiator that the water-cooled engine would require. At the time, the radial also developed more horsepower. But it was mounted in the vehicle vertically, and because of that imposed a high profile to the hull of the tank. But the M2 tank it first powered worked fine, allowing development of the "Armored" program to continue, and giving a large number of men the basic training on maintaining, maneuvering, and war gaming in a tank. (Later on, the British *did* try to use that Liberty aircraft engine to power their Cavalier tank, and it was an unmitigated disaster, as the engine wasn't up to the job.)

When the German Blitzkrieg rendered the M2 obsolete, the Army knew it needed a better tank. But it couldn't wait for the M4; it needed something yesterday. The M2 tank was quickly up-gunned by adding a 75mm gun in the M2 hull, and its chassis morphed into the basis for the M3 Grant. The Wright R-975 engine was carried over as part of the chassis and drive train. The M2 weighed 19 tons, and the Wright engine developed about 400 HP; while it could adequately drive the M2, it struggled trying to motivate the M3's 30 tons. The general consensus was that the M3 was underpowered and performed poorly.

Just after the start of WWII, on January 10, 1942, the Armored Force Board issued a project report that recommended a long range plan for engine standardization across all Army vehicles, and had specifically endorsed the use of commercial, in-line *diesel* engines for all Army vehicles – trucks and jeeps, but especially in tanks. Furthermore, the AFB had recommended *twin* engine installations in tanks of 20-30 ton weight, and had specifically said that radial engines using *any* fuel were *not desired*.

At the same time, the M3 engine situation was being studied and an alternative was sought. As single tractor/bus/truck engines were still not up to shoving 30 tons cross-country, the Army tried a tandem diesel setup, in accordance with the AFB's Long-range recommendations at that point. But in March 1942, the War Department overrode the AFB's recommendation and decreed that gasoline was the required fuel for tank engines, to simplify logistics. The Army was not going to be "Dual Fuel" per the War Department.

Chrysler offered for consideration a "Multibank" engine made from five, six-cylinder gasoline-powered bus engines mated up on a common drive. There were literally *five engines*, with five distributors, five fan belts, five water pumps, etc. In late 1942, the three engine configurations on the M3 Tanks were tested in a head-to-head competition.

The incredibly complex Multibank. This example is one of the later *simplified* Multibanks with only one water pump. Spot the distributors to pick out individual engines. (public domain)

None of the alternatives were ideal, and there wasn't a clear winner. The M3 with the Wright engine rated a "barely satisfactory" for performance from the Armored Force Board. The M3 with the twin diesels was preferred, but conflicted with the War Department's "no diesels" directive. The Multibank was a maintenance problem with even worse performance, as it only produced 370 HP when all 30 cylinders were running well, which wasn't often. Nonetheless, all three engines went into production – the Wright still being the most common, and the other two were on limited basis. Aside from a handful sent to and used in the Pacific, any diesels from that point on were used only for training, or were sent to Russian allies. Production of M3s stopped in late 1942, as the M4 "Sherman" came on line. (The name "Sherman" was a British nickname, and was never formally used by the U.S., but will be used here, as it has become an accepted moniker.)

M4 Sherman tank "Alligator Annie." (author, tank courtesy of the Wright Museum)

The Sherman is a large beast at about 9 feet tall, 8 ½ feet wide, and around 20 feet long. It weighs 30 tons, give or take a few pounds depending on the engine. (To put this in perspective, the average 2,000 square foot family home weighs 60 tons.) The rolling "half-house" had a crew compartment in the "basement" up front, behind which was the rotating turret with three more crew "upstairs," and the engine was in the back. A driveshaft ran from the engine, all the way forward under the turret basket, and to the transmission and differential, which was in the nose. The transmission drove the two sprockets that were outside and up front, and these in turn drove the tracks.

When the Army's newest tank, the M4, was being designed, the M3 chassis was again, unfortunately, carried over as an expedient, and with it again came the Wright aircraft engine. So the M4A1 debuted with the radial, now long in the tooth and still as cranky, along with the high profile that the radial imposed.

The Wright R-975 engine was a nine cylinder radial engine, designed to operate at a set rpm and drive an airplane's propeller. It was mounted vertically in the tank, with cylinder #5 at 6 o'clock. After sitting, oil tended to accumulate in the bottom cylinder (#5), and if it seeped past the rings it would pool in the combustion chamber.

If one then tried to start it and the engine was on the compression stroke for cylinder #5, it might hydraulic lock on the oil. (Oil, being a liquid, does not compress like air when the piston pushes against it, so the piston stops dead.) So, if you tried to start the engine and other cylinders started, and when the engine got to #5 it came up against the hydraulic lock, the engine would suddenly stop, and that would damage or destroy the crankshaft and possibly the engine.

Wright Radial R-975. (Factory Photo)

To prevent this from happening, if the engine had been off overnight prior to starting, the crew had to insert a hand crank (normally stowed on the rear apron of the vehicle) into a hand crank hole and turn the engine through five complete revolutions by hand-cranking the engine to make sure it wasn't going to lock. "Five Complete Revolutions" meant 50 turns of the hand crank. In the winter, when oil was thick, this was a back-breaker. If the engine turned through one complete revolution without locking up it was OK to start the engine with the starter. If it didn't go through one revolution, the crew had to remove the spark plugs from #5 (each cylinder had two spark plugs), let the oil drain out of the cylinder, clean the dripping wet oily plugs, reinstall them, and now try to start the engine. Even if it did go through one turn, the bottom cylinder might not start – it might have been filled with just enough oil to foul the spark plugs, but not enough to lock. Because of the oil puddling, cleaning spark plugs on the Wright R-975 was a routine chore, and the demand for new plugs outstripped supply. Any spare spark plugs were hoarded. Tanks sent back to Ordnance for repairs would typically have their spark plugs plundered before they left. Other endearing habits of the Wright Engine were that it did not like to idle, and if forced to do so it again fouled its spark plugs, which meant it started running on fewer and fewer cylinders until it just stopped running altogether. It made too much of a bellow at 1300 rpm to allow crews to sit and quietly listen for their opponents. Being so loud, it announced to all that an M4A1 was coming. Lastly, the dear thing also backfired loudly when it was throttled down. The ridiculous starting ritual was even more absurd, if you think of having to get out of your tank and hand-crank the engine, clean plugs, etc., when under fire.

The Multibank's starting drill wasn't a whole lot better if people were shooting at you: **Starting Instructions per Armored Force Board, Ft. Knox, KY**

Medium Tank M4A4 Gasoline Multibank

1. Make prestarting inspection as called for on daily report (Trip Ticket), Armored Force Form No. M1.
2. Open all doors of tank and air for 10 minutes.
3. Check supply of water in radiator and replenish if necessary.
4. Close battery switch. Check voltmeter (24 to 29 volts). Check ammeter. Should not show discharge.
5. Open fuel supply valves.

To Start

6. Turn engine over several times with starter with ignition switch closed. If engine turns over freely, proceed to next step of starting. If engine does not turn freely a hydrostatic lock had developed. Wait 10 minutes, then try starter again with switch off. Lock will have cleared itself by then.
7. Pull choke lever back all the way. Do not leave the choke lever in full choked position for more than 2 engine revolutions. Always partially close the moment engine fires.
8. Pull hand throttle lever out about 1/2 inch. Push clutch pedal in fully and hold until engine starts. Be sure shifting lever is in neutral.
9. Turn ignition switch on and press starting switch. Be sure choke lever is pushed forward to point where engine operates smoothly. Do not user starter to more than 30 seconds with allowing it to cool off for 15 seconds. Engine should start.
10. Reverse manual turning nut on full flow oil filter and note whether filter motor operates.
11. If oil pressure does not reach 40 lbs. in 30 seconds at 1300 rpm, stop engine.
12. Set hand throttle to idle at 1300 rpm.

Warming up the Engine

13. Warm engine at 1300 rpm until engine temperature reaches 160°.
14. If oil pressure drops below normal during warm up period, shut off engine and investigate cause.
15. Check ammeter and voltmeter and keep a careful check of water temperature of each engine.
16. As long as exhaust stack temperature signals remain lighted, the engine must be operated at 1300 rpm. Drive vehicle in 3rd gear at this speed until all stacks clear and all stack signals are automatically switched off. This engine warm-up period with the vehicle in operation also warms the transmission oil. (Armored Force Board Project #AFP-378, *Final Report on Special Test of 40 Medium Tanks, (10 Each M4A1, M4A2, M4A3, M4A4)*. Fort Knox, KY, Armored Force Board 1943)

As the war picked up and production was strained, the aircraft engine was needed for, naturally – aircraft, and shortages of the Wright engine made themselves immediately apparent, almost shutting down the M4 production lines on several occasions. To fill the gaps as an emergency measure, the proven direct-injected two-stroke twin-diesel arrangement was expediently copied from the M3, and so *another* less-than-satisfactory tank went into production as the M4A2. The Twin Diesel used two GM671 2-stroke diesels mounted in tandem and developed 375 HP. Although down on horsepower, the diesel wasn't as "fussy" as the Wright, and was much easier to drive and shift and easier to maintain, so crews loved them.

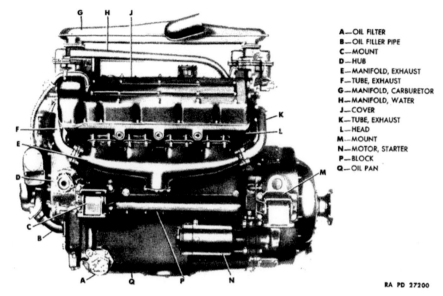

A—OIL FILTER
B—OIL FILLER PIPE
C—MOUNT
D—HUB
E—MANIFOLD, EXHAUST
F—TUBE, EXHAUST
G—MANIFOLD, CARBURETOR
H—MANIFOLD, WATER
J—COVER
K—TUBE, EXHAUST
L—HEAD
M—MOUNT
N—MOTOR, STARTER
P—BLOCK
Q—OIL PAN

RA PD 27200

Ford GAA Side view from the technical manual. (TM9-1731B)

The Army then approached Ford about the possibility of modifying an existing V-12 aircraft engine that Ford produced as an alternative to the Rolls-Royce Merlin and Packard engines. By cutting off the rear four cylinders, an 1,100 cubic inch V8 was born. This time, expediency and copying existing designs worked to the M4's advantage. The engine was designed to have an aluminum block, 4-valve per cylinder heads, and twin spark plugs per cylinder, and it developed 500 HP, which was much better than existing choices. This configuration of the Sherman was designated the M4A3.

The drill for starting the Ford V8 GAA-equipped M4A4 tank was a lot simpler than the Wright or the Multibank:

1. One of the turret crew had to open a fuel valve on the rear firewall, selecting a fuel tank to match the one chosen by the driver by the selector switch on his instrument panel. The driver would check how much fuel was in each tank as it was selected.
2. Driver turned the master power switch on the instrument panel to "ON," and checked that gearshift was in neutral and brakes were set.
3. The Driver held down the clutch pedal, checked the engine emergency shutoff valves were OK, and set the hand throttle to the "idle" position.
4. The Driver pushed the starter button and engine would start. The Driver did a quick gage check of tachometer and Oil Pressure, and then let out clutch in neutral to let the transmission warm up.

So there were four variations of the M4 going into production at once: 1) M4A1 Wright radial; 2) M4A2 Twin Diesels; 3) M4A3 Ford V8; and the 4) M4A4 Chrysler Multibank. This was a logistical nightmare in and of itself, but there were also myriad smaller variations in the rest of the tank. The engines weren't the only systems that had been expedited, "kluged," or carried-over. Cooler heads prevailed and a head-to-head test was conceived, to be run at the Armored Force Board testing grounds. Although by far the major focus was to be on the engines, this was the perfect opportunity to have "tests within a test," and many smaller items – suspensions, sprockets, tracks, turret traversing mechanisms, head lamps, instruments, bogies, bearings, oil seals, and more – were to be compared. The number of items tested made data collection and accuracy a primary concern.

The 781st Tank Battalion was detailed by the AFB to run the vehicles, collect the data, and provide feedback. The 781st was tasked to test the four M4 models for 400 hours or 4000 miles, or until catastrophic engine failure occurred, and was given 10 each M4A1, M4A2, M4A3, and M4A4 Sherman tanks. The tanks were the latest production version of each model, incorporating any improvements in place up to March 15, 1943.

"We did not test motors only. We had records on just about everything in the tank: gun mounts, the effectiveness of the gun's stabilizing gyroscope, turret traversing mechanisms, steel versus rubber tank treads, filters, and what-have-you. The Army wanted the best possible model tank to be rigged with the best possible equipment."
- Joe Graham

How the test became to be called the "Million Dollar Tanks Test" is unknown. A Sherman Tank cost approximately $47,000 in 1943. Being that there were 40 tanks tested, the value of the test mules was closer to $2 million, rather than $1 million, but the 781st referred to it from then on as the "Million Dollar Tank Test." In any case, it would be the biggest and most important test they would perform for the AFB, with far-reaching consequences throughout the war. Prior to the start of the test, each vehicle was inspected by the 781st, and a long laundry list of manufacturer's defects was compiled for each vehicle.

On the M4A1, which was the predominant model then in service, the test vehicles were manufactured by the Pressed Steel Car Company, which made railroad cars prior to the war. On top of finding hinges and buttons painted shut and other relatively minor bugs, the 781st inspectors surfaced a number of design flaws and serious manufacturing defects, including:

• The 75mm ammunition storage in the turret ring was defective, and the ready rounds hit the electrical junction box when the turret was rotated. 75mm rounds that were in the storage boxes wouldn't fit, or had to be pried out for use, or hit things when stored/removed.

• One tank supplied had a .50cal MG with it, but had .30 cal MG mounts and ammo boxes, so the .50cal MG was useless.

Considering that the suppliers knew that these vehicles were being delivered to the Army for testing, it might have been expected that the suppliers would have gone over them with a fine-toothed comb to ensure they were as close to perfect as possible. Maybe they had been? But this illustrates what the troops in Ordnance had to deal with to sort out a new M4A1 from Pressed Steel Car Company before it was ready to go into battle.

On the M4A2, a similar inspection yielded no discrepancies. These tanks were manufactured by Fischer Body Division of General Motors.

Five of the Ford M4A3s arrived late to the party, as they were being fitted with special test bogie bearings and seals at the factory. Two arrived on March 24th, and the test started immediately the next day. The pre-test inspections noted loose tracks that needed adjustment on four units and a few nitpicks. These were manufactured by Ford Motor Company at their Dearborn, Michigan, plant.

The M4A4s made by Chrysler Arsenal had problems, with lots of brackets welded in the wrong place or welded on backwards. All the oil dipsticks were incorrectly marked, causing each engine to be overfilled by 1-2 gallons of oil, which they all promptly regurgitated when started, making a mess of the engine compartments and fouling the fans.

Wherever possible, most of the functional discrepancies were corrected prior to starting the test. The tanks were then stripped bare, taken to a scale, and weighed empty. Each tank was then loaded to simulate a full combat load, and then each tank was re-weighed. The average tank weighed around sixty thousand pounds (30 tons, empty) at the start of the test.

The 781st started testing on Thursday, March 25, 1943, and the tests were run 24 hours a day for six days per week, so the 781st broke up into shifts to enable round-the-clock testing to continue. The tanks being tested were never shut off, except for maintenance or repairs. For testing, only two crewmen were used: a driver and a tank commander. Many of the 781st personnel who were normally assigned other duties were cross-trained to be a tank driver during this testing. While the test was running, when new officers and enlisted men joined the Battalion they were immediately assigned to the test, as it was a wonderful opportunity to get some intensive training. Two civilian representatives, one each

A Fort Knox Postcard shows Sherman tanks crossing the highway. (Courtesy of Rhodes family)

from Ford and GM, were on hand, and reported to Lt. Col. Kinne during the testing. The Ford rep in particular was very helpful in failure analysis and corrective actions for any observed defects on the Ford tanks.

The testing consisted of running the tanks for eight hours on unpaved roads, immediately followed by eight hours on the paved Highway 31W (which disintegrated from the pounding of the steel tracks), then followed by eight hours of rough, hilly cross-country trails, complete with muddy sections, dusty sections, and hilly sections.

During the testing, an unfortunate accident claimed the life of one civilian. The tanks were run day and night, one third on paved public roads. During one of the road segments, a local resident had parked his pickup truck half on and half off the road, and was in the bed of the pickup truck when it was struck by a passing tank, which tried to stop, but climbed into the back of the truck, crushing it and instantly killing the owner.

The ambient air temperature varied from 27 degrees on April 3rd to 87 degrees on May 5th, providing a nice test of the engine cooling systems. The auxiliary generators and turret traversing and gyro-stabilizing mechanisms were operated from two to four hours each day. Homer Turner drove several of the tanks, and quickly developed an affinity towards the Ford. He said: "the aircraft engines and Chryslers were hard to shift, because you had to keep the revs too high and they stirred up a cloud of dirt from their exhausts. You could see 'em coming by the dust cloud."

For every ten tanks there were two maintenance people from the Service Company. These guys were *really* busy, keeping accurate and detailed records about every minute spent on routine and corrective maintenance. On top of the normal items, like tune-ups and changing spark plugs, adjusting tracks, and oil changes, the maintenance guys removed and replaced engines, generators, water pumps, etc. To keep the tanks out on the course as much as possible, the Service crews were equipped with special half tracks that were outfitted as mobile maintenance shops, and the Service guys were expected to perform most of the maintenance in the field and get the tanks back circulating on the course as quickly as possible. Large repairs, like engine removal, obviously required the tank to be brought back to the maintenance bays. Despite the Service crews' best efforts, the majority of the 40 tanks were not able to complete the 400 hours or 4,000 mile test. On the plus side, the 781st maintenance crews became *very* familiar with the engine and equipment variations.

The testing was completed on Saturday, May 15th, a little over seven weeks after it began. It is interesting to note that it took 1,224 hours of round-the-clock testing to accumulate 400 hours on the test vehicles. The hundreds of pages of maintenance data sheets, manufacturer's failure analyses, fuel and oil consumption records, and comparison data were all boiled down and a preliminary conclusions report was issued a week later on May 22, 1943. But Jacob Devers wasn't there to see the end result. Just before the testing concluded, General Devers turned over the reins on May 11th to the third chief of the AFB, Maj. Gen. Alvan C. Gillem, Jr., an infantryman, and he issued the report.

4. "AND THE WINNER IS..."

So who won? After all the test data was collated and sorted, and the numbers were crunched, the final Test Report and conclusions were issued on August 2, 1943. The many sub-tests each had a findings and conclusions, but the main item of interest – the engines – got the most attention. The findings follow:

Drivability: The 781st once again preferred the twin diesel, as it was the easiest to drive and didn't raise a giant dust cloud behind it. The Ford was second. The Wright and the Multibank didn't have as much torque for low-rpm pulling as the Diesels and Ford, so the driver had to hold higher RPMs and slip the clutch more to get the tank moving. Once moving, the driver also had to run in lower gears to hold a set speed while moving cross-country. This, in turn, caused a tornado out of the exhaust, which raised a large "rooster tail" of dust behind the vehicle, enabling it to easily be spotted from quite a distance. The Ford was in the middle: not having the torque of the Diesel, but better than the other two. The Ford was much easier to drive than the Wright and Multibank, as it had more torque, it would idle, and it was flexible about revolutions. The troops later found out in the field that they could disconnect the Ford's engine governor, upping the rev limit from 2800 rpm to about 3800 rpm, when the valves would begin to float.

Suspension: The vertical volute spring suspension system (VVSS) on the M4 was rated as "very unsatisfactory," with these "major deficiencies" noted: excessive ground pressure, excessive maintenance requirements, and overloading of the bogie wheels, making service life of the bogie wheels "very unsatisfactory." It was stated that these defects could not be remedied without a major redesign. In early 1943, the Armored Force Board tested two first-generation M4 tanks fitted with the Horizontal Volute Spring Suspension (HVSS) system. But the tanks tested retained the narrow tracks used on the Vertical Volute Spring Suspension tanks, and this did not improve the excessive ground pressure, so there wasn't enough improvement to justify the change. In September 1943, they tested an improved Horizontal Volute

Spring Suspension (HVSS) system that had wider tracks and more bogies, and that was a success, being better in durability, having less tendency to throw a track, better flotation, and a better ride (the HVSS suspension had shocks and the VVSS didn't). The test results recommended that the Horizontal Volute Spring Suspension (HVSS) under testing should be expedited, and that actions be taken to fix what could be corrected on current design and production.

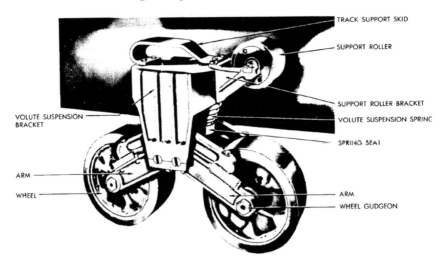

Vertical Volute Spring Suspension as used on early Sherman tanks. (TM9-759)

Tracks: The tracks are essentially large, endless chains that the tank runs over. There is a sprocket in the front, and several "bogie wheels," rubber-tired wheels that run on the inside of the track and support the tank's weight. In the rear is a return idler that is adjustable, like the rear wheel of a bicycle, to take up slack. There were three types of tracks in use: 19 vehicles had standard issue T54 E1 steel tracks; 18 had standard issue M48 rubber track with a chevron cleat molded in (which wore down), and three had a rubber track without a cleat (smooth-faced). The smooth rubber track had no traction, and the steel was too heavy and noisy, so the M48 chevroned track was preferred. The T54E1 steel track was rated "not satisfactory," as it wore out *ten times* as many bogie wheels per 1,600 miles of travel as the rubber-faced track. When the steel tracks failed, they abused the bogie wheels and track support rollers, causing rapid failure. When a rubber track failed, the rollers and bogies were not impacted. But when the rubber track won, another problem surfaced – the Japanese had captured all the rubber plantations and rubber was in short supply. Earlier in the war, the Army had directed that M4 tank tracks be converted to all-steel in an effort to save rubber and ease the shortage. The results of this test, and feedback from the field that the steel tracks were especially destructive to macadam (as supported by Kentucky's devastated Highway 31W), were so conclusive that the Army reversed itself and mandated rubber tracks. Another direct result of the test was that immediate corrective action was taken to improve the welds on steel track, so they failed less often. Tracks were also the great unspoken-of weapon on a tank, and were routinely used to run over opposing forces – especially by running down a slit trench.

Track Nomenclature; note horizontal volute spring differences.
(author, tank courtesy of Wright Museum)

Bogies: All tanks that had rubber tracks used regular-issue bogies. Six of the nineteen that used steel tracks tested special bogies made by Firestone, U.S. Tire, BF Goodrich, Goodyear, and Dayton Rubber. The ten Ford M4A3s came equipped with four different combinations of bogie bearings and seals, and data was collected to see which was best. Bogie manufacturers were a dead heat – all were equal when compared on the same type of track.

Bogie seals and bearings: Again, the test mules were the Ford M4A3s. Different types of grease seals for the bogie bearings were tested. The bearings tested were Timkin roller versus Timkin ball bearings, and the seals were leather vs. rubber. Seals were made by Ohio Rubber Co. (neoprene) and Chicago Rawhide (rawhide). A second test was folded in to extend the lubrication frequency from every 250 miles to every 500 miles, and see if that made a difference in seal lifetime. The combination of roller bearings and rubber seals was the worst (!), and the ball bearings with rawhide seals lasted the longest. The extended lubrication period did not make a difference, so the maintenance interval could have been extended, but the 250-mile greasing frequency was recommended to be kept, because there were so many roller/rubber bogies still in the field.

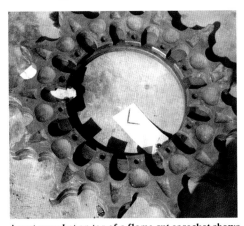

A cast sprocket on top of a flame-cut sprocket shows the cast unit has worn more. (U.S. Army, NARA)

Sprockets: 20 vehicles had flame-cut sprockets vs. cast sprockets, and 20 vehicles had flame-cut vs. forged sprockets. Flame-cut (or face hardened) sprockets were installed on the right hand side (RHS) of the tanks, and forged sprockets were installed on the left hand side (LHS) of test tanks. Some tanks ran cast sprockets as a baseline. Sprockets were reversed on the drive when they became worn and the teeth started to hook. The flame-cut sprocket had greater wear resistance than either the forged or cast sprockets.

Turret traverse mechanism: Westinghouse Electric's electric mechanism was compared to Oil Gear's hydraulic systems. Both the turret mechanisms were found to be satisfactory, but several improvements were proposed. Making sure the grease used on the turret ring was water repellent was the prime action required. Despite being "in general satisfactory," a lot of detail improvements were proposed and corrective actions were suggested.

Auxiliary Generator: The Homelite auxiliary generator (nicknamed "Little Joe") was a small two-stroke engine that lived in the left rear of the crew compartment and was operated by one of the turret personnel (usually the Loader, since he was closest to it and most often the junior of the Turret gang). This little beast needed to have oil mixed in with its gasoline, and came in two main versions, an upright cylinder version and an inverted cylinder version. Both types were oily, smoky gnomes that were miserable to start and keep running. The nice part of having "Little Joe" around was that the main motor didn't have to be running and making noise to power equipment – "Joe" could handle that. The two-stroke "Lil' Joe" was found to be unsatisfactory: they lacked reliability, required excessive maintenance, and having to premix the oil/fuel were all cited.

Electrical Systems: These were, in general, found to be unreliable, and required excessive maintenance. Tail lights were found to be flimsy and broke a lot. The main battery switches were in a difficult-to-access location and required the "crew to perform contortions in order to turn it on or off." Sealed beam headlights were tested in all tanks. Up to now, the headlight bulb was a separate plug-in unit. Sealed beams were placed in the LHS of tanks with odd numbers and in the RHS of vehicles with even numbers, and they were preferred. The radio tubes vibrated loose, killing the radio. The test recommendations included corrective actions to improve the electrical systems' reliability.

Instrument panels: Gauges were specially fitted in the Ford M4A3s and compared to see which was most reliable. The M4A3s were fitted with various gages made by five manufacturers: Stewart-Warner, A.C. Spark Plug, King-Seeley, Autolite, and Waltham. A second objective was to see which gauges weren't really needed, or didn't work. Any instrument that failed was sent to Ford for autopsy and corrective action, and was replaced by a like gauge in the panel. Right away, Service Company gave up on the clocks and stopped replacing them, as they were "practically useless, will not keep accurate time, and are constantly falling apart." The clock hands fell off, and then the adjustment knob vibrated off. One had to agree that a handless clock with no adjustment knob was not useful.

Other items of note: The front universal joint for the drive shaft was just behind the transmission, and was exposed without a safety cover. A few times during the test, this whirling beast caught radio or intercom cords and chewed them up. A guard was earnestly recommended and immediately adopted.

The M4A3 driver's and assistant driver's hatches were subject to damage if they were left open and the turret rotated. The turret could force the hatch beyond its open stop in one direction, and would slam it shut if turned in the other direction. This concussed drivers and assistants. Finally, if the turret jammed while pointing over the hatch, the hatch could not be opened, preventing escape.

Engines: Of the ten Wright-powered M4A1s that started the test, only *two* made it to the end. Nine major engine failures occurred, but one was replaced at the start, so there were really 11 engines in the test. Of the nine failures, six were caused by dirt being ingested through the air cleaners. Six units dropped out for excessive oil consumption (which was a harbinger of imminent rod failure). Three dropped out for broken generator drive gears, and two for failed master rod bearings. Every one of the M4A1s had their clutch replaced between 19 to 306 hours into the test. The A1s, because of their peaky power, needed to be revved hard to get going, and accordingly were really hard on clutches, as there were 78 clutch adjustments required and twelve clutches failed outright over the test.

"Sir, tank #926 will not be completing the test." This diesel suffered massive timing gear train failure during the test. (U.S. Army, NARA)

The performance of the GMC 6-71diesel-powered M4A2s was surprisingly similar to the Wright. Of the ten vehicles that started the test, only two made it to the end. Again, there were nine major engine failures, but one of the nine (#926) was deemed a manufacturing defect (a loose screw was left inside the engine when it was built, and it destroyed the timing gears), so an eleventh engine was allowed to take its place. Again, six of the nine failures were caused by air cleaners not doing their job, and all the engines, with one exception, suffered excessive ring wear, breakage, and/or holing of their pistons. Twelve clutches were replaced, and timing gears were destroyed on many of the test engines. One of the two engines that made it to the finish line was on the verge of failure, while the other was in remarkably good condition.

The Ford GAA-powered M4A3s had problems with their Cuno oil filters disintegrating and the intake manifolds cracked, which then bled air, leaning out the mixture and burning valves if not caught in time. One engine failure was caused by this, and Ford immediately instituted corrective action at their plant for the failure.

Fords break, too. M4A3 #944 coughed out most of its innards while on the cross-country course. (U.S. Army, NARA)

Several of the engines were repaired by pounding caulking into the crack and sealing it with Permatex gasket compound. They ran fine after the patch. Overall, twelve engines failed during the test. Interestingly, three engines were destroyed by crew errors or negligence. One had a stud dropped into the intake when a carburetor was being changed and that destroyed the engine. One was submerged in a ditch, and muddy water entered the intake and got into the engine, ruining it. The third was toasted when the crew forgot to reinstall the oil filler cap and the engine blew its oil out the filler; starved for oil, it burned its bearings. Two of these were replaced and continued testing, while the third was in the process of being replaced when the test ended. Several of the engines suffered from bearing wear and connecting rod or crankshaft failure followed.

The Multibank A4s at first all had a problem with their motor mounts flexing, which allowed the bottom of the engine to strike the hull, causing the oil pan to crack, dropping all the oil, and resulting in engine failure. One tank suffered an engine fire as a result of all the loose oil. The exhaust bellows tubes that connected

ARMORED FORCE BOARD 5580   P-378   FORT KNOX, KENTUCKY

Tank #944, Engine #1253: Showing connecting rods bent and broken in failure, wrist
pins bent, cap both broken. Note bent rod after terrible beating. 278:14 hours.

These pieces came out of the crippled Ford GAA.
(U.S. Army, NARA)

the manifolds to the exhausts also failed, which leaked the hot exhaust gases into the engine compartment and caused tests to be halted for fear of engine fires. There were 15 exhaust bellows failures which consumed the entire supply of available replacements, so crews were instructed that "unless the vehicle was in imminent danger of immolation the tests were to continue" with the broken exhausts. This was not a welcome directive. The engine compartments were already oily, as the crew had problems keeping the oil reservoirs properly filled due to inaccessibility of the filler pipe, so they spilled a lot of oil. On top of creating a messy fire hazard, the spilled oil also tended to be sucked into the radiator by the fan, where it then collected dirt that packed the radiator so it couldn't cool the engines. Finally, the spilled oil soaked the wiring so badly that the wire identification tags became unreadable, which caused nightmares when the engines were pulled – the mechanics had to trace the individual wires to find out which wire was connected to what. Finally, as if the job of driving oil-soaked fire-bombs wasn't bad enough, the fire warning systems on these tanks wasn't much solace, as it was deemed "useless" due to engine vibration causing numerous shorts! On two tanks, the vibration damper on one of the five "sub-engines" flew off and hit the distributor(s) on the adjacent engines. Burned valves and worn rings routinely caused engines to drop cylinders. (With thirty cylinders per tank, it was hard to tell if one was in trouble.) During the dry cross-country phase of testing, the clutches in the A4s would pack with dust and become "exceedingly hard to disengage." A new type of clutch was installed to solve the problem.

Of the ten Chrysler M4A4s, none made it as far as 300 hours of operation. Eleven engines failed: three ate their generator drive gears, two trashed bearings when they ran out of oil, and six were dead for excessive oil consumption, which meant one or more of the "sub-engines" in the cluster had died.

All of the above was noted, but the real heart of the test boiled down to two charts: maintenance time per tank and logistical requirements:

A Multibank radiator showing the effect of all that spilled oil clogging the radiator (note size of radiator compared to the person on the left.) (U.S. Army, NARA)

Type	Description	0-100 Engine Hours	100-200 Engine Hours	200-300 Engine Hours	300-400 Engine Hours	Total time
Maintenance hours on Engine, Clutch and Instruments Only (per tank)						
M4A1	Wright	46.9	143.6	57.0	NTC*	
M4A2	Diesel	30.3	52.0	93.1	37.7	213.1
M4A3	Ford	17.9	30.1	44.1	41.5	133.6
M4A4	Multibank	30.6	62.8	NTC*	NTC*	
Total Maintenance Time (per tank)						
M4A1	Wright	77.8	190.8	88.7	NTC*	
M4A2	Diesel	65.2	149.6	133.3	97.9	446.0
M4A3	Ford	38.4	87.7	122.5	112.0	360.6
M4A4	Multibank	39.0	102.0	NTC*	NTC*	

*No Tanks Completed this period.

Maintenance: The Wright reinforced its claim as the high maintenance creature it was already known to be, and couldn't reach the finish line. The Multibank and Diesel showed comparable maintenance needs up to 200 hours, and then the Multibank fell victim to its own complexity and disintegrated. The Diesel and the Ford

GAA made it to the end of the test, but the Diesel needed significantly more care than the Ford to do so, so the Ford took top honors in the engine department. Perhaps more significant was the total maintenance time spent per tank. The Wright took a lot of maintenance to make 200 hours and then tapered off, as the engine just died. The Diesel also soaked up maintenance time. The Multibank was second best until they died. The Ford had highs and lows, but turned in the lowest overall maintenance requirement.

FUEL AND OIL REQUIREMENTS:

ID	Description	Gallons of Fuel	Weight of Fuel (lbs)	Gallons of Oil	Weight of Oil (lbs)
100 miles of Highway Operation Requires:					
M4A1	Wright	2,237	18,907	89	868
M4A2	Diesel	1,546	13,069	28	276
M4A3	Ford	1,931	16,327	17	171
M4A4	Multibank	2,615	22,110	21	218
100 Miles of Cross-Country Operation Requires:					
M4A1	Wright	5,152	43,538	202	1,983
M4A2	Diesel	3,333	28,170	43	421
M4A3	Ford	4,359	36,835	48	476
M4A4	Multibank	5,862	49,540	47	468

Mileage: The weight of fuel and oil was a significant factor for the logistics and supply people, as they had to haul that fuel and oil to the front lines. The diesel won hands down, requiring significantly less fuel to operate, either on or off-highway. The Ford was 14% more efficient than the Wright on gas, and was positively great on oil use. The Multibank was a gas guzzler, drinking fuel liberally. The Wright was also a gas hog, but it additionally consumed a surprising amount of oil, over three times that of the next engine on highway, and it used four times as much oil as the next when going cross-country.

Choosing the Winner: So, when the chips were cashed in, the Ford GAA was the overall winner, which was really not much of a surprise. The Wright engine was included in the test as a baseline to compare others against. Unless the alternatives literally crashed and burned, its future was sealed. Following the War Department's decree of March '42, the Diesel was also a lost cause before it started unless the other gasoline engines self-destructed. So the test really boiled down to Ford's GAA vs. Chrysler's Multibank. The Ford won handily, finishing the test and turning in superior performance in all categories.

These tests proved to Generals Gillem and Devers that the Ford GAA-V-8 engine was *the* single medium tank engine for which the Army was looking. The Ordnance department would have settled on the GAA right there and then if Ford could have made enough of them to satisfy demand. Production started the very next month in June 1943 as the M4A3, and this became the preferred tank in the ETO. But even mighty Ford couldn't build that many tanks to supply everyone that soon.

So, *all* the other variants lived on! Despite the War Department's decree, 6,748 Diesel M4A2s were made anyway. The marines got a couple hundred for use in the Pacific (mostly to lessen the threat of fuel fires on landing craft), and most of the rest went to Russia, which did have a diesel logistics train to feed them.

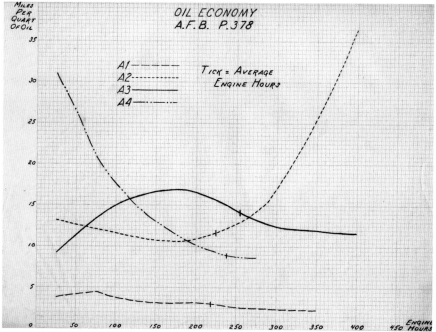

Oil mileage as the engines aged. Note that the M4A2 diesel improved radically while the Multibank deteriorated. The others were relatively constant. (U.S. Army, NARA)

Even the least successful engine, the Multibank, was also pressed into service again as the M4A4. Ordnance recommended that as soon as availability of other engines increased this configuration should be dropped. But Ordnance had jumped the gun. In November 1942, before the "Million Dollar Tank Test" was even run, Chrysler got a contract for and produced Multibanks for the U.S. Army, with 4,300 of these winding up in the Sherman. The U.S. Army, in what was surely a supreme sacrifice and a gesture of international amity and cooperation between allies, promptly sent most of these dogs to the British. The few Multibank engines that the Army did keep were restricted from overseas use and were relegated to training, parades, and exhibitions. It was widespread knowledge that the Multibank engine was full of bugs, and once the November 1942 order was filled, the production line would close. The Brits, being desperate for tanks, reluctantly accepted them, but only after a mandatory list of modifications were made! Chrysler continued to make improvements, and eventually got the engine to the point where it reached 400 hours between overhauls. The British eventually found them to be satisfactory if the maintenance and fuel consumption issues were overlooked, which was kind of like overlooking an elephant in a peanut factory. Closer to the truth, the British needed the 75mm gun that the Sherman carried, not because it was anything special, but because that gun brought with it a High Explosive (HE) round that was unlike anything available to the English armored troops, and a dual purpose gun was desperately needed by the British.

Production of the Multibank ceased in September 1943. Chrysler asked the AGF to consider signing a contract extension so they could build more engines. The AFB obligingly ran another test at Aberdeen Proving Ground from October 11, 1943, to February 10, 1944. Like the "Million Dollar Tank Test," it was done 24/7 in all weather. Four M4A4 Multibanks competed against four tanks of three other configurations. According to Chrysler: "3 of the 4 Multibank engines finished the 4,000-mile marathon. Of the other 12, only one finished. Ordnance reported that the Multibank gave the most reliable performance, its maintenance was lowest, and power loss was negligible. Its oil consumption was bettered only by a Diesel tank engine."

The Multibanks had all been shipped to England, and continued production was dependent on the British actually wanting more of them. But the Brits didn't want any more of an obsolete tank with a super-complex engine, so the production plug was pulled. As a final irony, during the Battle of the Bulge, Patton's Third Army was running out of replacement tanks and the British let him have some of their M4A4s, no doubt with a grin.

The final report of the testing did not get released until August 11, 1944. And with that report, the 781st contributed in testing and selecting the best available Sherman tank variant (M4A3), and along with that, they selected the best combat systems to make the M4 Sherman the best it could be. As a direct result of this testing and follow-on tests that were run, the Horizontal Volute Suspension System, the wider chevroned rubber-block track, longer-lived sprockets, and improved electrical systems came into being or were accelerated.

When all was said and done, this test eventually resulted in the release of the M4A3E8, or "Easy Eight" version of the Sherman tank, which incorporated most of the improvements suggested. So the overall winner of the "Million Dollar Tank Test" was the United States and the Armored crews of the U.S. Army. The "Easy Eight" saved untold crewmen's lives, and that tank significantly contributed to hastening the end of the war.

5. MORE TESTING

The AFB's "House Band" wrapped up the "Million Dollar Tank Test" and went on to other projects and other tests.

In November 1942, the AFB was testing the 105mm howitzer-equipped Sherman tank. At the final meeting to review the test results in February 1943, a host of modifications were proposed, mostly to improve the turret balance, which was so bad that the turret wouldn't rotate if the tank was parked on a slope! The gun barrel was so heavy, it would overpower the turret traverse and it would always point downhill. This made it useless in battle, as the ability to aim came in very handy. The 781st tested two pilot models with the modifications, and the M4 (105) was subsequently approved.

The M4 (105) Assault Guns in HQ Company of the 781st had 105mm howitzers, which were pretty much the same gun the artillery guys used. They were intended to be used to reduce fortifications with a large High Explosive shell by direct fire. ("Direct fire" was firing at a target you could see directly. "Indirect fire" was shooting at a target you could not directly see and relying on a spotter to help you adjust the aim.) The M4 (105) did not have the capability to elevate the gun as high as the artillery howitzers, so the effective range was much less. Also, the tank crews were nowhere as well trained, nor equipped as the dedicated artillery crews, so hitting a target with indirect fire was a long shot (pardon the pun).

Between February and April 1943, the AFB tested 76mm-equipped M4s and found the turret arrangement unsatisfactory because of inadequate turret space (that darned small turret ring!), and again because of bad turret balance. In July 1943, they tested a new turret design with the 76mm gun and found it to be satisfactory. In a letter dated August 17, 1943, the AFB recommended adoption of the 76mm gun.

The AFB also tested the M5 Light tank, to evaluate all the modifications and improvements that had been made to the vehicle. The M5 Light Tank was a well-rounded small tank that was well-suited to the reconnaissance, exploitation, and patrol roles it fulfilled. However, it was hopelessly outclassed in any armor confrontation.

M5A1 tested at Fort Knox with a test ID Number on it. (U.S. Army, NARA)

The M5 "Stuart" Light Tank had a crew of four: driver and co-driver, like the Sherman, in the hull; and a gunner and tank commander in the turret. This dispensed with the "loader" position as in the Sherman, causing the commander to assume that role. This posed a problem similar to early French tanks in WWII. The commander was supposed to choose targets, load the main gun, and maintain "situational awareness" – that is, he was supposed to know what's going on around him, where the enemy was located, where his forces were, and how best to position his forces to counter those of the enemy. As the French learned, the additional burden of loading significantly impacted the tank commander's ability to understand and control the fight. Captain Joe Graham, of "D" Company, agreed with this assessment, and during the later stages of the war he commanded his Company by riding alongside his Company in a jeep and speaking with the Platoon leaders via a radio. The British also used the M5, and they also ran into the same problem. For a time they tried operating the "Honey" (as they nicknamed it) with a five person crew, but the turret was simply too small to reasonably fit three people, so they abandoned the effort.

The main gun in the Stuart was a 37mm rifle that would have zero impact against enemy armor. About 1.5" in diameter, it was obsolete by 1943, as enemy tank development increased their armor to the point where the 37mm was ineffective. How ineffective? Well, by 1943, the Sherman's 75mm gun was becoming ineffective against the newest German tanks, so about the best the M5's 37mm would do was scratch the paint and make them mad. About 174 37mm rounds could be carried; loadout was about 60 High Explosive, 30 Armor Piercing, 10 White Phosphorous, and the balance in Canister. This reflects the main use of the rifle against infantry and Anti-Tank gun troops that might hide behind the AT gun's shield. The Canister round (100 steel balls in an aluminum tube) turned the 37mm rifle into a giant shotgun, and it was *very* effective against enemy troops at less than 100 yards.

The M5A1 also had two or three .30cal machine guns and carried 6,250 rounds on board. It was powered by twin Cadillac gas engines of 110hp each. The M5A1 was relatively agile and speedy, but suffered from the same narrow track problem the Sherman had and tended to sink in soft ground and snow. On the plus side, the Stuarts were quiet. The Shermans and Tigers bellowed and backfired their way into combat, and for them, the thought of sneaking up on their enemy with a degree of stealth was but a dream. However, the twins Caddys in the M5s were relatively muffled, and they *could* sneak up on the enemy. The M5s also used an automatic transmission, and were much easier to drive than the Sherman – the M5 driver didn't require three feet and a prehensile tail to operate his tank like in the Sherman. The other major strength of the Stuart was its speed. While the Sherman was hard-pressed to see 30 with a tailwind, the Stuart had a top speed of 36mph (designed), but could be coaxed to close to 50mph (with some baling wire on the governor.)

The M5 Stuart had undergone a great many modifications over its history, and the AFB wanted to verify that all those changes were effective. The AFB put a sample of the latest-configuration M5s through the familiar torture test, and the conclusion was that all the modifications worked.

The AFB also tested a light armored car in response to a request for a replacement for the obsolete M8 Light Armored Car. The 781st participated in this test of two candidates: the T27 8 x 6 Armored Car built by Studebaker competed against the T28 6 x 6 Armored Car built by Chevrolet. After another grueling round-the-clock test, the Chevy was declared the winner, and it was going into production as the M38 Wolfhound when the war ended and production was halted.

The AGF, with exceedingly bad foresight into German tank development, decided that the Sherman would be good enough to see the U.S. through the rest of the war. Part of this was due to General McNair's myopia regarding tanks fighting other tanks, and this was partly driven by a false sense of complacency.

General Devers had submitted a report in December 1942 that said the M4 and the 76mm gun were good enough, that the U.S. didn't need a heavy tank, and that the Army would make do with the M4/76mm for the rest of the war. This report caused the outright cancellation of the U.S. heavy tank program (and so doomed lots of M4 crews to death by newly-introduced Panthers and Tigers).

The 75mm gun in the M4 was the great-grandchild of a French artillery piece that was introduced in 1897. By 1942, it was long in the tooth but thoroughly de-bugged, and a year later it was pretty much ineffective against Panzer armor. The 75 didn't get weaker; the opponent's armor doubled or tripled in thickness. Something stronger was needed, but in General McNair's world, tanks didn't fight other tanks. The Sherman had been designated for close infantry support, and as such, it needed a dual-purpose gun that could fire High Explosive rounds for maximum impact on infantry. The 75mm gun had a superlative HE round, so the Sherman got a short-barreled version of the 75mm gun so it could shoot that round. It took a while for the brass to even acknowledge that there was a problem; that American tanks were indeed being forced to fight German tanks with predictably dire consequences. But even when the larger, stronger rifles appeared, they were at first earmarked for Tank Destroyers. When it was introduced for the Sherman, the 76mm rifle was sold as the cure-all for penetrating German armor. It was not. According to Vince Sutphin, a gunner in Company "B" of the 781st, the Sherman's main gun "proved to be far less than a match for the German guns."

And there was another catch. While the 76mm Armor-Piercing round *was* marginally more effective than the 75mm round, the 76mm High Explosive round was significantly *inferior* to that of the 75mm gun. So at first the crews wanted the 76mm, but when it was revealed that the 76 really didn't pack the promised knockout punch, they realized that it was actually better to have the older 75mm tank, because its HE round could knock the tracks off the opponents' tanks better than the new gun! A revised AP round for the 76 was developed, the M93 HVAP ("HyperVelocity Armor Piercing") – crews called them the "Hyper-Shot." These had a tungsten core, and finally allowed the 76mm Sherman to have a chance at killing a Panther or Tiger at realistic ranges, but they were always in very short supply, and tanks typically only had one or two on board. The other fault of the 76mm was its muzzle blast, which was so large the gunner was blinded by the dust cloud and couldn't spot where his own shot landed. Vince Sutphin's tank was equipped with the 76mm, and he thought it was an effective weapon "for what I ran into – thank God no German tanks!"

When the M4 Sherman was introduced to the African campaign, it was clearly the superior vehicle, easily besting the opposing Panzer IIs and IIIs. There was a British officer, one Lt. Colonel George Witheridge, who provided liaison services with the British Army. He fed glowing reports back from the field as the British introduced the Grant and Sherman tanks in the desert. At that point in time, the Sherman was quite possibly the best tank in the world. But that superiority was short-lived, as the Germans continued to improve their armor while the Americans pressed "pause." When the new Panzer IV was encountered, the Sherman was at least its equal, and could give as good as it got. When the Tiger I, then the Panther, and then the Tiger II showed up, the Sherman was severely outclassed, and yet the AGF still resisted new tank development.

Unfortunately, it also seriously delayed the development of the 90mm gun. The U.S. 90mm gun was tested, and was found to be roughly equivalent, or a tad inferior, to the excellent German 88. The British had an excellent alternative in their 17-pounder, which was equal to or better than the 88, and the Brits lobbied for its installation in the Sherman. They tried to prove their rifle was the best choice, but General Devers refused to attend a demonstration in England between the 76mm, 90mm, and the British 17-pounder. The U.S. Army, perhaps with a bad case of "not-invented-here," steadfastly refused to mount the 17-pounder in the Sherman. They also refused to mount the 90mm in the Sherman (the official position was entrenched that the 76mm was "good enough"). The decision not to mount the larger guns was impacted by the Sherman's small turret ring. Again, this later caused a lot of crews to die. The British didn't give up, moving ahead by themselves. They turned the 17-pounder on its side in a new turret and developed a new Sherman that could go "toe-to-toe" with a Panther. This became known as the "Sherman Firefly," and it was a true match for the Panthers and Tigers, in the gun department, at least. The Firefly's armor was still sub-par. The German tank crews soon learned to spot any attacking Fireflies and made every effort to take them out first.

One valid reason for stopping tank development was that the introduction of a new tank would cause a logistical problem. Large numbers of Shermans were being stockpiled for the upcoming invasion of Europe. If the Allies started to rearm with a new tank, the problems of retraining troops in use, maintenance, and other basics for the new model might impact the fighting effectiveness of the crews. The argument is lame, in that the Germans effectively fielded several different tank variants. The AGF also cited problems with building new tanks that were wider than the width of a flatcar. They cited problems with the lifting capacity of dockside cranes not being able to lift a new, heavier tank, and that of freighter holds not being wide enough to accommodate a bigger tank. Roadblock after roadblock was thrown up to block a new tank, and unfortunately, Allied crews died waiting for a competitive tank.

The feedback from the field indicated the Sherman was getting its ass kicked, and the Army finally resolved that they would just upgrade the M4 and try to keep pace with German tank development. There were many upgrades required, and the Armored Force had to test and evaluate all these suggested upgrades, but pretty soon there were just too many, and things spiraled out of control. This resulted in a decision to bundle a lot of the changes and release a second-generation Sherman. The design work started in December 1943.

The AGF's decision to overwhelm the enemy with quantity over quality certainly resulted in the needless loss of trained tank crews and lowered crew morale. Today, modern armies realize that the hardest thing to replace in the Armored Fighting Vehicle is the trained crew, and today's tank designs stress crew protection and survivability. Unfortunately, the U.S. Army just hadn't seen that light in 1944.

When the Army finally got motivated, the result – the M26 Pershing – was almost too late for the war, and was at best an underpowered "me too" design that didn't break any new ground, merely equaling the latest German and Russian designs and still carrying the sub-par U.S. 90mm gun. The Brits binned the Sherman chassis and released the Comet, which was also not a great tank, but at least it toted the 17-pounder, which was a better gun than the U.S. 90mm.

6. MEANWHILE, BACK AT THE WAR - 1943

By early 1943, the African campaign was over, the invasion of Sicily was complete, and the U.S. Joint Chiefs of Staff were discussing where to go next after Sicily. Some wanted to go to southern France right away, some advocated invading the Balkans, but the majority wanted to go right for the cross-channel invasion of northern France (in Normandy, which was later known as Operation Overlord).

At a Joint Strategy meeting between the U.S. and British staff called Trident, the British proposed the invasion of Italy, with the aim of taking Italy out of the war in 1943. After Italy fell, they argued, it would then be possible to go into southern France as a smaller-scale diversion for the Overlord effort. They were really driven by a directive from Winston Churchill, who felt that the Americans were not sufficiently experienced to mount such a major invasion, and proposed that they should carry out a couple of smaller "practice invasions" first. Second, the British also had plans for extending their postwar influence in the Balkans, and having Italy as a jumping off point would further those aims. The Americans, who were at this time somewhat of a junior partner in these meetings, conceded, and the Allied war planners had their next stop – Italy. Besides, the Americans thought, this might allow more resources to be sent to the Pacific, which was a welcome thought.

As was hoped, Italy surrendered in mid-1943, but the Germans then manned the lines in Italy and carried on the fight. Allied planners still thought that by mid-1944, the shouting would be over in Italy and there would be 12-14 divisions in theatre that would need to attack something before they got stale.

During the August 1943 War Planning Meeting, essentially the same discussion took place – what to do with the excess troops? This time, transportation – shipping, landing craft, and supply and logistics – were all in extremely short supply. Everything in existence and everything coming off the production lines was committed to

Operation Overlord, which in fact was postponed because of a lack of landing craft. There simply wasn't enough transportation to move all the extra resources that were currently in the Mediterranean to England for staging Overlord. And even if they could somehow be moved there, there weren't enough landing craft to get them across the channel as part of the invasion. So the War Planners had to find a local job for all those leftover troops – and southern France seemed as good a place to go as any. The strategic planners and Joint Chiefs officially bought into the invasion of southern France, now codenamed Operation Anvil. It was planned to be launched somewhat coincidentally to Overlord, enabling the Allies to attack the Germans on two fronts. And they strengthened the concept to be more than a diversionary attack for Overlord, because they had *a lot* of extra troops. This would be a full-scale effort, and the targeted landing zone was the Toulon-Marseilles area of southeast France. Everything was decided, except one thing: an endeavor this large needed a senior commander.

On May 11, 1943, General Devers had left Fort Knox and transferred to the ETO, which caused an old rivalry to resurface. General Devers and his new boss, General Eisenhower, disliked each other intensely, and were rivals in the post-WWI Army. About the only things they had in common were they both played polo and were nominally in the same uniform. Devers had graduated from the U.S. Military Academy at West Point a couple of years earlier than Ike, but in the post-WWI years Ike had risen a bit higher in rank, and was by this time one grade higher in rank than Devers. Initially upon his arrival, Devers worked for Ike prior to the big invasion, and when Ike was promoted to command the Supreme Headquarters Allied Expeditionary Force (SHAEF) he tried to torpedo his subordinate, trying to get Devers sent to a backwater post. Ike did not want Devers to command any of the Overlord invasion force.

Trying to get Devers reassigned right at that moment backfired on Eisenhower – it freed up an experienced senior officer just when the Joint Chiefs were looking for someone to command the invasion of Southern France. Devers was assigned to take that command. Eisenhower was not at all pleased to find out that Devers was assigned to command VI Corps and the whole second front in southern France. But all was not lost for Ike, however. Eisenhower did use the opportunity to offload a giant headache of his – the Free French Army (FFA). Eisenhower assigned the FFA to report to and through General Devers. While one part of the initial objectives for the southern France invasion was military – open a second French front – another objective was political. The invasion was aimed at capturing the seat of the Vichy government, and it was desired that the FFA play a large part.

The FFA was a smallish force, and was ill-equipped, having been reliant on their Allies for supplies, and was given mostly hand-me-downs, obsolete equipment, and spares. It was a motivated force in battle, but was definitely and openly distrusted. General Patton once said: "I'd rather have a German division in front of me than a French one behind me." That summed up the general feeling. The FFA leadership, in Generals DeLattre and DeGaulle, were rankled by that feeling, and they also possessed inflated egos, which was a bad mix to start. Eisenhower's move to have them report though Devers was viewed as an insult, and was met with dissatisfaction

General DeLattre (L) and General Jacob Devers with two French staff share a cordial moment. (U.S. Army Signal Corps, NARA)

from the FFA leadership about their chain of command. They wanted to report directly to Ike, President Roosevelt, or preferably God, with whom they felt on a more equal conversational level. This latest bit of effrontery didn't faze them, and if they suffered any further problems or insult – real or imagined – they would simply bypass the chain of command, jumping directly to Ike, George Marshall, President Roosevelt, or God, as needed. And to ice the cake, the French 2nd Armored was commanded by General Jacques Leclerc, who barely followed orders from his own commanders.

In Sicily, the U.S. Seventh Army was a "skeleton crew" under General Mark Clark. The Seventh Army had distinguished itself by overrunning Sicily while commanded by General George Patton, who at this point was out of favor and had been assigned to a backwater command to remove him from the public eye. Seventh Army was activated to take part in the Anvil invasion (now codenamed "Dragoon"). General Clark, who had done a fine job with the initial planning to reconstitute the Seventh, was seriously taxed to manage both the Seventh and Fifth Armies when the Germans blocked the Anzio invasions. To lighten his load, Seventh Army was transferred to Maj. Gen Alexander M. Patch. Patch had previously organized the Americal Division, which was sent to the Pacific Theatre (Guadalcanal), and they had done very well. Patch was a "soldier's general," and less concerned with trappings than results. Tall, with red hair, he was known to be very bottom-line oriented. He didn't provide great news copy and wasn't flamboyant like George Patton or Patton's arch-rival, British General Bernard Montgomery.

So General Jacob Devers began assembling his staff and implementing an invasion of Southern France, with an impatient Free French Army dogging him and demanding and threatening and wheedling on one hand, and a hostile superior waiting for him to trip up on the other.

7. 1943 THE "HOUSE BAND" DEPARTS

Besides performing tests for the AFB, the 781st was busy training personnel and developing efficient administration policies. The basic training given to soldiers at the Armored Force Replacement Center got them in good physical shape and taught them to march, basic squad battle formations, marksmanship, first aid, map reading, and how to use and care for items that had been issued to them. The 781st by this time was, in anticipation of the end of their tenure with the AFB, focusing more on combat readiness training for a tank battalion – firing practice, enemy vehicle (planes and tanks) recognition, map reading, maneuvering, gas mask training, first aid, and crew training.

Gas Training: Recruits were given a gas mask, which was carried in a sack, and the strap went over the shoulder. About the size of a large purse, the sack contained the mask, the charcoal canister that filtered the air, and a rubber hose that reached from the face mask to the canister. Recruits were taught how to put on their gas masks, fitting them tightly around their faces to prevent leaks, which would obviously render the mask useless. To drive the point home, the recruits were placed in a large gas chamber, and under actual gas situations (using tear gas), they had to hold their breath and quickly take their mask from the carry sack, put them on so they didn't leak (which was not so easy, as there were three belts that held the mask to your face: one went under your ears, one went over your ears, and one went around your temples), "clear" the mask (blow into it to clear any gas that got in while you were putting it on), and then sit back and relax. If they did it wrong, the tear gas would forcefully drive home the point. Instructors were on hand if someone got really out of control. Being an instructor was a really rotten assignment as after a few exposures it was reported that it felt like your skin was beginning to crawl."

By this time, the 781st adopted an unofficial motto of "Invictus" (Latin for "never conquered"), and this motto and an unofficial unit crest was found on the cover of the "Standing Operating Procedures" that defined the various tasks for the men. (In a reincarnated postwar 781st, "Duty before Self" was made the official Battalion motto with a formal coat of arms.)

In the 781st, there was a Standard Operating Procedure (SOP) for how to make your bunk and arrange your gear: bunks had to be alternated head/toe/head as one walked down the barracks aisle, four pairs of shoes underneath the bunk arranged service shoes/civilian shoes/slippers/shower clogs. Remember to make your bunk so the "U.S." on the blanket faces the aisle, the pillow is covered by the top blanket, and your field bag and gas mask bag are hung on the end at the aisle. You think that's picky?

How about the SOP requirement that all clothes hanging in the closets on the right side of the barracks must be hung *so the buttons face the rear* of the barracks? Clothes hung on the left side had to have their buttons facing the front... And God help you if you didn't hang your shirts all the way to the left, then your khakis, blouses, field jacket, overcoat, coveralls, and rain coat going towards the right in that order! The shelf over your bunk had to have certain items on it placed in a precise order. Each soldier was allocated the extreme right-hand side of their shelf for personal photos, but no pinups were allowed! Obviously, the arrangement of your uniform and belts and accessories for inspection was detailed, as was the contents and arrangement of your knapsack. An SOP governed everything. Even the out-of-sight stuff, like the contents of your footlocker, had to be arranged in a certain way, but at least there was some leeway here to hold some personal items.

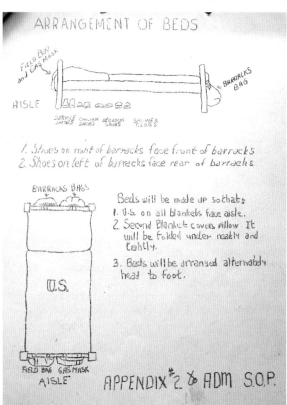

781st Admin Procedure Appendix #2 defines the proper way to make and arrange beds in the barracks. (U.S. Army, NARA)

The 781st SOPS do go way over the top in some areas. Examples: there was an SOP requirement for each mess to maintain six – not seven, not five – trash cans on a rack, labeled and in proper order: meat/edible/non-edible/trap grease/trash. Or the picayune SOP requirement for the proper way to hang mops and brooms on the outside of a barracks. Some of this admittedly smacks of an organization with too much time on its

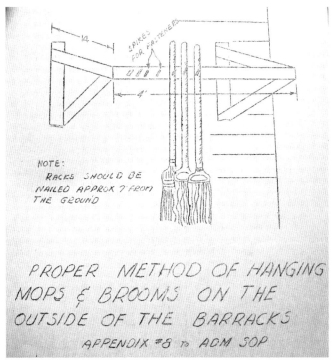

NOTE:
RACKS SHOULD BE NAILED APPROX 7' FROM THE GROUND

PROPER METHOD OF HANGING MOPS & BROOMS ON THE OUTSIDE OF THE BARRACKS
APPENDIX #8 TO ADM SOP

The proper way to hang mops per the 781st Admin SOP. (U.S. Army, NARA)

hands. Personal preferences of the CO were communicated via these SOPs, and while he obviously liked to run a "taut ship," Lt. Col Kinne's only personal restriction was against facial hair – no beards or moustaches were allowed in the 781st! This micromanagement by SOP did take its toll on the personnel. By the time the Battalion shipped overseas, only two Majors and one Captain had survived from the initial batch of Lt. Col Kinne's officers, as he relentlessly weeded out the "deadwood" and rewarded good performance.

These SOPs certainly covered the minutiae, and the benefit of these, other than keeping idle hands at work, could be debated. But they also covered complex tasks, such as marching formations, security, administrative tasks, and attack formations. These SOPs were deadly boring to read, but they had the benefit of hastening the learning curve for a newcomer, and made sure that everyone heard and obeyed the same rules. When the 781st finally entered combat, the time spent learning the SOPs increased their effectiveness as a fighting unit – the CO could call out for attack formation "X," and everyone would instantly know their proper position and movement to gain the objective.

There was a real incentive for learning your SOPs. During the war, the residents around Fort Knox ran a program wherein families would "adopt" a soldier and have them over for a Sunday dinner. But if you screwed up an inspection, you lost your home-cooked dinner. As the 781st stayed a while in the area, friendships were established, as soldiers and residents became attached to one another, and yes, friendships also blossomed into relationships and relationships into marriages. Needless to say, you were not going to miss a hot date because your buttons faced the wrong way in a closet.

Of course, a few of the craftier guys came up with other ways to get time off. Lt. Paul Shartel of "D" Company and 2nd Lt. Art Sloggatt of the Assault Gun Platoon were best buddies, and they had a great scheme. Lt. Sloggatt would go to his CO, Capt. Bill Rich, and say: "Captain Graham is giving a two-day pass to Lieutenant Shartel…I'd sure like to join him." At the same time, Lt. Shartel was giving the same song and dance to his CO, Capt. Graham. And the two drinking buddies scored their passes. This worked for about three months, until Captains Rich and Graham compared notes.

The standard U.S. Army training program started off by training the individual to be a soldier, followed by training that soldier to be part of a crew. As each goal is reached, the next goal involves larger and larger groups operating in harmony. New Tank Battalions were typically given three months to do their basic training, and another three to complete the combined-arms training. The 781st had a lot more time to train than the average Battalion, so they were very adept at Battalion-level tasks, and certainly had the most proficient mechanics in the Army.

The first step in training to become part of a crew would be in driving, gunnery, marksmanship, drill, and allied subjects for your assigned position. A Sherman/ Stuart vehicle crew – the "Squad" – would then train to become a cohesive unit. All crew members were given a leather helmet, copied from a football helmet and made by the Wilson Sporting Goods company. Squad training would include more driving, crossing mud, frozen ground, fording streams (checking the bed and banks), climbing hills, and knowing when to forge ahead and when to do some scouting. If the tank was the "command" or lead tank of the Platoon, the tank commander was either a first or second Lieutenant. A Staff Sergeant commanded the second-most senior tank. Sergeants commanded "regular" tanks in the platoon. The Lieutenant commanded a "section" of three tanks in the platoon, while the Staff Sergeant commanded the other "section" of two tanks. When the Squad had "gelled" into a team, wise squad leaders undertook to cross-train each member to do another's job. A squad could never have enough trained drivers, so that in the worst case scenario the last man standing could drive everyone else to safety. So just about everyone was trained to drive, and most trainees had gotten more than average "seat time" while the 781st was running the Million Dollar Tank Test.

Interior surfaces of the tank's crew area were white when new. Cleaning facilities were naturally limited in the field, and the floors suffered. After a death, the maintenance crews would clean up the blood/gore as best they could and repaint the surfaces that were stained. But it was common for bloodstained vehicles to be delivered back into service, and some of these smelled horribly when they got warm, because the blood/gore got under the turret basket or somewhere else where it couldn't be cleaned.

All during this time at Knox, new inductees were being assigned to the 781st. Homer Turner was transferred from one of the seed Battalions, and hadn't even completed his basic training when he was taken to a tank driving range and taught how to drive a tank. Homer had learned to drive his father's gas trucks when he was 12, so the whole driving "thing" came naturally. So naturally in fact that the training commander took note, and he was shanghaied and made a tank driving instructor for six weeks before he was allowed to finish his basic! Homer was eventually promoted to Gunner and then became a Tank Commander in HQ Company, commanding one of the Assault Guns under Lt. Yonkers. Homer transferred what he learned to his crew's driver, Adolph Hoppi.

Adolph Hoppi at Fort Knox, 1942. (Courtesy of Hoppi Family)

Adolph was from Simsbury, Connecticut, and transferred to the 781st with Homer from the 191st; he was assigned to "Hot Box," Homer's tank, as the Driver. As a tank Driver, Adolph sat in the left front, on a lightly padded seat which was adjustable both fore/aft and up/down in an initially claustrophobic pit. When seated, there was an instrument panel at shoulder height to his left front. In front of Adolph, the heavy front armor plate (Glacis) of the tank sloped away, and there were a couple of periscopes which allowed a limited view around the tank, but they were rather clunky to use. Being behind a periscope was great when the lead was flying, but all this periscope movement was pretty hard to manipulate with all the other levers and buttons calling for attention, so it was common for Drivers when not under fire to leave the overhead hatch open and use the U.S. Army Mark One Eyeball (adjust the seat all the way up and swivel your head to view your surroundings).

Once seated, Adolph found his feet were trapped in a narrow slot that was filled with pedals and levers. Under his left foot was the clutch pedal; under his right was the accelerator. And right about there is where any similarity to a car ends. In between Adolph's knees he found two long levers that stuck up to about chest height – the steering brakes. When underway, pulling on the right lever applied a brake to the right hand track, which caused the tank to slow down on the right and therefore turn to the right. Left worked the opposite way. Drivers could not "ride the brakes," or they would overheat and glaze. While the manuals stressed keeping the driver's hands off the brakes until needed, experienced drivers kept their hands lightly on the levers "just in case." The Sherman differential could completely stop the braked track and allow the track to make a tight turn, but it could not reverse one track while going forward on the other to pivot the vehicle in place like the German Panther could. Even then, only the strongest Sherman Drivers could hold the one brake lever hard enough to make a complete skid turn around a locked track. The normal minimum turning radius was 80 feet, so this was not a sports car.

For smooth operation, Adolph would apply more throttle when making a turn to maintain a steady speed and be smooth, or the tank would lurch around the bend and rough up the occupants. Slowing down was done by pulling both levers back equally and simultaneously. On Adolph's right side was a large casting that housed the transmission. The gear shift lever nestled next to his right knee. The transmission had five forward gears, but first gear was only used to creep, or to tow another vehicle. Normal operation started in second and progressed through fifth gear. Flat out the Sherman could hit maybe 30mph, unless the crew had diddled with the engine speed governor, and then Drivers could push the engine beyond red line until the valves began to float.

Adolph was schooled to notify the crew when he was going to turn or hit bumpy terrain so they could brace themselves and avoid impact with interior parts. Drivers were taught to "be kind to the Gunner" – avoid jerky starts and stops and turns, because the Gunner usually had his forehead against the sight and it would cause him to knock his head. Drivers had a lot of responsibility: place the tank in the best position to fire as quickly as possible, minimizing the vulnerability to enemy fire, and be able to start, move, turn, and stop smoothly when the crew was firing the gun. After the commander and gunner, the driver was typically the most senior crewman. Being a Driver wasn't especially hard, but being a *good* Driver took talent. Homer taught his tank's driver, Adolph Hoppi, to be a *good* Driver!

On June 14, 1943, Francis Mitzel was drafted. He reported to the Reception Center in his home town of Akron, Ohio, and received his induction and elementary training, and afterward was assigned to the Armored Force Replacement Train-

Half track. (U.S. Army, NARA)

ing Center at Fort Knox for basic training. After two weeks' training he then was assigned to the 781st and reported on June 27th. The reason for his assignment to a tank battalion is unknown, as he possessed zero mechanical ability and he knew it. He was nicknamed "Slats" for a while until the Army chow (which he *loved* if it was drenched in catsup) filled out his large frame, and then he became known as "Tiny" in deference to his size. He was assigned to the Mortar Platoon in HQ Company.

The HQ Mortar Platoon was commanded by a Lieutenant with seven noncommissioned officers and 17 Enlisted men, all mounted in four half tracks. The Mortar Platoon was led by the Lieutenant, who rode with a Staff Sergeant, a driver, and four riflemen in the first half track. Three mortar squads, each having a Sergeant, a gunner (Corporal rank), an assistant gunner, a driver, and two ammo handlers, followed in each of the three mortar half tracks.

The mortar half track M4A1 looked like the unholy mating of a Deuce-and-a-half with a light tank. The front looked like a very angular truck, and all the hood and fenders were thick steel. Where the rear axle *should* have resided was instead a set of tank treads, except instead of being steel, these were all rubber, very much like two giant rubber bands wrapped around the sprockets and wheels. There's a large rolling pin mounted on the front behind the bumper, and behind the cab was a large steel box. Inside the steel box was the mortar, which resembled a pipe that's about four inches in diameter and angled at 45 degrees toward the back of the vehicle. Most also mounted a .30 cal and a .50 cal machine gun for close-in defense.

The Half Track had space for eight, seating three in the cab. It was 20 feet long, had 4-wheel drive with a hi/lo range, and weighed nine tons. In two-wheel drive mode it could go 45mph, so it could outrun a medium tank. In 4-wheel drive mode, the transfer case was in high or low range, and the track was limited to 18mph in low range. The track had a four-speed transmission, but it was not synchromesh, so double clutching was required. The six cylinder engine got 3.5 miles per gallon, and its range was about 200 miles.

The light armor of the body would stop a rifle bullet, but the open top was a problem in the woods, where tree limbs would cause air bursts of rockets, shells, and mortar rounds. Engaging a tank, even a light tank, in a half track was suicidal. Like most things in the armored realm, the proper use of a mortar platoon was being developed. Mortar squads were typically placed at the rear of an advancing armored column, at the front of a retreat, and on the inside of a flank position. If an engagement occurred, the mortars were to find the nearest position to get shooting – don't waste time looking for the perfect firing position, just get shooting!

Once shooting, Mortars had two types of rounds to launch: High Explosive (HE) and Smoke. Smoke was intended to be used most often, and was used to blind hostile observation points, guns, and attacking forces. As was the case for the tank rounds, the mortar's Smoke shell was actually white phosphorous, and it produced smoke, but it also excelled at setting things on fire, which included people. The range for Smoke shells was 2,470 yards; it had a burst radius of 10 yards, it would produce smoke for 30 seconds after exploding, and provided a screen that was 75 yards long downwind. The Mortar team had a tough assignment to keep the enemy blind while making sure the smoke dissipated just at the right time for your attacking troops, or covering a withdrawal by blinding the enemy but not smoking out your friends. HE was used to take out enemy machine guns, mortars, and personnel, and was used to destroy barricades, structures, buildings, or other things that were "in the way."

Alternately, the mortar squad would be placed to cover an intersection or set point target where the enemy was most likely to appear. Usually mortars were placed on the top of a hill so the firing computations were easier and the tube could get into action faster with the fall of shot observed directly by the squad. When shooting, the front wheels of the half track were turned all the way to the right or left, so that the weapon could be traversed by moving the track forward or backward.

Pay: Up to 1943, Privates were paid $21 per month. Less than fully-honest recruiters tempted recruits with the promise of being paid $21 a day (which was huge money in 1941!), but they may have neglected to mention that it was only once a month that you were paid that $21! A song "Twenty-One Dollars a Day, Once a Month" came out in 1941 and people wised up. Starting in 1943, a private made $50 per month. But don't get excited, Private! That was what you had before the deductions started. Deduct laundry fees, life insurance fees, clothing fees, and repayment for the stuff you bought at the local post store (the Post Exchange, or "PX), and the average PFC didn't have too much to show for his labors. Overseas duty added between $2.75 to $5 per day, depending on the station and hazardous nature of the duty.

In August 1943, the annual inspection by the Army's Inspector General rated the 781st Tank Battalion as "Excellent." As a reward for the fine showing, Lt. Col

Kinne gave the Battalion a half-day off. The marksmanship of the Battalion was notable in the report, with 100% of the men qualifying with their principle weapon. Overall, "C" Company had the highest percentage of marksmen, and was designated as the Battalion Color Guard until some other Company dethroned them.

In September 1943, the Armored Force Board tested a Horizontal Volute Spring Suspension (HVSS) system that had wider tracks and more bogies, and that was a success; better in durability, less tendency to throw a track, better flotation, and a smoother ride (the HVSS suspension had shocks and the VVSS didn't). This test was a direct result of the "Million Dollar Tank Test" findings.

The AFB also tested an M4 with the 90mm gun in the fall of 1943, and recommended its adoption and installation on one thousand tanks. But General McNair turned it down (tanks didn't fight other tanks in his world, and he wanted the 90mm to go into tank destroyers). Also, the Infantry brass resisted the proposition to place 90mm guns in an infantry tank because the short-barreled 75mm had the better HE shell, which was what the Infantry divisions wanted.

Meanwhile, in Europe, the Germans were training their tank crews to lead off with an AP round as their first shot against U.S. tanks. High Explosive was only used in the German doctrine against infantry or artillery. At the same time, U.S. crews were being taught to shoot their machine guns at the enemy tank and watch their tracers to correct range errors (also giving away your position!) before they took their first shot. After that, they were supposed to watch the fall of their shot and try to bracket their opponent, then zero in for the kill. Meanwhile, the German crews relied on a magnesium tracer that was in the base of their AP shell to make corrections. They were trained to try to get a direct hit on the first round, and only fell back on the old "naval gunnery" tomfoolery when they failed on the first attempt. The German crews also adjusted for range errors by moving their tank, rather than changing gun elevation. They were trained to engage single tanks at 1,000-2,000 meters, and groups of tanks at 2,000 meters. More tellingly, they were taught that a Sherman could do no damage to a Panther or Tiger, and to not be afraid to engage Shermans even if the German crew was outnumbered two to one! The maximum engagement range was 2,500 meters, although in Russia it was common for the German crews to engage Grants and Shermans at 3,000 meters with good result.

And in return, the outgunned Sherman crews had to experiment and extemporize. Loaders in Shermans had a choice of three different types of rounds, and recognized the type of round by the color and markings: black tips with white letters were armor-piercing (AP). Olive Drab tips with yellow letters were High Explosive (HE). The last was White Phosphorous (WP) (nicknamed "Willy Pete") smoke rounds (grey). HE was most commonly used. (Since the Armor-piercing rounds didn't work so well, Sherman crews would fire High Explosive Rounds at Panzers routinely, because they might at least knock off a track at much longer ranges than they could penetrate the armor.) To use AP, the crew had to get *close* to the Panzer.

Another improvisation was using WP against armor. The WP round was then, and is still somewhat controversial, depending on how one looks at it. When the WP round impacted, it broke into pieces that burned with a bright, white-hot light at 2,750°F, and made dense clouds of white smoke. The burning phosphorous would readily start fires, wherein lies the problem, as the use of WP for illumination and smoke was "allowed" by the rules of warfare, but it was not sanctioned for use against people. The "rules of war" were broken; WP was used against infantry and armor, and it was expectedly really effective. The Sherman crews found they could use the WP round to trick the German tank crews into abandoning their vehicles. (They were just as afraid of a fire as the American tank crews.) The White Phosphorous shards would ignite any spilled oil or grease and cause a surface fire, and if you saw flames and you thought your tank was on fire, the one place you didn't want to be was *inside* it. Even if the German crew didn't evacuate, the WP smoke blinded the Panzer and gave the outgunned Shermans time to get closer and maneuver. The enemy then had to reacquire the Sherman when it exited the smoke.

Trained squads then learned to operate together with other squads in other vehicles, training at the "platoon" level. Tactical Platoon training took place: marches, firing positions, security, offensive action, defensive action, retreats (a.k.a. "retrograde movement"), and special ops, both as a squad and with platoon. The Platoons then repeated the training on a larger scale, as Platoons learned to operate as a Company. Again, Companies learned to operate together. Finally, the whole Battalion learned to move as a single entity.

Lastly, the 781st needed to train with Infantry. But Fort Knox wasn't big enough, and didn't house Infantry to facilitate that training. So the 781st had to move on to get combined training with other groups. When completely trained, the Tank Battalion would be proficient in operating with Infantry and *vice-versa*, which was what they were designed to do.

And after twenty-two months service testing armored vehicles and equipment for the Armored Force Board, the 781st got word that it was moving on to the "Big Show." The extended time at Knox gave them some huge advantages. This Battalion knew the current vehicles in use frontwards and backwards; they knew all their idiosyncrasies and how to maintain them. Better yet, they were also in a unique spot and knew about equipment that was in the pipeline. The 781st was well versed in Company, Platoon, and Squad-level operations. They also had a great administration and procedure set up. Most of the men were cross-trained, and all of them could aim and shoot.

Several long-standing relationships between the men and locals came to an end as families said goodbye to soldiers who had shared their tables and lives were now moving on.

8. MOVING OUT

The 781st underwent reorganization on October 18, 1943, and it changed from having an HQ Company with three mixed tank Companies (A/B/C) to having four tank companies – all the M5 Stuart Light tanks were collected from the three now medium-tank-only Companies and they formed a new "D" Company. This gave the Battalion a nice striking force with the medium companies, and let the Light tanks assume their more natural role as scouts, covering forces, and exploitation. Each company in the 781st Tank Battalion had 15 tanks, and the HQ Company had their own reserve of about half a dozen tanks.

The new "D" Company was largely staffed with men who were "nominated" by the A/B/C Company Commanding Officers. Even though they were not supposed to do so, the other company commanders naturally used this opportunity to clean house. Malcontents, slackers, wise-guys, dimwits, criminals, square pegs, losers, whatever – they were *all* sent to Company "D". As Joe Graham, who was at that point the Executive Officer of "C" Company under David Kelly, put it: "C" Company ended up as a better-staffed Company after we unloaded our transferees to 'D' Company." He would later be haunted by this.

In other words, "D" Company was "F Troop"; they knew they were castoffs, and they pretty quickly earned the nickname "The Raggedy-Assed Cadets" within the Battalion. There were other less flattering nicknames used, as well. Their first CO was Lt. William Kaiser, who had been XO in "A" Company, and he struggled mightily against the "RAC" and their ornery mind set for months, but wasn't able to make a dent. The "RAC" was belligerently proud of their nickname, and they wouldn't lift a pinkie to change it.

One man assigned to the new "D" Company to provide a solid core on which to build was Sgt. Frederick Williams. At thirty-three, he was the second-oldest man in the Company, and was known as the "Old Man." Well-respected by the enlisted men and officers alike, he was the man that everyone went to for advice and help.

He never bought into the "RAC" mind set, and he commanded a tank in First Platoon.

A Tank Commander (TC) was the heart and soul of a tank. As such, Fred was a great choice. In today's parlance, the TC was supposed to maintain "situational awareness," which is fancy speak for knowing what's going on around you. The TC had to keep an eye out for possible enemy activity, direct the driver where to position the vehicle, and call out targets to the gunner in order of their potential threat. When the TC spotted a target, he would alert the gunner and say the type of target and the ammunition to load (only for green gunners). The command sequence was supposed to be: "Gunner (announcing the crew position you are speaking to)/ Type of target/ Shot type to load / Traverse left or right (which way the gunner should turn the turret to see this target)/ "Steady" (keep turning) or "On" (when facing the target) / Range (estimate how far away the target is)/ "Fire." That was theory; in reality, whatever worked quickly was used. For example: "Gunner-tank-HE." The TC told the gunner which way to traverse the turret to acquire the target, because the TC had a wider field of view, so he guided the gunner to the target and gave him clues when to slow down (the word "steady") and when he was pointed at the target ("on"): "Gunner: Right..Right..Steady.. steady..on." The crewmember's last name was also used in place of the position. The TC also operated the radio, and in well-trained crews was backed up by the loader. Overall, the TC was the center of success if he did his job well and the reason you died if he didn't.

Vince Sutphin at last got his chance. He used the reorganization to get reassigned from HQ clerking to be in 1st Platoon of Company "B" as a Tank Driver in S/Sgt Elmer Shepherd's Sherman. Vince soon moved into the Gunner's seat for the rest of the war.

After reorganization the Battalion was sent to Camp Shelby, Mississippi, the Mississippi state National Guard training center that was taken over by Uncle Sam for the duration of WWII.

Gerald Mercier, 20, was working at the American Bosch factory outside Springfield, Massachusetts, and was engaged to be married when he got his draft notice. Gerry trained with the 8th Armored at Camp Polk, Louisiana, so he was well acquainted with the weather. He was then assigned to the 781st, and joined up with them when they reached Camp Shelby.

Gerry was trained to be a tank gunner and was assigned to "A" Company. Gunners were senior crewmen next to the tank Commander and had great responsibility to shoot first, accurately. The Gunner was seated on a padded seat immediately in front of the tank Commander on the right side of the main gun. Gerry's main job was to aim and fire the main gun and the turret MG. A monocular telescopic gunsight was to his front left, and a binocular observation periscope immediately to his front. Both had reticles to aid aiming. The British universally decried the periscopic sight, as it got loose and wiggled about in its mount, and gunners took to jamming them with matchsticks to tighten them up in order to have a chance at hitting something. The telescope was preferred, and the periscope was used as the backup. The Panther Gunner lacked a secondary sight, and his scope had a narrow field of view. In a moving fight, the Sherman's wider field of view was an advantage, but at rest it was

Camp Shelby, Mississippi, in 1941. (U.S. Army, NARA)

moot. The Sherman sight was less complex and easier to use than the German sight for a less-expert Gunner, but an expert gunner in a Panther had a real advantage.

The Gunner used a foot pedal to fire the guns. In Gerry's left hand was the elevation crank for raising or lowering the barrel. In his right was a pistol grip-like handle: turning it right to traverse right, left for left, and how fast to turn was controlled by how far the handle was turned. If the electrics failed the gunner could hand-crank the turret, but that was painfully slow.

The Gunner looked for the target as directed by the Commander, acquired it by rotating the turret, and acknowledged finding the target (he was trained to say "Target acquired!," but this degenerated in the heat of battle to "I see it, I see it!," "Got it!," or whatever came out). The Gunner then aimed the gun with the aid of the sight, placed the firing switch in the "on" position, yelled "Ready," moved his eye away from the eyepiece, and then pulled the trigger on the joystick or stepped on the foot switch to fire the gun. (Hopefully the loader had already loaded the gun.) Yelling "Ready" was supposed to give the commander the opportunity to respond "Fire!," but it was one of the "Book" instructions that was often eliminated to save time in combat – the gunner just pulled the trigger. Another time saver was allowing the gunner to specify the type of round instead of the commander. He would use a hand signal to the loader: a fist or one finger for AP, spread hand or two fingers for HE, etc. If the first round missed, the crew kept loading and firing until the target was destroyed or the commander yelled "Cease Fire!" Gerry's crew didn't get much practice in reloading because Gerry Mercier was a very, very good gunner.

Jim Grantland was the loader for Gerry Mercier. Jim's station was located inside the turret to the left of the main gun. As the name implies, Jim's main job was to retrieve the proper round for the main gun from one of the storage bins and load it into the main gun. To load the main gun, the loader grabbed and pulled the breech block handle, which opened the breech. This was usually left open to save time, and sometimes the gun was loaded with Armor-Piercing or High-Explosive ammo before sighting the enemy, again as a time saver to get off that very important first shot. The type of round to be pre-loaded was selected by reading the mission orders and the type of target the tank was likely to meet. (While the lead tank of the platoon might pre-load, some platoon leaders didn't want the following tanks to pre-load for fear of being accidentally shot by a trigger-happy following unit.) The loader selected the correct type of round as called for by the Commander or Gunner and pushed it home in the breech with a healthy shove. When it was fully inserted, the shell's rim tripped a catch and the breech closed and set the firing pin. The Loader had some sort of signal, such as yelling/punching/kicking the gunner to let him know the gun was ready, but most gunners just listened for the breech block to slam home and then pushed the fire button. The empty casing was ejected as part of the recoil when the gun was fired. After firing the gun was open and ready for reloading.

Rounds for the main gun were located in several places inside the tank. Some locations required help from the gunner or commander or assistant driver to pass the rounds to the Loader. There was a space for a few ready rounds at the Loader's feet, but these were saved for emergency/short notice use. In reality, because the Loader couldn't ask other crewmen to stop what they were doing during a battle to help pass rounds, it was common for a loader to have several rounds out and ready, piled at his feet. Being unprotected, they would readily light up if the hull was punctured by an incoming round and they were hit by shrapnel. This tendency for unsecured rounds to burn was blamed on the gasoline fuel, and caused a rumor about the flammability of a Sherman that persists to this day. It wasn't the gas, it was the ammunition.

The inter-tank and intra-tank communication situation bears note. When tanks were first fielded, the Army tried using the bugle as an approved means to communicate between tanks. Then they tried semaphore flags, and they finally copied the Germans and used radios. Eavesdropping on your enemy's radio chatter was common and scrambling was not invented yet, so for secure messages, a human messenger would have been used. The on-board radio was used only when other means was unavailable. The radio was in the turret "bustle." Most M4s had an FM set that had a range of 5-20 miles, depending on weather conditions. Power came from the tank's batteries. Some M4s had an AM radio (walkie-talkie) so the tank could speak to the foot soldiers outside on the "walkie-talkie" frequency. Only the commander or loader could speak on the walkie-talkie. (Oddly, German tanks, for all their sophistication in other areas, lacked this.)

To communicate inside the tank, the crew had an intercom. To speak, the crewmember had to press a button on his chest to turn on his mike. This was OK, but the result was pretty unintelligible, and the crew — especially the driver — needed all their hands. The commander had a handheld microphone to transmit clearly (nicknamed the "Pork Chop," as it did resemble a pork chop in shape). Chatter was discouraged, as it would talk over incoming radio messages, so most crews communicated to each other by simply yelling at each other.

At Shelby, the basic military training subjects were completed and small-arms training was emphasized. But almost 100% of the men in the Battalion were already officially qualified on their primary weapon. Those who were qualified used the opportunity to achieve higher rankings. With the exception of "D" Company, there were a high number of marksmen, sharpshooters, expert riflemen, etc., in the line Companies, and even the HQ and Service Companies produced some really good riflemen. Most of the Enlisted men were exposed to the .30 and .50 cal machine guns, many were also qualified in their use, and quite a few became first class marksmen on the heavy weapons, as well.

The Machine Gun on top of the tank turret was either a .50 or .30 cal. These fired bullets that were one-half inch (.50 cal) or one-third of an inch in diameter (.30 cal). The M4 started off with a .50 caliber, then changed to a .30 in late '42, then went back to the .50 in April '43. The .50 caliber was a wonderfully powerful gun, and was used to flush targets, reveal hidden AT gun teams, set fire to things (houses, barns, haystacks), and scare the hell out of the Krauts. The Commander would fire the gun at a seemingly innocuous target – a haystack, for example. If the .50 slugs ricocheted off something in the haystack, they then used the main gun to obliterate it. The half-inch diameter slugs could punch through everything short of a tank, and the hydraulic shock when it hit the human body meant a man was down no matter where he was hit. The .50 caliber did have downsides: it required the Commander to be significantly exposed to shoot it, .50 cal ammo was not as plentiful as .30, and the .50 was not very effective as an anti-aircraft gun due to its size and bulk. So crews swapped both ways according to preference.

Alas, "D" Company was notable only for their almost complete lack of mention when the marksmen awards were given out. It was not for lack of motivation, as everyone was motivated to be a good shot as a primary means of self-preservation. Nor was it lack of talent, as they later proved they could hit their mark when called upon to do so in battle. The consensus of opinion holds that the damn "Raggedy Ass Cadets" simply *chose* to "miss" the target when they were being tested! This entire Battalion, "D" Company included, knew how to shoot and hit a target with all the weapons in their inventory.

In November, the 781st didn't have to deal with the steam bath that Mississippi became in high summer. But with the winter rains, Shelby was a muddy mess and not suitable for combined operations. The armor couldn't go off road without miring, and the only part of the battalion that got a good workout at Camp Shelby was the tank retriever section. As for personal comfort, Homer Turner remembers that "Shelby was tick city – the bunks were infested!" The only good thing about Shelby was that it was close to New Orleans when it came time for leave. Col Kinne raised a ruckus and tried to get the 781st out of there. While they waited, the companies got their initial training in tank gunnery and practiced operating in sections, platoons, and company-level groups, but kept to the roads.

EW Rhodes and his tank "Dynamite" at Camp Shelby. (Courtesy of Rhodes family)

Whom do you call when your 30-ton Sherman tank breaks down or gets stuck? Triple A? A normal tow truck isn't going to budge it! Enter the M32 Tank Recovery Vehicle. Take an M4 Sherman, remove the turret, and add a large winch and a large "A" Frame that pivoted at the front of the hull. While the TRV was armored, it could, and frequently did, recover vehicles while under small arms fire, but since the armor was just as vulnerable as the Sherman's, they couldn't expose themselves if the antitank rounds were still flying. Towing a Sherman required two towing cables, one on each front or rear corner. Look at pictures of Shermans, and you will see that each Sherman carried one cable, on the theory that if one tank was going to tow a second tank, they would have the two required cables between them. So don't forget that the Sherman tank's version of "Triple A Service" still required someone to dismount and connect the towing cables and fasten the tow eyes to the tow loops. Snipers knew this, and frequently waited quietly until they could get a shot at the TRV crew.

In December 1943, production of the second-generation Sherman pilot vehicles began. This was the "Easy-Eight" version, which incorporated many of the improvements tested and proven by the 781st while at Knox. (Better hatches, better suspension, providing a commander's cupola for better visibility and protection, thicker armor, and wet storage of ammo.) The first of these vehicles were delivered for test in February 1944.

In March 1944, the Sherman tank's Horizontal Volute Spring Suspension (HVSS), tested and recommended by the AFB while the 781st was at Fort Knox, was adopted for use by the U.S. Army. Right after this, Lt. Colonel Kinne finally persuaded the brass that Shelby wasn't suitable, and the 781st got orders to move. They were originally bound for Fort Rucker, Alabama. This was an outstandingly bad choice as an alternative to Shelby, as Fort Rucker's 58,000 acres were also wet farmland that was just itching to swallow a tank or two. Everything was set, and then someone came to their senses and those orders were revoked. On April 16th new orders came, sending the 781st to Fort Jackson, South Carolina. Fort Jackson had 52,000 acres of land in the midlands of South Carolina near Columbia. Best of all, it wasn't a swamp.

Combat training at Jackson built on what they had learned at Shelby. Here they continued to learn the finer points of tank gunnery, and learned how to maneuver in larger and larger groups, up to and including learning the ins and outs of tactical operations at the Battalion level.

Around this time, Lt. Col. Kinne decided that the so-far incorrigible "Raggedy Ass Cadets" were in need of a new CO. Their first CO went back to Company "A," and Company "D" was reassigned to Lieutenant Joe Graham. Lt. Graham struggled to find a way to break the "RAC" mind set of his new Company, instill some healthy pride, and bring them back into the fold, but he knew that he was also reaping what he had sown when he "unloaded" his dregs of "C" Company back in October.

On June 6, 1944, the Allied forces in Europe successfully landed via amphibious assault on the beaches in Normandy, in northwestern France. This was huge. The Allies had been making significant advances in Italy after the Italians had surrendered the previous fall, and in the Pacific, the Japanese tide of expansion had at last been stopped at Guadalcanal. The Russians were engaged in a brutal slugging match on the Eastern Front, but the European Western Front had yet to be challenged. Hitler had his Wehrmacht build an impressive string of defenses along the coastline from Norway to Spain, commanded by none other than Erwin Rommel (a.k.a. "The Desert Fox" of Africa fame), and was boasting that his "Fortress Europe" was invincible. Breaking through Hitler's "Atlantic Wall" created a second front, which took pressure off the Russians, and was a tremendous morale boost for the home front, as well as for the 781st.

Lt. Joe Graham was Officer of the Day for the evening of June 5th/6th, and was keeping guard over a quiet Battalion while they slept in Fort Jackson. He was listening to a Columbia, South Carolina, radio station early in the morning when the news broke. (The invasion started in the early morning of June 6th in Normandy, which is five hours ahead of South Carolina. By the time the news broke – around noon in London – it was about 7 a.m. in SC.) First Lieutenant Joe Graham called Lt. Colonel Kinne, sent guards to awaken the camp, and generally spread the news: "It's on the radio…We're in France… The Invasion is on and we're moving inland!" He recalls "The Entire camp came alive with yells and whoops!"

Later on D-Day, the Mortar Squad was on maneuvers with the command half track riding down a sandy, wooded stretch that came to a fork in the road with a single pine tree standing in the center of the fork.

A classic "Three Stooges" episode followed – "Go left – No, right, no, left!" – that ended up with the half track center punching the tree. This comedic error was most likely abetted by the driver violating the rule that the hand throttle was not to be used as a sort of "Cruise Control." A rather common thing to do despite the rules, if the driver had set the hand throttle, when he lifted off the gas and stepped on the brake the half track would not slow down. (When one thinks about that, this is probably why there was a rule about that!)

The roller on the front of the half track hit the tree and started pushing the tree over, and the momentum of nine tons *kept* pushing. But the half track wasn't going fast enough or wasn't heavy enough to push this tree *all* the way over – it leaned to a 20-degree list and there it stopped, but the half track kept gliding up the trunk, guided by the trunk between the front wheels, until it stopped, unable to climb, unable to push the tree all the way down, and most importantly, unable to back down off the tree. The crew spent most of D-Day stuck up a tree in a half track, waiting for a tow to come and yank them back down. Fortunately, the incident was forgotten or overlooked in the D-Day excitement.

In the meantime, someone in Washington had gotten a request that a light tank company be detailed for special duty. Shortly after, an order arrived on Lt. Col. Kinne's desk. Lt. Col Kinne was no doubt having heart palpitations as he passed the orders down. Lt. Joe Graham received the orders to take his Company "D" and report to Camp Wainwright, in Alberta, Canada, for temporary duty. Their mission? Secret! What's more, they only had three days to prepare and pack the Company for movement! The men of Company "D" had scattered for the weekend. Troops were detailed to find and collect the RAC from furloughs and their normal haunts.

The Raggedy Ass Cadets (who to this date had also successfully resisted all of Lieutenant Graham's reform efforts), and their justifiably nervous CO, boarded their train and departed for Wainwright on time. But a funny thing happened. By this time, "D" Company's men had started to believe that they had been selected for this special assignment, not because they just happened to be available, or they were the light tank Company that was closest to being fully trained, or for some other more likely reason, but they believed they were selected because they were the best light tank company in the U.S. Army! The rest of the 781st just prayed sending the RAC to Canada wouldn't result in an international incident.

"D"/781st and all their equipment arrived in western Canada and learned their assignment: the Allied Army Top Brass wanted to explore if tanks and infantry could be employed successfully together while operating under a thick smoke screen. The idea was to use large smoke screen generators that billowed a steam and diesel smoke mix to blanket the area where an attack was planned. Under the smoke screen cover, the combined teams were supposed to attack, with their movement and noise masked by the smoke. They were supposed to arrive at the objective *en masse* and unscathed just as the screen would dissipate, and take the objective from a startled and overwhelmed foe. This was what a tank battalion's Mortar Platoon routinely did on a small scale, but this was expanding the scope to enormity, at a Brigade-level scale. "D" Company would join the Royal Canadian 6th Infantry Brigade to make it work.

And by this time "D" Company, who were now positively convinced that they were the best damned light tank company in the U.S. Army, pitched in and tried to prove it! The RAC set up their tents in the camp in precisely straight rows, parked their vehicles in meticulously straight lines (they aligned the front bumpers with taut lengths of string!), and erected a birch wood archway with the U.S. Armored triangular emblem and the company name on it over the pathway to their area. To cap it all, they gathered stones and lined all the pathways in their camp, and then they *whitewashed the stones*! (The transformation from devils into angels wasn't complete, however; the mischief makers didn't entirely reform.)

Because the best time to test the smoke generators was at sunrise or sunset, when there would be little wind to blow away the smoke, the test location made a lot of sense. Camp Wainwright was so far north, in June the nights were very short and the sunset/sunrises were very long, so the tests could run from 9:00PM to 4:00AM. The tactics that evolved had the tanks and infantry "riding" a radio beacon toward the target while cloaked in smoke. The radio receiver would emit a steady "eeeee" when on the correct path, short "beeps" if they were to the right, and long "beeps" if they were too far to the left. The biggest challenge was for the tanks and infantry to stay close but not collide, or worse, have tanks flatten the GIs. They conducted close to 20 trials over the six week time period they were at Wainwright and developed some useful tactics. The tactics were later improved by having the infantry ride on the tanks (as the Soviets commonly did).

Deemed successful, this technique was later used in several operations in Europe, the most famous being operation VARSITY, conducted on March 24, 1945. VARSITY was another joint American-British effort, and was the largest single airborne operation in one day at a single location, with its objective of crossing the Rhine River in western Germany. The VARSITY operation was a success, and it used the combined arms training using smokescreen cover pioneered by "D" Company of the 781st. The 781st also had a couple of opportunities to use this technique themselves in the upcoming months.

D/781st were becoming the best damned light tank company in the U.S. Army for real! The Canadian General at Wainwright inquired of Lt. Graham if, in their spare time, the light tanks might participate in some exercises, and Lt. Graham agreed. So in their spare time, when they weren't developing smoke tactics, D/781st worked with the Canadians to improve the two groups' teamwork in regular tank/infantry roles. At times, these team building sessions were "live-fire" exercises that were amazingly real. The reality may have been augmented by the RAC devils still having some "fun" – during live-fire exercises, some guys thought it might be fun to shoot a round or two close to their leader's helmet to see if he would notice! In his memoirs Joe Graham mentions that "there was a lot of lead flying close," so apparently he did.

As an aside, during this session the members of "D" Company were paid for "Overseas Duty" and got an extra 10% pay. While the local area didn't offer too much for recreational facilities, the men enjoyed the extra 10% on top of the favorable exchange rate for the U.S. dollar at the time. When they had time off, the men boarded a train and headed to either Saskatoon, Manitoba, or Edmonton, Alberta.

When the trials were over, a newly-cohesive "D" Company left Canada with fanfare, well wishes from the Canadians, and a newly promoted CO – Lt. Joe Graham received his promotion telegram and new Captain's bars as the train was pulling out of the station!

"D" Company also left with a new mascot – an eagle they somehow kidnapped and named "Saskatoon" in honor of their favorite Canadian watering hole. Saskatoon was fed a steady diet of hot dogs while in captivity. On his first opportunity after arriving at Fort Jackson, Saskatoon escaped and was last seen winging northwest, probably in search of a decent meal. On their return to the railroad station near Jackson, the conquering heroes expected to be met with fanfare, but due to a scheduling snafu nobody was there. So "D" Company marched from the station to the base, and they were congratulated by Lt. Col. Kinne for their *outstanding* performance.

From the actual message from Major General Ganong of the Canadian Army to Col Kinne, which triggered another memo from the Canadian Joint Staff in Washington to the U.S. War Department (!), and was endorsed by just about everyone in the U.S. Army chain of command and flowed down to Lt. Col Kinne, who probably passed out:

**"Officer Commanding
781st U.S.A. Tank Battalion**

I would like to express to you my appreciation of the splendid co-operation given by Lt. Graham and all the ranks of "D" Company of your unit during the time they were in Wainwright Military Camp.

On attachment here for a certain specific purpose, they nevertheless went all out in assisting our training in every way possible, and co-operated in a most whole-hearted manner in all our exercises and manoeuvres.

The efficiency of the Company was very marked, and their conduct during the entire period of attachment was exemplary. They reflected great credit to your unit and your corps, and made a splendid impression on all ranks of this Division. Such contacts are of inestimable value to both nations, now and in the years to come.

My personal thanks to you, to Lt. Graham, and all the grand lads in his Company.

**Sincerely,
H.N.Ganong Maj Gen 6 Cdn. Div."**

While "D" Company was in Canada, the rest of the Battalion went to Fort Pickett, VA, for a month. Pickett was new in 1941, and had 45,000 acres set up with infantry training in mind to be done at the divisional level, which required the space. It had 1,400 buildings, its own airfield, four movie theaters, a gym, several "Officer's" clubs, and lots of "PXs." The 781st conducted combined arms training there, supporting the 78th Infantry Division in its pre-deployment training. Here, the 781st learned to operate with infantry, and the infantry learned to operate with tanks. This training was later to prove invaluable. Toward the end of July, the Battalion got its combat alert and had to cut short this exercise, and returned to Fort Jackson and prepared to deploy.

While they waited for deployment details, the tank companies were schooled in indirect fire techniques using their main gun. ("Indirect fire" refers to the technique of shooting at a target when you can't see the target. Hits are obtained by lobbing shells instead of shooting like a bullet.) The men could now shoot their 75mm rifles as well as their small arms. By this time, when compared to a "normal" independent Tank Battalion, the 781st would have been spectacularly trained, and familiar in the use of the new equipment being thrown at them. They had been together for two years and were very familiar with each other, as well as their equipment and its foibles and maintenance. They helped develop some of the tank/infantry tactics in use. They had so much time together that most crew members would have been cross-trained on other positions and could fill in when someone was injured. On the other hand, tactical training was a waste, as it wasn't based in reality – it was based in 1918, because armored units hadn't seen battle since then. When the units arrived overseas, they had to pick up the training on the fly or literally die trying. Upon arrival, they were hopefully given enough time for a face-to-face session with a veteran unit to let word of mouth training improve the odds of survival.

By this time in the war, their German opponents would have been a mix of the battle-hardened and exhausted veterans and very poorly trained replacements. The best replacements were wounded Panzer corps vets returning to action, followed by ex-Kriegsmarine or Luftwaffe people who were being reassigned – they were probably gun shy, or exhausted or demoralized because their aircraft and ships were decimated, but at least they knew what service life was like. The raw recruits were grim. They would receive basic training and not much else. Most had never fired the main gun, or even been in a tank when they reported to their unit. Drivers were passed with only a couple of hours seat time (this inexperience led to increased transmission failure rates in Panthers), and what meager time the trainees got was usually spent in captured or obsolete vehicles, which wasn't always of use. There was no fuel or ammunition with which to practice, and because of allied air superiority, the tanks couldn't move around very much anyway. Additionally, since the service life of the Panther was so low they didn't want to use them up in practice. Veterans tried to teach newbies by word of mouth, but the casualty rate among officers caused people to be promoted before their time, and the leaders were struggling as they tried to learn their new tasks.

The average panzer regiment suffered higher casualties than the worst case U.S. tank units. Especially hard put were new Panther gunners, as the Panther gun sight, although superior to the Sherman's for a well-trained gunner, was tough to use for an untrained gunner. Estimating range and crossing speed of a target was done by comparing the target's apparent size and movement to a series of small etched triangles in the reticle. All well and good for a trained gunner, but this was *waaay* too hard for a newbie. So they tended to use the coax MG to gage range, but this gave away the first shot, just as the Americans were trained to do. Also, the gunner had to rotate the reticle to adjust for the type of projectile being fired. (Different shot needed different trajectories – if the loader loaded one and the gunner adjusted for another it would be an automatic "miss.") Shermans didn't have this problem – they had to fire at less than 1,000 yards to get a hit, and at those ranges the different rounds had the same trajectory. So the untrained German gunners were giving up one of the most important advantages they had over the Sherman – the ability to stand off at long range and kill their opponent while they were out of range themselves.

The Operation ANVIL Landings started August 15, 1944, with Generals Devers and Patch commanding. The Germans expected any invasion to be concurrent with D-Day. Since ANVIL was late, events in Normandy caused the Germans to withdraw troops from the south of France to support their counterattack at Mortain, France. When that counterattack also failed to repel the Normandy invaders, the Germans considered withdrawal of all troops from France to defensive positions within the Reich. For some reason, the Germans never considered using the troops in Italy to flank attack the ANVIL landings.

The Allies first destroyed all the bridges over the Rhone River, which runs northwards from the Marseille area, cutting off the invasion site from the west and making German redeployment of what resources were available really difficult. On the eve of the landing, the German defenses were woefully unprepared to resist an amphibious assault. On the Allied side, capturing Marseilles quickly was imperative, as it was the only port that could handle the anticipated supply volumes. Anything less and the bad supply situation would get radically worse, as there weren't enough landing craft yet available. The landings went very well, and the Allies pursued a weakened and shattered foe north toward Germany.

The first phase of the "Champagne Campaign" drove the Germans back to the Franco-German border faster and at less cost than expected, but instead of praise from his boss, Devers was criticized by Ike for not completely destroying the opposing forces. By the third quarter of 1944, the Allied troops were very tired. The logistical lines for the Allies were now much longer, while those for the Germans were correspondingly shorter. German opposition in Southern France had a lot of PzKw IVs and few Tigers or Panthers, as the first-line equipment had largely been sent to repel the Normandy invaders. This front was heavily equipped with captured vehicles from other theatres. While there were a few odd tanks roaming about, this was especially true for artillery and transport vehicles, where there was a hodgepodge of everything – Russian, Czech, Polish, French, etc. This made the logistical problem for the Germans much worse, and saw a resurgence of horse transport as the mélange of vehicles broke down. The Germans needed a break to regroup and resupply to mount an effective border defense. The Allies paused to reorganize their command structure and realign priorities, which provided that break.

Back at Jackson, overseas preparations for the 781st got into full swing. As part of shipping out, worn equipment was exchanged for new. Companies A, B, and C got to turn in their Wright radial-engine M1A1 tanks for new ones, and now the 781st realized some of the fruits of their labors at Knox. They received new M1A3s with the Ford GAA engine, but some were still armed with the now-outdated 75mm gun. The HQ Assault Gun Platoon had to keep their "old" 105mm tanks, as they weren't being made with the better engine. (They eventually did get new tanks, as we shall see.) The Preparation for Overseas Movement requirements dictated, in conjunction with the Table of Organization and Equipment, everything that a tank battalion should have packed prior to departure, down to spare parts and toilet paper. They also required everyone to be certified as physically fit. So tanks weren't the only new equipment the 781st received: Jeeps, trucks, tents, cooking equipment – everything that an outfit of that size needed to function. Colonel Kinne even got a new trailer that would serve as his command center while they were overseas.

Speculation as to their destination was ended when a shipment of wool winter uniforms arrived – the men knew they were headed to Europe. Along with receiving all the new equipment and training in its use, the men were actively involved in becoming the best soldiers they could be at the individual level, learning and proving

The Colonel's Trailer (Up from Marseille).

proficiency on all the weapons they were likely to encounter. Once all the equipment was received, all the training absorbed, and all the checklists were checked, the men were allowed brief leaves to prepare their family and home life for extended overseas duty. It was quite common for the men to have portrait photos taken at this time in their best uniform as hand-tinted images for the family mantle.

At this point, Lt. Colonel Kinne received a top-secret letter from Washington, but not too much should be made of it. Every unit commander that was about to take his unit overseas received a copy of their required operational maps under a Top-Secret-Bigot procedure, as was used for the Normandy invasion planning. The recipient had to have a top-secret clearance. Lt. Col Kinne was restricted from opening his bundle of maps until he was in the final marshalling area at Camp Shanks or on board the ship as it left harbor.

They departed Fort Jackson for Camp Shanks, NY, October 7, 1944. Nicknamed by the G.I.s "Last Stop, USA," Camp Shanks was where troops staged for overseas deployment. It was brand new, having just opened January 4, 1944, and about 30 minutes from Broadway via the Erie railroad. The barracks where the 781st lived while undergoing the processing were each 20' x 100', and had two rows of bunks with three coal-burning stoves (at each end and middle) to provide heat. The objective was to put the battalion through an inspection and make double-sure everything worked and everyone was equipped. A final physical check of persons and equipment took place, and then everything was covered in grease and Cosmoline, wrapped, crated, and packed. The tanks were dropped at a port depot, where they would have been sealed to prevent water entry during the trip. And every square inch of exposed metal got sprayed with Cosmoline. For a great deal of the equipment it was the last time they saw it.

67

Each soldier received two vomit bags and anti-seasickness pills. There was also a last-chance facility where the soldiers could purchase Service Life Insurance and prepare their wills. When the soldiers were done processing, they would be waiting to be placed on "Alert" status, which meant they were leaving within the next 12 hours. After the 781st Tank Battalion had finished processing, everyone was supposed to get a general pass, as a train had been scheduled to take the boys for a visit to Broadway, but it had to be cancelled at the last minute, since they were placed on "Alert." The disappointed soldiers removed their insignia, and their helmets would get marked with chalk with a letter and a number, indicating the proper marching order from the camp to the train and the railroad car to ride in. That train went to Weehawken, NJ, where the troops received doughnuts and coffee, then were ferried out to the proper ships.

The 781st was transported to "ship number 461," which turned out to be the *USS LeJeune*. The *USS LeJeune* was formerly and recently named the "SS *Windhuk*" (pronounced "Vent Hook," named for the capital of Namibia), and was a captured German supply ship for the German pocket battleship "Graf Spee." SS *Winhuk* was built in 1936, and sailed between Hamburg and South Africa until 1939 in a semi-luxury liner mode. She was good-sized, weighed 12 thousand tons, and was 577' long. After the German *Graf Spee* was sunk, the *Windhuk* put into Rio to hide December 7, 1941. Hiding quietly in Rio worked until 1942, when Brazil severed ties with Nazi Germany and *Winhuk* was interned. However, the crew tried to

U.S.S. LeJeune (AA-74). (U.S. Navy Photographic Center, NARA)

sabotage her, ruining her turbines by pouring concrete into them and generally wreaking destruction with cutting torches, etc. She was purchased by the U.S. Navy in May 1942 and new engines were installed, and she was commissioned April 15, 1944. Renamed *USS LeJeune*, she carried about 4,500 men on each trip, and she made ten trips total during the war.

"Our 'stateroom' had been converted from holding two passengers to a total of six (with all our personal combat gear). Poor Lieutenant McIntyre, my Executive Officer! 'Mac' became seasick immediately and 'heaved' all night long. But wait! When we were sent up on deck the next morning for exercise, we found we were still tied up to the dock in Staten Island! 'Mac' stayed seasick the entire voyage."—Capt. Joe Graham

---

The *USS LeJeune* sailed October 13, 1944 – Friday the 13th, as a matter of fact! – in convoy number UGF.16. UGF.16 was a large convoy of 20 ships. The *LeJeune* was the largest vessel in the convoy, which was largely composed of troop ships, tankers, and a few fast cargo ships protected by seven Gleaves class USN destroyers. A "baby flat top," the *HMS Reaper*, also sailed with the convoy, but not as an escort, for she was packed with planes being transported to the UK. The convoy had smooth sailing for the two weeks *en route* across the Atlantic. (Despite what Lieutenant MacIntyre may have thought.) Joe Graham deduced that their route took them south of Bermuda, and hence eastward.

There was the usual hi jinx gambling and interplay between the soldiers and swabbies. Service Company's dog took great delight in soiling the decks to the dismay of the Navy, and this was not the only dog that accompanied the 781st on the *LeJeune*. One of the leaders in "D" Company also brought a dog along. This particular person decided to sleep on deck each night with his dog. Setting up his cot caused a minor disruption each night when everyone else went below deck to sleep. Neither the master nor the dog was much liked by the "RAC," one of whom took the opportunity one dark night while the master went below deck to use the head to launch the poor dog overboard! The deceased dog's master then took the hint and started sleeping below decks like everyone else.

Homer Turner recalls: "The LeJeune had big open troughs for urinals, and a great many men got sick in them. When it came time to select a bunk in the hold – grab a top bunk or get puked on!"

They recognized the Rock of Gibraltar on the 27th, and under a virtual umbrella of Royal Air Force fighters, they turned north for the final high-speed dash to the southern coast of France. When they reached the port of Marseilles it was back on its feet, and the *LeJeune* was able to unload the 781st right onto a dock on the 28th/29th. Marseille had only been "open" for a little over a month. It had been heavily destroyed when the Germans left, and the first Liberty ships began unloading on September 15th. The logistical system was still immature, and areas to receive the supplies being offloaded were also just being set up, moved, etc. Trucks and support vehicles were in especially short supply. Offloaded supplies were piled up haphazardly so the fuel and ammo could be shipped out first, and it was quite common at this point for the logistics personnel to be "digging for the good stuff."

The 781st Tank Battalion arrived in France, walked off the *USS LeJeune*, and headed for their bivouac area outside of town.

9. THE "CHAMPAGNE CAMPAIGN"

Glad to be on dry land, the 781st trudged eight miles out of town to a nameless, barren, windy hillside, erected their shelter halves (pup tents), and set up temporary camp. This was intended to be a short stay in a staging area; staying only long enough to collect their equipment, clean off the Cosmoline, and then move out to join the fight. But due to some misplaced baggage and equipment the stay was extended. Anyone who has done any traveling would expect that, in making a move of this magnitude, a few pieces of luggage might go AWOL. But imagine the shock and dismay when it was found that a few of the Battalion's *tanks* and *one thousand crates* of equipment were missing! Despite all the efforts at tracing the lost items, the missing tanks and crates never turned up. All six of the 105mm tanks belonging to the Assault Gun Platoon were MIA and the Platoon had to wait for new ones to be issued. When the supplies were given up for lost, this so totally screwed up their inventory that the Battalion had to go through a complete resupply, which took about a month.

As a result, the short stop on the little nameless hill turned out to be an extended stay in an area that just wasn't well-suited to extended residence by 700 men. By the time the Battalion mercifully left, the nameless hill was a ruined, muddy shambles and indelibly etched into the Battalion's memory. It just needed a name to remember it by for the Battalion's history record. A contest was suggested by the HQ staff with a pass to Marseille as the prize for the winning suggestion. However, the men presented a unified front and refused to enter the contest! Except for one lone anonymous entry from – you guessed it – Company "D." The entry read: "Chicken Shit Hill and you can stick your pass up your ass!" Nice rhyme, actually. Knowing they were licked, the HQ staff decided that the hill's new name was "Goat

Hill," despite the total absence of the species in the area. Perhaps they named it that because they had been made goats of with their contest?

Goat Hill (Up From Marseille).

But what about the missing supplies? There are several possibilities:

1. The supplies were deliberately routed to the French. Logistical support was under the command of General Thomas Larkin, who commanded Services of Supply. Besides supplying the American Seventh Army, Services of Supply was also responsible for supplying the French Army, and General Larkin had to make up supply shortages for the French by drawing from the American supplies. At times he literally "robbed Peter to pay Paul." The possibility exists that the missing supplies were "siphoned off" to give them to the French. Since September 28th, Truscott and Patch needed the French 3rd Algerian division to assume responsibility for some additional real estate to the south of Truscott's position. This would allow the U.S. to resume the offensive. The catch was that the French Algerians needed supplies to assume that responsibility. If Patch and Truscott diverted the 781st supplies to the Algerians, allowing them to get up to speed, it would allow Patch/Truscott to resume the offensive in their sector. Another incitement for this was when French General DeLattre wrote a formal complaint on October 1st, in which he charged that his troops had been short-changed on supplies and that his troops were being constrained from attacking by the unfair treatment and short supply situation. Citing "inexcusable unfavorable treatment," he charged that the situation "seriously endangered his army's existence and operations." This was written in draft form to be sent over Devers' and Eisenhower's heads to General Marshall. (This unprofessional behavior was exactly what Eisenhower expected when he assigned the French to Devers. It was jumping several levels of command, and was basically uncalled for, as DeLattre could readily see that

Patch was operating under equal supply problems!) The memo wasn't signed, but the draft was waved in Devers' face as an obvious threat. So, to get DeLattre off his back, Devers may have ordered 7th Army to divert the supplies, in order to satisfy the French general. But in a couple of weeks, DeLattre met with Marshall and launched into a tirade that embarrassed Patch, Devers, and Marshall. At that point the supplies might have been "appropriated" to quiet the French. These were not rare circumstances, and were called "special supply allocations" by the logistics personnel.

2. The supplies were genuinely lost. Cargo was shipped via a process known as "flatting." Cargo for Operation Anvil was stowed in the hold of a ship, and then a floor was put on top (the "flatting"). The area below the flatting in a hold was a sort of "reserved space" for a special destination, but cargo above the "flatted" section could go anywhere. If the 781st's cargo was incorrectly stowed *above* rather than *below* the flatting, or if the flatting was not correctly installed, the cargo could have gone anywhere. This might account for the lost crates, but does not account for lost tanks, which were on deck.

3. The supplies were stolen. Marseille became a center of the "black market" for southern France, and it was estimated that at one point 20% of all the supplies offloaded were stolen. Again, while this works for the crates, it's hard to imagine a large black market demand for six 105mm Sherman tanks.

4. The supplies were a victim of "moonlight requisitioning" themselves and were "diverted" to other U.S. units. There were shortages of equipment, especially engineer, transportation, and signal equipment. Anvil was planned *knowing* that there weren't supplies enough to go around. If the invasion went well, they would outstrip the supply situation. And Anvil had gone *very* well. The possibility exists that the supplies could have been "rerouted" – "moonlight requisition" writ large.

5. The supplies were deliberately routed to other U.S. Army units. In mid-October, General Devers was being pressured by SHAEF to shift some of his supplies to Patton's 3rd Army to their north. SHAEF may have benefitted from reading the German ULTRA Code, and may have had advance notice of the Bulge offensive and wanted those supplies where it was going to strike. Devers, who was short of supplies already, and tired of being reined in so that Patton could benefit, tried to placate Eisenhower, and promised this could be done in November. Devers might have sent the supplies as promised by diverting the 781st supplies.

6. The ship carrying the supplies sank. One of the 781st vets said that he saw the ship onto which the 781st had loaded cargo and the tanks for the assault gun platoon keeping station next to the *LeJeune*. The tanks were stowed on deck forward, and he remembered the vessel pitching to the point of lifting its propellers out of the water. He recalled seeing it there one day, going to bed, and when he got up the next morning that ship was nowhere to be seen. Records for convoy UGF.16 indicate that none of the convoy was lost, but it remains possible that the ship in question did not go to Marseille, and parted company as previously planned during the night. A second vet supports this theory, and recalls the Mediterranean being very rough, but posits that the tanks and materiel were simply swept overboard rather than the ship sinking.

While waiting for the resupply, the 781st Battalion S-3 officer and all the platoon leaders were sent forward and observed platoon leaders and staffs of the 753rd and 756th Tank Battalions in action. This was wonderful experience, and significantly shortened their learning curve when they stepped up to the plate. The Basic Rule they learned was: "Spot first, engage first, hit first." Training was key – the well-trained commander was able to keep situational awareness and spot the enemy first. The well-trained crew would be coordinated and maneuver to engage first, and the well-trained gunner could get a hit first.

That wasn't all. Lt. Col. Kinne also observed operations, and he implemented a novel reorganization of the Battalion as a result. HQ and Service companies were split into two halves – one half of each was designated a "Forward Command Post (CP)." This unit would be on the spot, up front and ready to command and support the fighting Companies in "real time." Commanders would be on the spot; tank servicing could take place immediately, etc. There would be no wait while information was passed rearward and forward. The rest of the HQ and Service Companies formed the "Rear CP," comprised of heavier items, administrative functions, and functions that weren't required to be close to the front lines. Furthermore, the Assault Gun and Mortar Platoons were combined, yielding a strong platoon able to place indirect fire where needed. Lastly, the Transportation Platoon was split up and spread amongst the line companies, so each company had their own supply capability. These changes gave the 781st a unique ability to act and react quickly, and each company was configured to be fairly self-sufficient.

The Transportation Platoons used the "Deuce-and-a-Half." Denoting its cargo capacity (two and a half tons), the Deuce was the premier supply truck used by the 781st. It was a 6x6 with a driven front axle and two driven rear axles. No speed demon, it was typically used at 25mph in convoys, spaced 60 yards from the truck in front, and driven by a two-man driver team. A large 6-cylinder engine drove a standard transmission, and it typically had a stake body and a soft top. They were wonderfully reliable and easy to drive for the amateur soldiers who drove them through all types of roads and conditions.

And while waiting on Goat Hill, the unit used this time to prepare their vehicles for the coming winter. For the tanks, they attached new track widening devices called "Grousers" or "duck bills" to the tank tracks. The width of the track was an important factor, as narrow tracks put more pressure per square foot on the dirt and would mire faster in snow or mud. These devices were bolted to the end of each track link, and because they spread the load over a wider footprint (like a snowshoe), they lowered the tank's footprint pressure, so they wouldn't bog down in mud or snow as easily. Unfortunately, "Grousers" were in short supply. Besides the tanks, the other vehicles would have been serviced for cold weather operation. Unlike today's cars and trucks that shrug off winter with little maintenance, there was a lot to do to enable your vehicle to survive the winter in 1944.

Winterization kits for vehicles were installed (they consisted of an engine block heater and a shroud to cover the front/radiator) when they were available. This engine block heater wasn't some plug-in electrode like modern engine heaters – it

Deuce-and-a-half. (U.S. Army, NARA)

was gasoline powered! The operation of the heater went as follows: "If built-in engine heater is supplied, drop bottom cover of heater. Make sure valve in gasoline supply line is open to heater. Open lighter hole in base of heater. Remove lighter tool from clip on side of heater, soak lighter tool with gasoline, ignite, and insert lighter tool in hole, lighting heater. Close lighter hole." This was basically setting your vehicle on fire in a hopefully controlled manner. The shroud was put over the engine and weighted at the edges with stones or snow to trap the heat. Heating the engine in this fashion kept the motor oil thin enough so the starter stood a chance of turning the motor over. This was before the advent of multiweight or synthetic oils, and the oils in use in 1944 would thicken to the consistency of grease when cold.

Some vehicles had a battery warming coil to warm the batteries for easier starting – it too wasn't electric; it ran off the radiator. The gasoline fire that was heating the engine block also heated the water in the radiator, which then circulated through the coil and heated the batteries. The battery warmer was to be turned on 45 minutes before trying to start the engine.

For vehicles without heater kits, starting was more of a challenge. The oil in some vehicles was diluted with gasoline to thin it out – there was even a valve on the side of the engine to send gas into the crankcase. In really cold situations, the motor oil was drained out of the engine into cans and was warmed over a campfire before pouring it back into the motor and starting the engine. Alternately, the engine was covered with a tarp and small fires were built under it, or blowtorches could be played on the sump. The transmission oil would thicken up so that the gears would stick on the shafts and it wouldn't be possible to get out of neutral without gear grinding. To fix that, the gear oil was also diluted to thin it out - six-to-one with gasoline. Antifreeze was used in the radiator. The spark plug gaps were closed to .020" to cope with the weaker voltage that the cold batteries delivered. The air filters were of the oil bath type, which wouldn't work in the winter, so troops drained the oil from the air cleaners. Emergency brakes were not set when parking during the winter, as they liked to stick "on." Even the normal vehicle brakes were sticky when cold, and might need to be warmed with a blowtorch to free them up. Troops finally had to disconnect the speedometer cable, as it would break. Winterization was a large task!

While on "Goat Hill," the supply sergeant of "D" Company, Sgt. Waldron, proved to be especially adept at "moonlight requisitioning" items from other nearby outfits. This is really not very surprising, coming from "D" Company. Sgt Waldron, who, prior to the war, had been a prison guard at the Pennsylvania State Penitentiary in Danamora, took the opportunity and relieved the U.S. Tenth Mountain Division of their great winter sleeping bags, and distributed them amongst the "D" Company officers and his friends.

And then there was the mail. Mail from home was the highlight of every soldier's life. The mail was delivered to the Battalion 781st "rear CP" and parceled up by Company, and was then delivered to each Company via a jeep. Soldiers got letters, handmade items – knitted mittens, hats, and scarves were favorites - newspapers, and food. The use of "V-Mail" (short for "Victory Mail") was encouraged – this was a method where folks wrote their letters on a standard form which was then photographed, put on microfilm, and the film was then transported to a processing center, where it was "reconstituted" back onto paper and delivered. The recipient got a miniature envelope which unfolded and the letter was on the inside. Shipping just the film saved weight.

Soldiers' outgoing mail was censored after writing, and any forbidden passages were blacked out or physically cut from the letter. If the passages were too big, the letter was confiscated and the soldier was probably not notified. If the soldier strayed from the rules a lot, he would most likely get a scolding for being careless. The Censor was usually an officer in the unit, and this was not a popular assignment.

Thanksgiving 1944 for the 781st. (Up from Marseille)

Censors removed any reference to locations (even saying "somewhere in France" was specifically forbidden!), unit names, or numbers; troop strength or anything that might be of value to the enemy; and even phrases the sensor thought were morally offensive. The Censor also looked for signs of declining morale or weakening of the will to fight. Officers' mail was self-censored and occasionally looked at by ranking officers, but not very often. Before departure, Gerald Mercier and his fiancé had devised a coded system so Gerry could write to Gisele and mention locations, and "Gee" could decipher the location and know where Gerry was.

On November 15, 1944, the Battalion received orders formally attaching it to the 7th Army and further to the VI Corps. They were scheduled to start moving in about ten days.

The 781st celebrated Thanksgiving November 23rd, eating a real turkey dinner out of their mess kits. At this point, the 781st had 720 people, 40 officers, 220 NCOs, and 460 enlisted men. They had 53 M4A3 Sherman tanks (Ford GAA V8s and 75mm gun), 17 M5A1 Stuart light tanks, six assault guns (Sherman M1s with a 105mm gun), and three self-propelled 81mm mortars mounted in half tracks.

While on "Goat Hill," the men were allowed to go into Marseille on passes for recreation. On November 24th, the day after Thanksgiving, the 781st suffered its first combat casualty – a sniper shot at a truck that contained a number of men who were returning from a pass to Marseille and struck two people, killing T/5 James D. Mitchell, a Headquarters Company driver, and wounding Pvt. Salvador Gaglio from Company "C." The sniper was never caught.

On the 25th, the Battalion started to move forward, and an advance detachment left at 0700. The Battalion split by company, and each company rode a railway train to the front. Shipping the entire Battalion required several trains, which were run by French engineers to French schedules. This meant that the trains stopped when it was time for the engineers to eat lunch, or they stopped so the engineers could chat with buddies. This Gallic indifference to the war was astonishing, as they preferred to stop and eat or chitchat, rather than deliver liberating troops to the front line! The troopers amused themselves in return by practicing their sharpshooting from the tops of the moving railcars. One stop they didn't mind was in Lyons, when the train paused on an elevated track immediately next to a brothel, and during the all-too-brief stop the "ladies" made quite an exhibit of their wares to a very appreciative train.

The 781st, upon their arrival at Padoux, was quickly assigned to the 100th Infantry Division and had to move out immediately to catch up with them. Having left the U.S. shortly before the 781st, and not having been delayed by missing equipment, the 100th Infantry Division had recently arrived and relieved the 45th Infantry Division, taking over the northern portion of the VI Corps line. Being new and untried, they were considered, along with the similarly untried 103rd, as the "junior" infantry divisions in the 7th Army. The 3rd and 36th were the "seniors." The 100th was already on the advance, being tasked by Devers and Patch to lead the November advance across the Meurthe River. If the 100th was successful, then the rest of the offensive would be successful – with so much riding on them they were being put in the deep end of the pool. The 45th Infantry Division had experienced great difficulty in advancing in the same region, so it was a bit ambitious for Patch to expect the new guys to succeed where the veterans had stumbled.

On December 5, 1944, the advance elements of the 781st departed for Hangviller, France, to catch the 100th Infantry Division. The Battalion left in two sections: the first under Lt. Souders, comprised of the administrative, maintenance, and supply

M4 of the 781st moves out. (U.S. Army Signal Corps, NARA)

vehicles travelling at 25-30mph. The second section left 30 minutes after the first, traveling at 12-17mph, and was under the Executive Officer (XO), Maj. Tindall. It comprised all the tracked vehicles: Companies B, C, D, and A in that order, with the HQ tanks and half-tracks interspersed. Each company was to be spaced exactly ten minutes apart, and each vehicle was to be exactly 88 yards apart in convoy, under strict radio silence.

The German infantry defenders facing the 100th Infantry Division were generally weakened after being chased up from the coast. They augmented what strength they could muster via liberal use of land mines and booby traps, and they tried to use the rugged terrain to their best advantage. Using landmines to block the roads was a great stratagem, as it brought entire advancing columns to a halt. The Meurthe river crossings were incomplete and thinly manned, but the terrain behind the river favored the defense, with high, rugged hills that caused an uphill fight all the way for the offense. It was just not good terrain for armor – the vehicles were forced to keep to the few available roads because going cross-country just wasn't an option in the mud and hilly terrain. Weather also favored the defenders, with heavy snow and freezing rain being common. The winter of 1944-5 was one of the worst on record for that sector, and once the snow started falling, most tanks and infantry were trailbreaking in deep snow. Lastly, the Germans had recently gotten reinforcements in artillery and had a goodly supply of ammunition.

The "new kids" of the 100th were anxious to show their stuff to the seniors, but had not yet seen the type of uphill fight into well-honed delaying tactics that they now faced. The German defenders delayed as much as possible, but the Meurthe river was eventually crossed. Soon the 100th and the 3rd Divisions were in a race to see which division would be first to liberate the large eastern French city of Strasbourg. There was a rumor circulating that whichever division secured the city first would win a 72-hour pass for all members of that division. The two divisions raced across the countryside, mowing down all opposition, sometimes in plain sight of each other. As the 100th neared the city, they were overtaken by a messenger and were given the unwelcome news that the 100th Division was being redeployed to the north and reassigned to the XV Corps, leaving the 3rd unopposed to win the race to Strasbourg. The 100th was justifiably dejected, with all dreams

Generals Devers and Patch.
(U.S. Army Signal Corps, NARA)

of a three-day pass gone, but soon they recovered their spirits when they heard the news: when the 3rd Division arrived on the outskirts of Strasbourg, they were informed that the city had *already* been liberated by the French 2nd Armored Division. Justice was served!

The 7th Army was elated by its fast drive to the Rhine and began planning for a crossing. Amphibious trucks (DUKWs) were started moving from the rear assembly areas toward the front in anticipation. The little 6th Corps, which was really not expected by Ike to do much on the right of the Allied line except tie down some German forces, had presented Ike with a ready, intact Rhine crossing and a chance to flank his opponent and drive north to the heart of Germany. Bottom line: the 7th Army exceeded expectations and presented SHAEF with a golden opportunity - and SHAEF didn't know what to do with it, because it didn't "fit" their preordained plan.

So SHAEF intervened. A drive by the 7th Army on the right/southern end of the line would take away the spotlight on British General Montgomery, who was *supposed* to be the focus of the Allied drive into Germany. Also, it is possible that, via reading of the German secret communications, SHAEF had some inkling that there was an enemy buildup and potential German counterattack in the works. If that was the case, then SHAEF didn't want to divert major strength to the south at this time.

General Montgomery had flubbed his offensive through the Low Countries (Operation Market Garden, a.k.a. "A Bridge Too Far"), and Patton's 3rd Army had stalled in its advance. General Eisenhower wanted to give Patton a boost, so the 7th Army was only going to push Patton's swing again. Supporting Patton's advance into the Saar basin was given priority. Eisenhower ordered Patch to shift his focus from the Rhine crossing to a northward direction, which would hopefully divert German forces and take pressure off Patton, so Patton's forces could begin to advance again. As part of the order, the XV Corps was given a portion of the line that was Patton's, a move that allowed Patton to narrow his front and concentrate his forces. This thinned out the XV Corps, causing Devers and Ike to disagree over these orders, and Devers was fairly public in his criticism, leaving Ike furious.

But XV Corps turned north as ordered, and by December 6th, the 100th again found itself in the center of the advance, outside a French town called Bitche, which was in the center of the French Maginot line of fortifications. And now arrived the 781st Tank Battalion, fresh and spoiling for a fight. The unofficial motto of the 781st by this time was "Advance when Possible," and they aimed to do just that.

As the 781st got closer to the front, helmet chin straps were tightened, conversation lagged, people got more introspective, and equipment was checked and rechecked. The sound of gunfire for the first time caused most men to momentarily freeze, and then collect oneself, and finally continue. Going into battle the first time was mechanical, mindless, no thought, just training taking over and advance if you can. During the fight it was all din – explosions, sharp cracks of small arms, yelling, cursing, smoke, smell of ammo, recoil, the ground heaving and the smell of earth, cries of the wounded – then it was over and the objective reached, and all that was left was exhaustion and relief, cold and wet. Fear? It was a constantly lurking companion. Everyone was afraid while in combat. All the tank crews were afraid of getting hit and burning up in a tank. But the fear retreated when the first rounds started flying and then training took over, and fear was kept at bay by trusting in your crewmates and yourself. Most of the enlisted men were driven by two basic motives: "don't let my buddies down" and "survive." The Hershey's chocolate bars each soldier carried did have a purpose other than satisfying a sweet tooth. They were to be eaten after combat to offset the intense adrenaline "crash."

The weather aggravated the troops more than the enemy. This was one of the coldest winters in 10 years to hit the area, and most of the winter was spent wading through snow that was "up to your fanny!," per Homer Turner. Despite all the time the battalion spent resupplying on Goat Hill, many of the men still wore leather shoes and didn't have "shoe pacs," which were high, insulated rubber boots (unless you were lucky or knew Sergeant Waldron).

December 7, 1944, was seasonally cold, with intermittent rain and fair visibility. First Platoon of Company "A" went into action at 1700. Their Commanding Officer, Lt. William Kaiser, was the officer that was moved out of "D" when they were still firmly entrenched as the "Raggedy Assed Cadets." Reassigned as a platoon leader in "A" Company, Lt. Kaiser and his tank platoon were assigned the mission of spearheading an advance across a strongly-defended slope and into the enemy-held town of Lemberg. Intense fire from enemy machine guns, mortars, and artillery was focused on the Allied forces right at the scheduled time of departure. Without regard for the intense fire, Lt. Kaiser, occupying the lead vehicle of the platoon, ordered his forces forward, and the charge got off to a tepid start, as two of his four tanks almost immediately struck landmines and threw tracks. Firing continuously as they advanced, the remaining two tanks demolished enemy twenty-millimeter gun emplacements, and using constant bursts of fire kept opposing riflemen pinned to the ground while U.S. infantry crossed the open terrain. Entering the town of Lemberg itself, the tanks attacked building after building, sending direct muzzle fire through doorways and windows with devastating effectiveness which caused the surrender of fourteen enemy infantry in one structure and eleven in another. One tank of the remaining pair was damaged when it went off the road into the soft shoulder on the right-hand side, sank to a 45-degree angle, and couldn't get back on the road – it had to be towed out by the Service Company. (All that practice tugging tanks out of the Mississippi mud was paying off already!) For this effective attack Lt. Kaiser won a Silver Star –for the first time he met the enemy in France!

Sergeant Daley's tank needs a tow at Lemberg. (U.S. Army Signal Corps, NARA)

Sgt. Dan Daley, Cpl. William Lindsey, T5 Boyd Broadhead, and Pvt. Santiago Gomez earned Bronze Stars for their work at Lemberg following Lt. Kaiser's tank. They advanced through two hostile road blocks and mine fields, entered the town, and disrupted the enemy, allowing the town to be gained by the infantry.

One of the tanks that were disabled in crossing the first field also contributed three *more* Bronze Stars, as the crewmen – T4 John Anderson, Cpl. John Szywalski, and Pfc. Robert White – remained with their disabled tank for a 24-hour period waiting for rescue, and prevented the vehicle from being captured. While those three crewmen waited in the first tank that was disabled during Lt. Kaiser's attack by hitting a mine, Pfc. Mario Slavich tried to reach the other disabled tank, but was driven off by the intense mortar and sniper fire. He took cover, waited a while, and tried again. He made it on his second attempt and was able to relieve the crew, and then he stayed with this vehicle for 24 hours until it was recovered by Service Company. He too won a Bronze Star for his actions.

December 9, 1944, broke with intermittent rain and fair visibility. First Lt. Donald Crane of 2nd Platoon "A" Company was assigned a mission with the infantry troops of clearing Lemberg of remaining hostile troops. The four tanks under Lt. Crane's command emulated what worked for Kaiser's charge, and by firing at point-blank range into houses and buildings they routed the German delaying forces, enabling the rifle companies to secure the town. At this point his mission was accomplished, but Lt. Crane didn't stop – he led his platoon forward in pursuit of the retreating Nazis, who were in full flight on the road out

Getting ready to clean up in Lemberg.
Note the fourth vehicle in line is the tank retriever.
(U.S. Army Signal Corps, NARA)

of Lemberg toward Bitche. Lt. Crane and 2nd Platoon were now traversing unfamiliar terrain, leaving their infantry support behind and ignoring the danger from mines. As they advanced 2nd Platoon came under fire by anti-tank and machine gun fire, but the platoon continued to advance and charged headlong into the enemy troops, who were reinforced by three flak wagons. The charging Shermans overran the enemy position, and Gunner Gerald Mercier destroyed the three flak wagons by shooting off their tracks. The others in the group took care of two seventy-five millimeter field pieces, two howitzers, and other weapons and equipment, along with causing seven casualties and completely routing the enemy. At that point they stopped the charge and returned to their bivouac.

While Lt. Crane's attack was taking place, Second Lt. Pascal Riddle of Service Company and his crew (Robert Brown, George Rice, William Turner, John Bradish, and Harold Alexander) were engaged in retrieving the two tanks lost to mines the previous day. The recovery team had crept in under cover of darkness to avoid heavy enemy fire and managed to reach the tanks. They succeeded in rescuing the three crewmen in one tank and Pfc. Slavich in the second tank, and repossessed both vehicles without loss or injury. The Service Company then really outdid expectations by having both vehicles back on the line the next day! The six men in the recovery team each won a Bronze Star for their efforts.

Lt. Crane won a Silver Star for his leadership and aggressiveness in his attack. The other nineteen crewmembers of Lt. Crane's four tanks each received a Bronze Star for their efforts in supporting the attack out of Lemberg. They were: John Brennan, Robert Johnson, James Sublette, Raymond Carter, Joseph Marzucco, Frank Miller, Herschel Rogers, L. Beauchamp, Gerald Mercier, Charles Wolf, Donie Blea, Berger Johnson, Ramiro Aguilar, James Grantland, Warren Parrish, Sidney Schrieber, James Sirginnis, Marvin Spitzer, and Bernard Donnelly.

Charles Wolf was wounded in the action on the 9th, so he earned a Purple Heart as well. So, in two days the 781st, in its debut actions, racked up two Silver Stars, 33 Bronze Stars, and one Purple Heart!

Meanwhile, "D" Company was at first assigned as what Joe Graham referred to as "Palace Guard," which meant they were setting up roadblocks at entrances to the towns where the 100th Division HQ was located. In this mission, they would intercept any enemy probe before it could impact the HQ, but there was little chance of any real action, as the HQ was typically a safe distance behind the Main Line of Resistance (MLR, a.k.a. the "Front").

December 10, 1944, saw the rain change to snow, and the Battalion was following up its recent action. "A" Company was clearing the country NE of Lemberg. The other Companies were performing the ever-required maintenance and resupplying. The reinforced Assault Gun Platoon was joining up with the 375th Field Artillery and preparing to support them. The Rear CP joined the forward CP at Zittersheim. Company "D" was detached from "Palace Guard" duty, and was attached to the 399th Infantry Regiment.

The next day, the snow turned back to rain, and while Company "A" got their chance to resupply and perform maintenance, the rest of the 781st got into the fight. First Lieutenant Francis Coolican's second platoon of "B" Company attacked on the road north out of Mouterhouse, but in a now-familiar pattern, the enemy retreated again before the tanks could make contact, and so his tanks obliterated an enemy road block. Staff Sergeant Elmer Shepherd's tank led the assault, and gunner Vince Sutphin fired the first shot of the war at the enemy for "B" Company. Soon after, Lt. Coolican's tank was disabled by a mine; the force of the explosion blew him up and out of the open turret hatch, and he landed on the rear deck of the Sherman. The situation got worse when the tank was taken under mortar fire – the tank's crew abandoned the vehicle and, thinking the Lieutenant was certainly dead, ran for a nearby ditch to take cover while shells fell all around. At that point one of the crew noticed that Francis Coolican was moving – he wasn't dead after all! When they realized he was still alive, Sgt. Joseph Polizzano, T4 George Rinaldi, and Cpl. Morton Hoch left their shelter and retrieved the Lieutenant, carrying him through intense fire back to safety. For this heroic act, the three men earned a Bronze Star.

The 2nd Platoon of Company "C," commanded by 1st Lt. James E. Walsh, was patrolling the road North of Mouterhouse when it too was stopped by a roadblock.

Chow!

Five different types of rations were provided for the soldiers' dining enjoyment: the "A" Ration, "B" Ration, "C" Ration, "D" Ration, and "K" Ration. "A" Rations were the best: a hot meal with some fresh components, cooked in a base kitchen. "B" Rations were provided by the battalion and cooked in a field kitchen, and were usually a good hot meal composed of canned or preserved items.

Individuals carried "C" Rations, "K" Rations, and "D" Rations as single-serving meals that were generally eaten on the fly, cold, or frequently heated on the engines of vehicles.

"C" Rations were a prepared meal that came in two cans – an "M" unit that contained the main course and a "B" unit that contained bread and dessert. The "M" unit came in a tin can about 3.5 inches tall and 3 inches in diameter. Inside the can was one of the entrees:

1. meat (a mix of beef and pork) and beans (a favorite with the 781st)
2. ham, egg, and potato hash (universally reviled in the 781st)
3. meat and vegetable (potatoes and carrots) stew (another real loser meal for the 781st)
4. meat and spaghetti in tomato sauce
5. meat and noodles
6. pork and rice
7. franks and beans (the favorite meal of the 781st!)
8. pork and beans (second favorite)
9. ham and lima beans (loser! – everyone hated lima beans)
10. mutton stew (loser)
11. Chicken and vegetables

The predictable aftermath of five healthy men eating a lot of beans and then being cooped up in an enclosed tank beggars description.

Inside the "B" can were three hardtack biscuits, compressed cereal, candy, cookies or fudge, jam, a couple of sugar packets, and some

This time the defenders didn't retreat, and Second Platoon then poured 75mm and MG fire into the enemy positions, suppressing them so that 24 POWs were captured by the advancing infantry. An opportunity to inflict greater damage on the enemy was missed because faulty information was conveyed from the infantry to the tanks about the location of friendly troops, causing the tanks to hold fire when they could have let loose. The infantry did not have SCR-300 radios, which would have allowed communication between tanks and infantry, and this was painfully noted in the tankers' after-action report.

1st Platoon of "D" was assisting the 397th in trying to advance, but soon their advance was barred by a German 20mm Flak Wagon. "D" Company immediately swarmed and attacked, and the German crew abandoned their vehicle, whereupon "D" Company dismounted and used thermite grenades to destroy the vehicle. The instant drink mix (coffee, lemonade, bouillon, cocoa, or grape or orange drink). The "key" for opening the cans was attached to the bottom of the "B" can. Each soldier got three rations per day, so the lack of choices quickly became a problem! Stew for breakfast, lunch, and dinner for a week could get old.

If the soldier was lucky enough to get to a mess hall and eat the hot food served there – well, it was meat hash, meat stew, or meat and beans! The Army intentionally copied and canned the meals served in messes. Also given out were packages of "accessories" – water purification tablets, salt tablets, a flat wooden spoon, chewing gum, cigarettes (Camel, Chelsea, Chesterfield, Lucky Strikes, Old Gold, Phillip Morris, Raleigh, and others), matches, a can opener, and toilet paper.

"K" Ration: this was an austere combat ration that was originally intended for paratroops, tankers, and mobile forces for use as an emergency ration for not more than three days. There were three types of "K" Ration for breakfast, dinner (lunch), or supper. They were in a box that was produced by the Cracker Jack Company, and were in a box about that size. Inside were such delicacies as breakfast: a tin of chopped ham and eggs or veal loaf with biscuits, a dried fruit or cereal bar, water purification tabs, sugar, cigarettes, matches, gum, and powdered coffee. Lunch? A tin of cheese, ham, or ham and cheese, biscuits, candy, sugar, salt, cigs, matches, gum, and powdered drink. Dinner? Canned meat, biscuits, chocolate bar, toilet paper, cigs, gum, and bouillon cube or powder packet. Repetitive, and around 3,000 calories per day if you could eat it all. The "C" Ration was heavier, had more calories, and was better for you, as the "K" Ration was deficient in vitamins (esp. C) and about 1,000 calories short per day for an active male.

Lastly, there was the "D" Ration, which was an emergency ration made of compressed chocolate bars with energy boosting ingredients. They provided about 600 calories and were specially made to taste like a boiled potato, so the troops weren't tempted to gobble them down.

It was therefore no wonder that this diet was supplemented from local sources whenever possible!

Reinforced Assault Gun Platoon was also active, firing 44 105mm rounds on five targets, the last three targets being enemy tanks.

Despite the rugged and forested terrain, the 100th and 781st teams used their prior combined arms training and "clicked" – and as a result, they made better progress than expected, tearing through Lemberg. As the weather cleared over the next two days, the 781st and the 100th continued their advance northward toward the Maginot Line and the fortress town of Bitche. But suddenly, when about four miles short of Bitche, the German resistance stiffened, and artillery and mortar fire supported by aggressive infantry counterattacks stopped their advance. The German troops turned every farmhouse into a fortress, and when they begrudgingly gave ground, they left landmines and booby traps, cratered the roads, and destroyed any bridges to hinder pursuit. They strung almost-invisible piano wire at neck height across roads, hoping to decapitate soldiers who were riding in jeeps with the windshield folded down (which was commonly done, as the windshield hampered firing your gun when aimed ahead of the jeep). The mines were especially troublesome, as many were the new German Topfmine, which was just being introduced. It was a completely nonmetallic mine, and used glass and pressed sawdust in its construction. As a result, it was not detectable by current Allied minesweeping techniques. It was primarily envisioned as an antipersonnel mine and lacked the destructive power of the Tellermine. While a Tellermine could easily damage tracks and belly plates of tanks, the Topfmine would most likely damage a track, and perhaps disable a tank. At the same time, rain, snow, and fog moved in to add to the discomfort, and the poor visibility severely limited any possible air and artillery support.

The 781st and 100th were now consolidated in and around Lemberg, and the Companies executed short missions: 1st Platoon "D" advanced ahead and then took up a defensive position south of Bitche, but clearly wasn't welcome, as they were subjected to heavy German artillery fire. After Sgt. Patrick Perry was wounded "D" was withdrawn back to Lemberg. 3rd Platoon "B" went out to clear a hill ("Hill 427") that was holding up the 398th advance, but for the second time the enemy bugged out before they arrived, so the hill was taken without fuss. 2nd Platoon "C" advanced on the road North of Mouterhouse, but was again stopped by a roadblock. They lost one tank disabled by a mine and said "thanks" by shelling the town of LaPapeterie. 2nd and 3rd Platoons of "B" then advanced on Reyersviller, which was halfway between Lemberg and Bitche – again meeting no enemy resistance (the Germans had all fallen back to Bitche), and the town was occupied. During the attack on Reyersviller, one tank became stuck in a field and was subjected to artillery fire. Pvt. Alfred Blanchette left his immobile tank and hooked up the tow cables between his tank and another that had come to assist. The second tank was then able to tow Blanchette's tank to solid ground and Blanchette got a Bronze Star for his efforts, which enabled his tank to rejoin the fight and make the mission a success.

U.S. vehicles that were knocked out or broken down were recoverable by the Allies, but any German vehicles that were abandoned were forever lost to the Germans, as they were captured by the advancing troops. The superiority of the U.S. Service Companies in retrieving tanks and getting them fixed and back on-line was remarkable, but it bore a heavy price. The Germans soon noticed that knocked out tanks were being quickly hauled off for repair, and they recognized these "recycled" tanks as ones they had already killed. The German gunners soon tired of having to repeatedly kill the same tank. The only way to totally destroy a tank was to make it burn, which ruined the heat treatment of the armor and rendered it useless. Knowing this, the Germans started a new deadly tactic: don't stop shooting once a Sherman was hit. *Keep* shooting Shermans after they were immobilized until they caught fire and burned, so they couldn't be fixed.

10. SONS OF BITCHE

The fight for Bitche was on. The American commanders thought that the Germans might once again retreat after offering token resistance, but the Germans had at last found a suitable strongpoint and decided to make a stand. The Maginot Line fortresses at Bitche offered a feature not often found elsewhere in the Line. The Maginot Line was originally constructed to defend France from attack by Germany, and the defenses generally pointed in the wrong direction for use by Germans in their defense. A lot of effort was required on the German's part to turn the defenses around to point toward France, and in many cases the forts were simply destroyed if they couldn't easily be modified. But at Bitche, the defenses also offered excellent protection against an attack from the south. So the Germans occupied the forts at Bitche and prepared their defense.

The linked chain of forts at Bitche ran for approximately eight miles on a generally east-west line along a highway north of town. Farthest west was Fort Simserhof, which was a large complex of ten mini-forts that were mutually supporting. A mile and a half east of Simserhof was Fort Schiesseck, the largest of the Bitche defense forts – which had guns up to 135mm in a combination of steel turrets and concrete casements. There was a moat around the fort, and it even had built-in chutes down which the defenders could roll hand grenades onto the attackers. Almost across the highway was Fort Freudenburg, a small installation with only one unit. Next Eastward was Fort Otterbiel, which had five mini-forts. Then was a string of comparatively lightly defended single units until one reached Camp de Bitche, which was the German garrison. The line of forts ended about one mile further east with Fort Grande Hohekirkel, which had five mini-forts. Lest the moniker mislead, each mini-fort had walls and ceilings of reinforced concrete up to ten feet thick. The mini-forts were interconnected underground, and when attacked, the defenders could retreat deep underground (some went five stories deep!), then return later through the tunnels and re-engage, much like the Japanese tactics employed at Iwo Jima and

Okinawa. To confound attackers, some of the units didn't have an entrance door and could only be reached via tunnel. Another nice touch was the "disappearing guns," which would rise up from their casements, shoot, and then lower back underground.

Fortress Bitche looks down on the area. (U.S. Army Signal Corps, NARA)

This was a tough nut to crack, but then add the normal barbed wire, mines, covering field positions with anti-tank guns, machine guns, and supportive artillery and mortars in the surrounding countryside. The forts were impervious to bombs and shrugged off indirect artillery fire. All of which meant that the tank-infantry teams were the only viable way to conquer the forts. The Bitche sector forts were never taken by the Germans in 1940 – despite many attempts, the French defenders were able to hold on, and the forts were only surrendered after the German-French armistice. However, the German high command also helped. German Field Marshall Gerd Von Rundstedt had ordered the defenders to withdraw to the West Wall defense line once the Ardennes offensive started on the 15th. If this had not happened the contest would have been even tougher.

The Allied forces closed on the Bitche fortifications as the weather turned clear and cold. The 781st was getting into position to support the 100th Division Infantry regiments as they assaulted the Maginot Line. Employing a typical American assault plan of flanking a heavily-defended position, the 100th Division's plans for taking Bitche required taking the high ground to the left (West) and rear of the town, then reducing the forts in the sector. The plan for taking fortified positions was for close-in direct fire from the armor to keep the defenders occupied while the infantry eliminated the *Panzerfaust* teams and hopefully found time to advance. The Engineers would then set explosive charges to blast the forts.

Company "B" was tasked with securing the high ground, and they launched their initial attack on the 14th, with 1st Platoon "B" overrunning a roadblock and a pillbox. The attack netted some prisoners, and Sgt. Richard Ogilvie's tank was escorting the prisoners back to the American lines for interrogation when it was hit by anti-tank fire. Four of the crew were wounded: Sgt. Ogilvie, PFC Henry Rodwell, Pvt. William Goodman, and Pvt. Frank Scafide. Sgt Ogilvie was standing with his head out the hatch when the shell exploded and he was hit by shrapnel, which destroyed his jaw, knocked out his teeth, and lodged in his neck. His crew was rescued and Ogilvie had to be evacuated and flown home, where he faced extensive reconstructive surgery over the next seven months. (He then went back to school and earned a history degree, then a law degree, and eventually entered politics and later became the Governor of Illinois.) Not as lucky, Pfc. Goodman was seriously wounded and held on for a week before succumbing to his wounds on the 21st.

"D" Company was split up among the Infantry regiments. 3rd Platoon "D" moved to another position southeast of Bitche and carried out a patrol on the right flank. They were still unwelcome, and once more were treated to heavy mortar and artillery fire, this time killing Pfc. Raymond McGaughey. The next night, 3rd platoon of "D" Company was blundering around in the darkness, trying to find the Infantry unit they had been assigned to, when they wound up supporting the wrong regiment,

Looking over Bitche (Up from Marseille).

helped them ambush a couple of enemy patrols, and helped take 16 prisoners. They found their correct regiment the next morning. The very next night, 2nd platoon "D" took on machine gun nests and seized some local high ground 1 km south of Bitche, with three enemy killed and 12 POWs taken. "D" Company also participated in a few "snatch and grabs," where the light tanks would dart into a German position while carrying infantry, grab a couple of Germans as prisoners, toss them onto the back decks of the Stuarts, and be gone before anyone realized what hit them. Joe Graham credited the silent running twin Cadillac engines with aiding success on missions of this sort.

GIs examine Fort Simserhoff after its capture December 22, 1944. (U.S. Army Signal Corps, NARA)

The Reinforced Assault Gun Platoon fired 16 rounds, killing four Germans in one volley and allowing the infantry to capture 14 more Germans after a direct hit on a pill box. Meanwhile, to the west, the opening attacks in the Ardennes took place, and Hitler launched part of his reserves toward the west with an eye towards recapturing Antwerp.

On December 17, 1944, the attack on the Bitche fortresses began in earnest. On the 17th, "B" Company attacked the forts west of the town with the 398th Infantry and augmented by part of the Reinforced Assault Gun Platoon and a couple of 90mm Tank Destroyers. "B" Company First Lieutenant Augustus "Gus" Sitton's platoon was given the mission of supporting an attack on the Maginot line fortress, but two rifle companies of the 398th Infantry were quickly pinned down by the ferocious defensive fire and couldn't move. Lt. Sitton led his platoon as part of a combined infantry, artillery, and armored thrust on the enemy position to rescue the rifle companies. Sitton's tank platoon charged down an unscouted road and quickly drew heavy enemy artillery fire. The U.S. artillery put down a rolling barrage, and the pinned infantry rose to join the attack as the relief reached them. The combined weight of the infantry and charging tanks drove the enemy back two hundred yards and allowed the infantry to move and occupy the fortresses Freudenburg and Schiesseck. The only loss was two tanks that got bogged down in the mud. For his role in planning and leading the attack, Lt. Sitton won a Bronze Star.

The 3rd Battalion 398th received a Presidential Unit Citation for their work in reducing the fortifications at Bitche. The Citation was awarded to the 3rd Battalion and also applied to B/781, as they assisted in the mutually attained results. Quoting from the citation:

> 3rd BN was assigned the mission of breaching the formidable fortifications of the Maginot line west of the town of Bitche, France. With no terrain features for protection and only shell craters for cover, the 3rd Battalion, taking advantage of a forty-five minute barrage, moved in to the attack. Under intense enemy artillery, mortar, automatic weapons, and small arms fire, the 3rd Battalion pressed the attack and, after fierce fighting, captured Fort Freudenburg, along with units ten and eleven of Fort Schiesseck. At this point, the enemy increased their artillery and mortar fire, forcing the Battalion to dig in for the night. At 0930 hours the following morning, 18 Dec 1944, the attack was continued behind a rolling barrage laid down by supporting artillery. Fighting their way up the steep, barren slope of the difficult terrain through heavy barbed wire entanglements, the assault detachments, despite harassing enemy fire, rapidly wrested the remaining units of Fort Schiesseck from the enemy. The fighting aggressiveness, courage, and devotion to duty displayed by member of the 3rd Battalion are worthy of the highest emulation and reflect the finest traditions of the Armed Forces of the United States.

The Presidential Unit Citation was awarded March 12, 1945. Following this, the entire 100th Division and their attached battalions referred to themselves as "Sons of Bitche."

The techniques for neutralizing the forts evolved into a set method. The tank/infantry team would deal with the outlying field strong points, which typically were abandoned when the defenders went inside the fort. The tanks would then fire their main guns at whatever openings, doors, slits, or ports were visible to keep the defenders under cover. The tanks employed in the attacks on the forts were successful in that, while the 75mm and 105mm HE rounds did little direct damage to the concrete structures, they caused enough concussive blast damage to keep the defenders inside and hunkered down, which in turn allowed the infantry to advance. The Assault Gun Platoon fired 42 rounds of 105mm HE and AP at Fort Schiesseck alone as it was taken. Then the infantry/engineers would drop explosive charges inside the forts to cut off the tunnels and stairs. But, somewhat understandably, the infantry seldom descended into the forts to weed out the hiding defenders. So the tactic was not always successful, and troops would move on only to find later that the fort was again active and in enemy hands as the defenders came up from the basement.

In an effort to enable the forts to be neutralized remotely, some logic was applied – if a 75mm HE shell worked OK as a door knocker, and a 105mm HE shell worked better, then a 155mm shell might just be the ticket, so U.S. troops didn't have to approach and enter these casements! The few self-propelled 155mm guns available in theater were lumbering beasts that had virtually no armor protection for their

crew; they were designed for indirect fire missions from safely behind the lines. The idea of using these guns in a direct fire mission was thinking outside the box, but they could not be risked, nor could they face tank or antitank opposition. But it was decided to give them a shot, literally, and three Self-Propelled 155s were brought up on the 18th. A noisy

M12 firing its 155mm rifle downrange. (U.S. Army Signal Corps, NARA)

artillery barrage masked the engine noise during their approach and they were covered during the advance to their firing positions by "D" Company's light tanks, which took the opportunity to take some target practice and fired 20 rounds of their 37mm ammo at enemy pillboxes. The 155s punched their way through the casements, and as they backed off infantry ran up and dropped explosives into the holes. The infantry then scrambled onto the M5Stuarts and they bugged out to the next site. This was repeated at four or five positions.

Over the next couple of days, the 781st Tank Battalion was scooting from position to position, mopping up, firing on pillboxes, scouting, and providing flank support and other support missions assisted by good visibility and clear, cold skies. "B" Company scouted out the location of some enemy artillery which had the 398th pinned down, and on the 20th, the Assault Gun platoon moved up to cover the 398th. Their 105mm fire into the trees was devastating and kept the German defenders pinned down, allowing the 398th Regiment to successfully withdraw, along with the Reinforced Assault Gun Platoon.

Ronald O'Donnell caught up with the 781st while it was at Bitche after suffering seasickness during a long, stormy trip from the U.S. to England, and then to Lehavre, where he was squashed into a boxcar for the long slow ride to Bitche. The odd French railroad timetables had not improved: "It seemed like we'd go forward about two miles, and then back a mile!" Upon arrival he was assigned to "B" Company as Driver in Sgt. Earl Brownell's M4.

Since August 1944, Hitler had been stockpiling a secret reserve to launch another offensive. As veteran units were chewed up on the East or West Fronts, they were pulled back, and the core group of veteran survivors was brought back to operating strength by adding raw recruits. These recruits were pretty much the bottom of the barrel, being children, old men, displaced navy or air force personnel, and foreign draftees that agreed to serve in lieu of imprisonment. The training was minimal and their physical conditioning was abysmal, but the recruits were given a large number of *Panzerfauste* and automatic weapons. On balance, they still could put a lot of lead in the air when they needed to. Hitler launched this offensive in mid-December, and it rocked the Allies back on their heels.

Withdrawal was on the Allied high command's mind more and more, as the German Ardennes offensive was uncoiling and powering through the Allied lines to the west. A general withdrawal was anticipated, and word-of-mouth rumor of a possible retreat was getting through to the GIs. The 100th was in an awkward spot, with a portion of the Bitche defenses taken and some still in German hands. The 781st was being used more for defensive and flank protection, holding onto what they had rather than grabbing more territory.

During the day of the 20th, one tank from "C" Company was hit by anti-tank fire, killing Sgt. Henry Roberge and wounding one of his crew. On the night of the 20th, "D" Company's Lt. Paul Pais and his platoon were moving to Freudenburg Farms, but missed it in the darkness and made a meandering loop almost around it. They backtracked, then took a wrong turn, and found themselves barreling straight toward the enemy front. They were in the very same area that the 398th Infantry had evacuated the day before. Realizing his mistake, Pais' lead tank stood on the brakes and stopped, but the next tank behind couldn't stop in time and rear-ended the lead tank. The third tank rear-ended the second, etc., etc. As a result of the multi-tank pileup, all four tanks were immobilized and two tanks were disabled with broken tracks. They came to rest about halfway into "no-man's land," a little closer to the German main line of resistance than the U.S. GIs at Freudenburg Farm. Realizing that they would have to retrace their path to get help, the men quietly withdrew and a four-man volunteer guard was posted on the disabled vehicles. They disabled the tanks' main guns "just in case," and dismounted the machine guns to new positions on either side of the road to cover the tanks. And if they weren't having a bad enough night already, the disabled vehicles came under aggressive German artillery fire, and one of the guards, Pvt. Richard Van Winkle, was wounded in the cheek by a flying splinter. The guard team evacuated when the shelling stopped and spent the night in the cellar of a 45th Division field hospital.

The two tanks lost from "D" Company had their tracks broken but were otherwise OK, so they wanted to recover those vehicles pretty badly, especially since it was anticipated that a general withdrawal might be imminent. Captain Joe Graham, who owned those tanks, and Captain Vinnie Donise, who owned the tank retrievers, personally went to scout the situation. The tanks were in a fairly "hot" zone, and the two COs had to take every advantage of cover from the same German artillery, who were certainly earning their pay. They were finally forced to take cover in a roadside ditch. This was not out of the ordinary, but the ditch had previously been home to the immobile 398th for quite a while and they hadn't the luxury of latrines. The ditch was pretty much an open sewer in spots, and the Captains were forced to use the ditch as cover to crawl back to safety. Upon getting back to safety, Captain Donise sent Lt. Cohen and his retriever crew to retrieve the tanks. Captain Graham received a summons to immediately see Lt. Col Kinne and he obeyed, although he didn't have time to change his clothes. Captain Graham was the "butt" of many jokes over the next few weeks. His two tanks were recovered, and his ego eventually recovered, but his thoroughly soiled and very aromatic uniform did not. Lt. Jason Cohen was provided with another friendly artillery barrage to mask the noise of his tank retrievers as they waddled up to the disabled M5s. The barrage also covered the crews as they dismounted, hooked up, and remounted. Only one German 88mm shell was sent in their direction, but it "missed by a mile" and the tanks were successfully retrieved.

While it patrolled surrounding roads, "C" Company had encountered booby traps in trees that were designed to be activated by trip wires. The wires were at such a height that all vehicles except the tall Shermans would safely pass. The Division then issued a directive that all radio masts were to be tied down immediately. This wasn't very popular, as this caused a delay in getting into action, since the radio mast had to be untied before rotating the turret or it would snap off. The Battalion also ordered that hatches of all tanks were to be closed down when stationary or when under artillery fire. This was ordered because, if hit by High Explosive, the tank crew was faced with not just the impact, but the pressure wave. Open hatches, ventilators, periscope holes, etc., all let in the overpressure wave. Concussion to crew, disorientation, and loss of interior lights, radio tubes, etc., were the usual result of a near miss.

In order to stop the German defenders from reoccupying deserted and conquered forts by means of the tunnels, a new strategy was formed – bury them! To achieve this, a 781st HQ Company tank that had a bulldozer blade was brought up with the intention of heaping dirt over the captured forts, preventing their re-use. But the enemy defensive fire was so intense that the tank was kept in the wings. Finally, after several days of impatient waiting for the defensive fire to ease, T/5 Joseph Anderson volunteered to drive the dozer tank and seal Fort Simserhof once and for all. He first buried Unit #9 under earth and rocks; he next filled the moats and sealed the exits of Units 2 and 4, and finally blocked the turrets of Units 6 and 8. While attempting to cover Unit 7, his tank became mired down and got stuck. Anderson escaped, but unfortunately, his tank was in a position where the recovery vehicles couldn't get close, because the German defenders had the area covered with 88mm AT fire and were glad to demonstrate that to anyone who doubted them. For his bravery in manning his tank, T/5 Anderson won a Bronze Star. When the 100th Div withdrew from the area, this tank had to be blown up and abandoned by 100th Div engineers. It was the only tank lost by the Battalion during December.

11. WITHDRAWAL

Many miles to the Northwest of Bitche, the Germans poured across the Allied lines in the Ardennes region and the Allied front lines fell back, forming a large "Bulge" in the Allied MLR (hence the "Battle of the Bulge"). As the strength of the German offensive became surprisingly apparent, Ike ordered Devers to make the VI Army Group assume a defensive posture and halt offensive operations until the Bulge could be stabilized. This was unprecedented, as the top commander was actually ordering one of his armies to retreat if attacked. But Ike didn't trust Devers. On the 20th, Gen. Patton began to disengage his 3rd Army from the front and swing to the west to pitch his forces into the "Bulge." Because the 3rd Army was charged with counterattacking the Bulge, the 7th Army was ordered to spread out and cover the area vacated by the 3rd. Patton's disengagement and movement to counter the Bulge has become legendary. The 7th Army *enabled* Patton to make history by covering the territory his army vacated, moving with equal speed and dexterity to shift westward, which allowed Patton to leave. As he left, the 7th Army had to spread and stretch its lines to the west to cover Patton's departure. The thinness of the lines meant that the 7th Army had to be careful about advances and use resources wisely. Rather than getting any praise for the maneuver, the Seventh Army was viewed as being "wasted." After all, Ike reasoned, if Devers had destroyed the German forces instead of merely pursuing them, then the Seventh could be productively used in the Ardennes instead of guarding them.

As part of this "thinning" of the lines, the 781st was detached from the 100th Division and XV Corps, and attached to VI Corps by direct order of General Patch. Commanding General Wade Haislip of XV Corp also sent a memorandum to General Burress of the 100th Division, asking Burress to convey the route and intended destination (Soufflenheim) of the 781st directly to Lt. Col Kinne. The 781st moved to Soufflenheim, and was then attached to the 79th Infantry Division and put on line at Hatten, France, seven miles west of the Rhine. The 781st was broken up upon arrival: company "A" was attached to the 313th Infantry Regiment; "B" to 314th; and "C" to the 315th. The Assault Gun Platoon was attached to the 315th as well. Company "D" was back in Division reserve, with instructions to look for German paratroopers dressed in U.S. uniforms who spoke perfect English. The Battalion's mission was to strengthen the Main Line of Resistance (MLR) occupied by infantry, and to prepare plans for withdrawal to a secondary line. On December 23, 1944, elements of C/781st were the first units of the battalion to enter Germany in support of the 79th at Rechtenbach, just north of Wissembourg.

The 79th Infantry Divisional reports for December 21st through January 3rd record that, aside from some light, occasional harassing fire, the sector was "Very Quiet." On the other side of the lines on the 21st, Hitler and his generals had agreed that a new attack was necessary. Having failed to reach objectives in the Ardennes, the Germans *recognized* Patton's 3rd Army as part of the Allied mass that was pummeling their offense in the Bulge. Knowing that up to last week the 3rd Army had been 120 miles to the east, they drew an obvious conclusion. They concluded that Patton couldn't still be there if he was here. They then started to plan a new attack named "Nordwind" and aimed it right at the lines where the 3rd Army used to be. That target was right where the now-stretched-thin 7th Army held the line.

The German high command continued planning and massing troops for Operation "Nordwind." Its aim was to split the 7th Army in half between the XV and VI Corps, and relieve the German troops that still hung on to northern Alsace, in the Colmar Pocket, which had resisted all attempts by the French to push back that salient. It was lastly hoped that the offensive would blunt the Western Front for a time and gain enough of a respite to allow the Germans to toss resources at the Eastern front, where the Russians were pressing hard. The German offensive would start in the vicinity of Bitche and progress to the southeast, and was scheduled to kick off on New Year's Eve, 1944. Nordwind would be the last major German offensive of the war.

Allied intelligence detected this buildup opposite the 7th Army, and SHAEF ordered Devers to prepare the 7th Army to pull back, as it appeared to be faced with a new attack. The 7th Army, at this point, was in a bad defensive situation. Patch's front lines looked like a looping, backwards "S" shape that joined two bulges. The top of the "S" was joined to the Allied lines and bellied eastward over the Colmar Pocket to the south, leaving a large salient in the north. Bisected by the Vosges Mountains, with roads that generally lead in all the wrong directions and impeded by winter weather, it was not a good position.

Eisenhower wanted to withdraw the 7th Army and straighten the lines, but that would mean that Strasbourg would have to be evacuated. SHAEF probably had solid intelligence information from broken German codes, but they weren't sharing; Devers and Patch didn't want to pull back and give up hard-won ground based on rumors. Losing Strasbourg would mean the loss of the largest industrial center and capital of Alsace, and its possession was a tremendous psychological asset to the French. When the French got word of the proposed withdrawal they got in *everyone's* face, because leaving Strasbourg was simply unacceptable to them. They issued a strongly-worded protest to Ike. They issued a strongly-worded protest to Churchill.

And Roosevelt. General Charles DeGaulle, ever the team player, threatened to withdraw the French 1st Army from under Devers' command, and at the same time issued orders to it to defend Strasbourg "no matter what" the rest of the Allied armies did! (This pretty much equates to withdrawing your Army from under SHAEF control.) Devers wanted to follow orders and evacuate; but Patch sided with the French, which endeared him permanently to the FFA. After more back-and-forth threats, DeGaulle then escalated the conflict and threatened to cut *all* the American supply lines in France! Faced with complete disintegration of the Allied effort, Eisenhower then relented. The 7th Army would not abandon Strasbourg, but that meant the bulge outward in Patch's lines remained.

Christmas Eve and Day were clear, cold, and relatively quiet. Other than the Assault Gun Platoon, which rained 170 rounds of 105mm High Explosive Christmas cheer on the Germans, and "A" Company, which likewise fired 280 rounds of harassing fire, the rest of the battalion saw no action. Joe Graham attended Midnight Mass (which was held at 2:00 PM due to curfews) in Hatten and sang "Stille Nacht, Heilige Nacht" with his Tommy gun on the church pew next to him the whole time.

On the 26th, the pattern repeated itself: "A" fired another 240 rounds and the Assault Gun Platoon unleashed 70 rounds. The Battalion HQ received a recommendation for a field modification to the U.S. tanks for increased protection from *Panzerschreks* and *Panzerfauste*. The bulletin recommended that crews surround their tanks with a mesh wire screen (like chicken wire) mounted 11" from the hull and supported by a frame. The theory was that the warhead's detonator would hit the wires in the mesh and detonate prior to striking the hull. If predetonated in this manner, the warhead's chance of penetrating the armor was (it was hoped) lessened. Crews looked for alternatives to the wire mesh and used whatever was handy.

To combat the *Panzerfaust/Panzershreck* shooters, the Sherman crews slapped all kinds of stuff over the armor to ward off the warhead – the favorite was sandbags, although spare track links, cut up plate from recovered tanks, and logs and boards were used. Some units even poured reinforced concrete on the front of their tanks! There wasn't solid proof it worked, but there was *some* evidence, and the psychological value and crew morale boost it gave was worth it. General George Patton would later upbraid his tank commanders for having too much of the homemade protection on the tanks. The downside to hanging all that extra "armor" on the tanks was it overtaxed the suspension, which was none too great to start with, and caused early failure of the bogie wheels and tracks.

There was a dustup during the night of the 29th, when 3rd Platoon "D" encountered a German patrol during the night near Mothern, losing two tanks to *Panzerfaust* fire, which blew their tracks off, fortunately without crew injury. On the 29th, Company "A" was detached from the 79th and also from battalion control, and was reattached to a special Task Force Linden, which was tasked with covering the familiar area around Bitche. They left taking six M4 Shermans mounting 76mm guns, eleven M4 Shermans mounting 75mm guns, and their T-2 Tank Recovery Vehicle. The Battalion's remaining armored assets were reshuffled in the 79th to cover their departure.

The year-end Armored Report for the 781st showed 644 effective personnel out of 671, with eight sick and one wounded over the previous week. Intelligence reports coming in to the Battalion noted a "possible build-up of enemy armor in the Bitche area." It was noted that enemy activity was notably lacking armor, and that many tanks were stationary, with the prophetic guess that they were "perhaps being conserved." However, as the 781ˢᵗ manned the lines, much movement of tracked vehicles was heard at night. The Germans were forced to move at night due to the overwhelming air superiority enjoyed by the Allies, and movement during the day was suicidal. The battalion received word that three tanks equipped with flame throwers were to be issued to the battalion in the near future. These, it was hoped, would provide another method of taking strongpoints and gun emplacements.

As part of his December monthly report, Lt. Col Kinne passed the following suggestions based on their experiences during the month of December up the chain of command for consideration:

1. Tanks and infantry units have to use the SCR300 radios for proper communication.
2. In order to do #1, the radios have to be convenient. (To this end, the 781ˢᵗ was mounting field telephones on the rear of their tanks.)
3. Cooperation in the initial planning phases of attacks and movements is vital.
4. Making a specific infantry unit responsible to protect the tanks against bazooka attack is required.

Along came New Year's Eve, and so closed the year 1944. After hitting the front lines with a "bang" being on the offensive alongside the 100ᵗʰ Division, the 781ˢᵗ now found itself in a mostly static defensive position on a relatively quiet front line, occasionally lobbing harassing fire onto the enemy with the 79ᵗʰ Infantry Division. Ominously, the fireworks that were stored by the townspeople in Wingen for their New Years' Eve celebration mysteriously exploded the night before.

12. THE ADVERSARIES

The two major enemies facing the 781st at this time were the weather and the German Army; each of which inflicted a lot of pain and death. The winter of 1944/5 in France's Alsace region was one of the harshest on record, being cold, wet, and deep. The supply problems through Marseille had still not been rectified and many of the men were still without shoe paks, and bare leather boots didn't cut it in slush and snow. As a result, trench foot and frostbite were a common problem, aggravated by the cold and the numerous stream and river crossings. Tank crews were trained to scout all water crossings before trying to cross, which resulted in wet feet. Soldiers without access to vehicles would try to dry their socks by carrying them inside their shirt; vehicles provided a ready source of heat to dry clothes over the engine bay. Fresh socks were issued with daily rations, and were just as important to the men as the food.

Infantry used the warmth of the tank's rear deck to get warm or dry clothing, and they slept over the engine compartment heat. Whenever the tank or vehicle was stopped, the crew covered the engine compartment with a tarp, and with luck, it might stay warm for several hours. If the stop was longer, the ritual of lighting off the engine and battery heaters was performed. There was a field stove (M1942) that was part of the kit carried on a tank, but it wasn't used all that much in winter – the engine manifolds heated more rations with less fuss. Rather than having to wait for the Assistant Driver to light off the stove and wait for things to heat, the crew just grabbed their rations off the hot engine, opened them, and chowed down.

The tanks had two heat settings – hot in the summer and cold in the winter. When 30 tons of steel drops below freezing it becomes a large, very effective freezer. Despite that, if crews couldn't commandeer a barn or farmhouse, they would rather sleep in the tank when it was cold, rather than shoveling space for sleeping bags and shelter halves outside. The interior of the tank did shelter crews from the wind, but the freezing surfaces would ice up from condensation when breathing. There was some heat transmitted through the engine bulkhead. Rather obviously, there wasn't room for anyone to stretch out, so this wasn't a comfortable arrangement. During operation the interior was still very cold, and frozen feet were a common problem among Drivers and Assistant Drivers – their station was cramped and didn't provide much room to move.

When the tank was operating, the air intake for the engine could be ducted to come from outside through the turret (which caused an intense draft and sucked out any heat. While nice in summer, in winter, this just added a wind chill to the cold.). Alternately, the outside air could be drawn in directly to the engine if the inside flaps were closed (in which case the interior was just *cold*). When firing the main gun, the turret was ducted by fans to help sweep fumes from the gun out of the turret, which was tolerated because being cold beat choking. The "Little Joe" two-stroke engine inside the crew compartment that charged the batteries was air-cooled, and was a small heat source that was welcome in the winter.

The icy roads played no favorites. The rubber-tired wheeled vehicles used tire chains to gain traction. Despite their weight, the half track's and the Sherman's rubber tracks slid badly on ice. While there was not much that could be done for a half track because of the all-rubber track, tank crews tied barbed wire or chain, or fitted bolts to the tracks to get some traction; they welded things to the tracks, and they mixed steel track sections into the rubber tracks on the M4s. There were no snowplows at the front. The tank dozers were called to clear roads, but since the dozer blade could not be angled the snow just piled up in front. As a result, plowing a road was a long and laborious effort.

The heavier German tanks also slipped on the icy roads, and the Tiger II and Jagdtigers' great weight and lack of maneuverability made them harder to stop sliding

Panther crew servicing road wheels. (German Federal Archive)

once they got started, and harder to retrieve when they got stuck. Panthers and Tigers had a problem with failure of the rim bolts on their dished road wheels. Fixing an inner road wheel was a problem due to their overlapping design; on some tanks there were six layers of wheels. Service techs had to pull two outers to service one inner. The deep snow and ice also compounded the problem when slush would freeze the tightly-packed wheels together. Trying to move without checking for free movement could damage the road wheels or worse, immobilize the vehicle.

The Panther transmission was also weak, and was frequently sabotaged at the factory. (The impressed laborers would intentionally weaken a gear tooth so it broke under load.) Again, metal quality was deteriorating, as the war denied Germany the alloying metals to strengthen the steel and poor gear strength became a problem. Panthers were prone to strip their 3rd gear, and the entire final drive was prone to strip if the tank was put through many pivot turns. Unlike a Sherman, the Panther's final drive was not a bolt-on unit, but was housed inside the frontal armor. A broken final drive could only be removed after stripping the driver's compartment and removing the transmission first, a far more involved task than the Sherman's "package unit." Average engine life in a Panther was only 650 miles, and over the course of the war more Panthers were disabled by movement than by battle. The best way to defeat a Panther was to make it move and hope it would break down. Homer Turner related that the Sherman "couldn't hold a candle to a German tank, but the Sherman was all we had. The Sherman was fast and we tried to outmaneuver them."

Panthers also liked to catch fire due to carburetor backfires, which ignited hydraulic fluid leaks from the transmission and fuel leaks from the complicated fuel plumbing. Shermans got twice the gas mileage that Panthers and Tigers got, and the Shermans' tracks were good for 2,500 miles, while the Panther and Tiger averaged about 500 miles. The Sherman's gun tubes also had a longer life expectancy than that of the German tanks, but the battle life of the tanks was shorter than the gun tube life expectancy, so it mattered little.

The German Panther had a long 75mm gun that had a higher muzzle velocity and greater penetrating power than the Sherman's gun. Tigers went one better and had a long 88mm gun that could poke holes through Shermans at will from great range. As Homer Turner said: "You respected that 88!" The Allied troops respected many German weapons and tended to lump them together. All antitank weapons became "88s," and all German tanks were "Tigers." Oddly enough, the Panther was actually physically bigger than the

Panther Tank. (German Federal Archives)

Tiger! The Panther generated less panic in opponents, but it accounted for more kills. The Tiger had the superior reputation. Sherman tank crews actually became "gun shy" about engaging German tanks, because they knew their ineffective guns couldn't take them out, while they in turn were a sitting duck.

Shermans had the following advantages over the Tigers and Panthers:
1. They were more reliable, easier to service, and their crews were generally better trained than their German counterparts at this point.
2. They were more maneuverable over hard ground.
3. They had greater range, both on road and cross-country.
4. Speed: Of the Panther, Tiger, and Sherman, the Panther was theoretically fastest on straight roads, but in reality, the Sherman and Panther were in a dead heat, because German fuel quality was deteriorating and Sherman crews were wiring their tanks' engine governors open.
5. Higher quality armor. The Sherman's armor was tougher and less prone to cracking, but there just wasn't enough of it.
6. Quantity – there were oodles and oodles of Shermans for every Panther.

Panthers had the following advantages over Shermans:
1. Low flash powder: the U.S. rounds had such a big muzzle blast and smoke that the gunner, at times, couldn't see through it to mark the fall of his shot. The German rounds went off clean, only marked by a dust cloud if the round passed over dirt.
2. A better gun with higher penetration. Ricochets had been seen that *went through* a Sherman at 3,000 yards.
3. Thicker armor. The 75mm and 76mm rifles of the Sherman couldn't penetrate the front hull of a Panther. Shermans could penetrate a Panther or Tiger from the side, and since the Panther stowed rounds in the sides, they would frequently light up if hit from the side. Panther armor, though thicker, was becoming brittle; as the war dragged on, supplies of critical alloying elements – molybdenum in particular – were being cut off. The Panther armor was prone to fracture.
4. Superior gunsights that had two magnifications: 2.5x and 5x. (Sherman had a fixed 5x.) The Panther and Sherman sights were lit, and gradations could be seen during low-illumination times. But the Panther also had a flip-down shade for shooting into the sun that the Sherman gunner didn't. However, the German gunner's sight didn't have a brow pad, and having his forehead anywhere near the sight while moving was dangerous. So the Panther gunner was blind until the tanks stopped, then he had to reorient and reacquire. The gunner also had to flip his right earpiece out of the way when sighting, because the gun was so close to his right shoulder. (The Panther and Sherman gunnery crews were positioned differently. The Sherman's gunner was to the right of the gun with the loader on the left. The Panther crews were in the opposite positions.)
5. Superior floatation. The Panther could outmaneuver a Sherman in wet and muddy terrain due to the Sherman's higher ground pressure. On mud, where a Panther would leave track marks five inches deep, a Sherman would sink until it stuck.
6. Lower silhouette. The Panther was 9ft tall, vs. the 11ft Sherman, which could easily be seen from 200 to 3,500 yards away.
7. The commander's hatch on the German tanks opened by popping up five inches and then swinging to the side. This permitted the commander to ride with the hatch popped up but not swung open, which provided superior visibility and

ventilation, and still gave overhead protection from air bursts, shells, snipers, grenades, weather, etc. Allied Commanders had to look through periscopes or go into danger with an open turret hatch. Most chose to go with the hatch open, which of course made them prime targets for snipers and bazooka teams.

Tiger and Panther crews knew the 75mm Sherman couldn't touch them, and they would sometimes show themselves, daring the Shermans to advance! They were taught not to fear Shermans, even if they were outnumbered 2:1. The first Panthers did have a weak spot in the gun armor, but the odds of getting close enough to accurately place your round in that spot were pretty remote. Most often the Tiger or Panther would just sit in a prepared position and make the Shermans advance. The Allied forces developed a technique to kill a crouching Tiger or Panther. When Shermans faced off with Panthers or Tigers, there were hopefully two or more Shermans to each German. The first Sherman would try to shoot off a track, which was about the most they could hope for without being punctured themselves. The Panther or Tiger could then only move forwards or backwards a few feet on the remaining track, which also caused it to turn. While this was hopefully happening, the second U.S. tank maneuvered for a side shot. This technique worked better with Tigers, because the Shermans could outrun their slow, hand-cranked turret traverse, but not so much with Panthers – they had a power traverse.

To offset this tactic, the Germans developed the doctrine that "Tiger never works alone." Sometimes two Tigers worked together, but more often a Tiger was paired with a *Sturmgeshutz*, or another lesser tank. The *Sturmgeshutz* (German for "assault gun," a.k.a. "Stug") were great defensive vehicles, but the lack of a turret greatly hampered them on offense. When the Sherman troop slipped around the flank, they discovered the second team member lying quietly in wait on *their* flank, quite often augmented by infantry teams armed with *Panzerfauste* who were hungry for Shermans. When faced with a Tiger team, options were few. At that point, the Tiger would

German Tiger I. (German Federal Archives)

have to be isolated. It would be hit with a White Phosphorous round to blind it. Then artillery was used, with Allied tanks and infantry fighting through defensive lines of infantry and hull-down sniping Panthers and Stugs to clear the German supporting infantry and clear a path for Anti-Tank fire. Of course, while all this was going on, the poor Shermans were out there dodging rounds, which was horrible, and it didn't improve the longer it went on. The Shermans had a gun stabilizer that maintained elevation on the gun while moving. The Sherman would rush in to get close, shoot, then scoot. But the odds were still long. There was a report of one Tiger that polished off six Shermans single-handedly, while it shrugged off being hit *15 times* at a distance of 700 yards. German tank crews were taught to fear the U.S. Bazooka and the M-36 Tank Destroyers with their 90mm gun, but not the Sherman.

Allied 75mm tank guns had to be within 100 yards, or hit the rear of the turret, or the vertical plates on the flanks of Tigers or Panthers – the 75mm could not penetrate the frontal armor of a Tiger at *any* range. A 76mm had to be within 300 yards to make a dent. This was getting ridiculous to the Sherman team – having to get that close to the enemy before you can fire meant that for every round you put in the air, there were two German rounds in the air coming back at you! The Russians had a similar problem, and solved it by having one tank sacrifice itself by *ramming* the Tiger and immobilizing it so the others could then shoot it! The Sherman Firefly, which mounted the British 17-pounder, was in demand, as it could penetrate a Tiger I in a frontal engagement at ranges up to 1,900 yards. They could not penetrate the frontal armor of a Tiger II, only the side. But Fireflies were in short supply. On the other hand, German Armor Piercing rounds could go through a Sherman front armor plate, the transmission behind it, the ammunition boxes behind those, through the engine behind that, and out the rear, and would typically kill two crewmembers doing so. Allied crews joked that shooting at a Panther or Tiger merely scratched the paint and made them mad.

The antitank guns in use by both sides were pretty even. The German "88" had a reputation that was fearsome, although to the Allied troopers, *all* German AT guns were "88s," even if the majority of them were really 75mm. The bazooka, 37mm, and 57mm guns that were organic to the U.S. infantry divisions couldn't touch a Panther or Tiger from the front. The AT team hoped to knock off a tread, or a periscope, or an antenna, or something that would render the German tank ineffective, or at least "ring the bell" enough to make the crew nervous and bug out.

The hand-held antitank weapons, Bazookas, and *Panzerfauste* were feared on both sides. *Panzerfaust* gunners always aimed at the engine compartment to cause a bailout, and the crew would be cut down by the infantry supporting them with submachine guns. The *Panzershreck* was an unabashed copy of the U.S. Bazooka, just larger and more powerful, but also pretty unwieldy. The *Panzerfaust*, a smaller, easy-to-use single-shot weapon, pioneered shaped-charge technology, and its warhead torched a molten jet of copper through the armor. This molten jet squirted into the crew compartment where all the ammo was stored, or was held in the crewmembers' arms (remember that crew had to pass ammo to the loader unless he was using the emergency store or his close locker), and perilously ready to ignite. It made a mess of crewmembers as well. Crews almost instinctively bailed out when the tank was hit – the great fear of being burned alive was a constant in the crews, and they wasted no time getting out. Regrettably, an ammo fire typically happened so quickly that the crew didn't have enough time to evacuate.

GI with Bazooka. (U.S. Army Signal Corps, NARA)

Popping smoke was also effective, especially White Phosphorous, as this could cause engine fires, which the Panther and Tigers were prone to have, and as a result, the German crews were afraid of the smoke, thinking their tank was ablaze. It also caused claustrophobia and anxiety. Most times the tank would turn and run or the crew would bail out. At the very least it blinded the German gunner, and allowed the Shermans to work closer. If the Tiger/Panther advanced through the smoke to attack the advancing Shermans, it became a perfect target against the white smoke backdrop for the Anti-Tank fire and artillery.

So the 781st faced a grim job ahead. The really decisive factors in tank-tank battles seemed to favor the enemy. Range favored the Germans exclusively. Being on the defense helped. First to shoot – the side that gets the jump and fires first – usually wins, and American crews were giving away the first shot advantage by firing ranging shots. Only numbers – the theory that material advantage will eventually win – favored the Allies, and that wasn't a pleasant prospect if you were part of the cannon fodder being thrown at Gerry tanks. The trump card to all of those factors that favored the 781st was training! The coordination between the 781st tank-infantry team and their supportive artillery evened out the disparity between the tanks when it worked. Experience was the key – especially if house-to-house combat was involved, where street fighters with experience made all the difference.

13. "NORDWIND"

Generals Devers and Patch were rushing reinforcements to the front lines. Three green Infantry divisions (the 42nd, 63rd, and 70th) had their stateside training cut short before they even finished their twelve-week basic training, and they were herded on board ship. They had *zero* combined arms training, and had barely disembarked at Marseille when they were whisked to the front. They were not given time to collect their organic armor nor artillery units before the move; they each had just their three Infantry regiments and a portion of their HQ. This Infantry was also nothing to write home about, as the Divisions had previously been stripped of their best rifle-men to solve an earlier crisis, and what remained were men at best partially trained in basic weapons. These guys were basically uniformed civilians who just about knew which end of a rifle the bullet came from. To take advantage of their Infantry strength, but also to give them a chance of survival, Patch formed three task forces, mixing them with experienced support units and placing them under the command of an experienced assistant Division commander. This was good news for the raw troops, but bad news for the support troops, especially the armored battalions, as these troops were totally clueless when it came to supporting tanks. Task Force Linden was formed around the 42nd Infantry ("Rainbow") Division, and Company "A" of the 781st was selected to provide experienced armor support. Patch also formed Task Force Harris, which contained the 63rd Infantry, and Task Force Herren, which contained the 70th Infantry ("Trailblazers"). Task Force Harris and Task Force Herren still needed some armor.

The major part of the 781st (now with the 79th Division) faced north in the upper-right corner of the salient in the 7th Army's line. They held an east-west line from Wissembourg to Lauterbourg, along the Lauter River. "A" Company, with Task Force Linden and the 42nd Infantry, faced east on the west bank of the Rhine River north of Strasbourg, at a right angle to the 79th. The German planned attack formed a pincer that hoped to lop off a large portion of the 7th Army and relieve the Colmar-

Pocket, but to be successful, they had to get through the 781st Tank Battalion.

And where was the Allied Air Force? During January, the Air forces were grounded for half the month by fog, snow, sleet, and rain, so Allied air superiority could not be called upon, and as a result, this was largely a ground campaign. Luftwaffe planes led off with a big bang when their offensive started, but most of the effort supported the Belgium front and very little was used in Alsace. On the Allied side, there were a few deep air raids that prevented German supply and reinforcement movement, but not much close air support for the ground troops.

General Patch knew from intelligence reports the exact day and even the time (early AM) when Nordwind would launch; he just didn't know exactly where it would hit. Bad weather had stopped aerial recon, and signal intercepts didn't reveal details. Just to tighten his lines, Patch directed a withdrawal from the corner where the 781st was stationed. This proved to be lucky, as the 781st was saddled up to withdraw with their Infantry Regiments to a new Main Line of Resistance, so they were ready to roll and could quickly respond to threats.

The German "Nordwind" attack was launched on time, and hit the Allied lines precisely as planned just before midnight on New Year's Eve. The U.S. 44th, then the 100th Infantry Divisions near Bitche were hit first, and hard. The 44th started to buckle to the left of the 100th, but they gave ground slowly. The Nordwind plan was perfectly executed, and the German attackers didn't allow themselves to get bogged down when faced with resistance. They rolled off any strongpoints from west to east across the 7th Army front and kept probing for a weakness or hole in the U.S. lines. The 100th held firm, but to their right, Task Force Hudelson crumbled. The 100th was in serious jeopardy of being cut off! Off to the east, the 781st was nervously watching as their infantry got orders to withdraw per General Patch's orders, and they wondered if were being left behind. The tankers fired harassing rounds to discourage any possible German advance and to mask the Infantry movements. 1st Platoon of "D" Company intercepted and broke up one such probing German patrol of 18 men, capturing one wounded POW.

On January 3, 1945, the movement orders at last came for the 781st. Most of the Battalion was relieved from attachment to the 79th Infantry Division, and was immediately assigned to Task Force Herren. Task Force Herren was assigned to move to the east to shore up the lines just as Nordwind was probing the same lines. 1st Platoon "D" was left still attached to the 79th Infantry Division as a mobile reserve. The move started under cold and cloudy skies with fair visibility. Any movement at this time was being seriously impeded by the throngs of civilians that were fleeing the oncoming German assault. They clogged the roads in all directions as they did their best to stay away from the fighting.

The clogged roads delayed movement, and as a result, the 79th still was in the process of withdrawing to their new assigned position when the 781st started moving. Under the timetable for the withdrawal, division artillery was to pack up and leave at 1830, January 3rd. Infantry was to pack up and leave at 2000, and the rear guard was to stay in place and provide cover until 2400, midnight. "C" Company was the last of the tank-infantry groups to depart. One of the 781st vets remembered: "As we withdrew, the people stood in groups on street corners and looked scared. French flags weren't hanging from the windows anymore, and no little kids waved. Moving back was a new and unwelcome experience."

The Reinforced Assault Gun Platoon, consisting of six M4s with 105 mm Howitzers and the Mortar Platoon, were tasked with being part of the rear guard covering the withdrawal, and, as rear guard, they had to stay until midnight. The night turned clear and cold, and the snow was waist deep. From their vantage point, the AGP could see three approach roads, and each was filled with approaching German advance units. The AGP would zero in on one road and would rain shells on that road, scattering the enemy and stopping their advance. They would then shift fire to another road, where another column was approaching, and scatter them. Then they would shell the German troops on the 3rd road and disperse them. By that time, the advance on the first road had gathered itself back up and they would start over, but each time the advance got a little closer. The Platoon fired 240 rounds this day in this manner.

Adolph Hoppi and Homer Turner standing on Hot Box. (Courtesy of Hoppi Family)

Night dragged on, and the hostiles were getting pretty close, but at last the clock crept past midnight, and the Assault Gun Platoon could bug out. In Homer Turner's tank "Hot Box" his driver, Adolph Hoppi, fired up the engine and they moved out, following the rest of the Platoon. The roads were cold and icy, and they could barely see in the dark, so they slowly crept rearward. As sunlight appeared, they cleared the patch of wood they were in, sped up, and were going up a hill when Hot Box hit an obstacle that was hidden, buried by snow, and "high-centered" on it. The tank was balanced on its belly pan on the obstacle – not able to go forward and not able to back off – and was stuck fast, with the German Army not far behind! Homer and his crew radioed for a tow, but the Tank Recovery vehicles had already left, and would have to "swim upstream" against the withdrawing troops and fleeing civilians to get back to Homer's position.

While they waited for rescue, Homer's crew dismounted the tank's .50 caliber and .30 caliber machine guns, traversed the main gun to the rear, and prepared positions to defend their tank until help arrived. Just in case help didn't arrive, they also set demolition charges on the engine and breech of the gun (each tank carried two pounds of TNT in the turret and two pounds of TNT in the bow gunner's position for this eventuality). While this was going on, the last of the rear-guard GIs were streaming by on their way to the rear, pointing in the direction of the oncoming enemy and calling "You'd better get going!" Homer and his crew replied "We aren't leaving our tank!," and those five men prepared to take on the entire oncoming German Army to make their point. One sympathetic truckload of soldiers stopped and set up to provide cover just as the Tank Recovery Vehicle appeared. On the first try, the TRV hooked up the tow cables and tried to winch Hot Box free, but instead of dragging the tank free, the TRV started to drag towards Hot Box! This got the TRV crew somewhat peeved – Germans or no Germans, this bastard was coming free! They then anchored the front of the TRV by tying it to a nearby tree and tried winching again, and this time Hot Box conceded defeat and popped loose. Also by this time, the enemy was so close that their tracers were flying overhead! The Good Samaritan GIs quickly mounted up and the TRV scooted out, with Hot Box providing cover for their withdrawal. Homer Turner and the crew of Hot Box were the last of the last to withdraw that day! They caught up with Task Force Herren and the rest of the Battalion at La Petite Pierre, which was about seven miles southwest of Wingen-sur-Moder. As a result of the changes in strategy ("we aren't protecting Strasbourg." "Oh yes we are."), movement orders for the portion of the Seventh Army in the northeast salient were confused. Task Force Herren was now on its way to assist the 45th at Bitche and shore up the right flank of that Division in the Wingen area. However, the blow was not to come at Bitche, but to the east. This would place the 781st exactly where one of Hilter's pincers would strike.

This whole Alsace region had a schizophrenic quality to it. Sandwiched between Germany and France, and over time claimed by both, this area was called Alsace Lorraine by the French when they owned it and Elassas and Lothrinnen by the Germans when they owned it. Germany took this territory from France when they won the Franco-Prussian war in the late 1800s, but then lost it back to France as part of reparations for World War I. Germany then reclaimed the region in 1940. The populace, who were understandably bilingual, needed to look to see which flag was flying each morning, and loyalties and sentiments were mixed and confused. Hitler was determined to hold on to the area, and he demanded that the area "Germanize" and convert everything – language, names, customs, signs, and clothing – to German. Towns that had French names like La Petite Pierre (which means "The Pebble" in French) were now called by their German name ("Lutzelstein").

"Bonjour" was forbidden – "Guten tag" was the only approved greeting. Berets were forbidden. The name changes meant that all the road maps didn't match the road signs. A 781st vet remembers that: "more than one tanker was billeted in a house that had the French tricolor sticking out the window, and a photograph of a Nazi soldier standing on the mantle."

So there was a large percentage of the local population that didn't mind being under German control and who were ambivalent at best toward the Amis who were "rescuing" them. And when they were liberated and placed back under French control, there was the inevitable round of recriminations and retributions, such as occurred not long after General Leclerc arrived in Strasbourg and proceeded to root out the collaborators and dispense "justice."

14. WINGEN-SUR-MODER

On the 3rd, the townspeople of La Petite Pierre saw the U.S. troops arrive and took to their cellars in expectation of the coming battle. The citizens of Wingen-sur-Moder, a couple of miles to the north, who still felt the outcome of the war was anything but certain, also decided upon discretion and went into their cellars. The 781st was gathering itself at La Petite Pierre as part of their assignment.

As the "Hot Box" crew navigated the icy, hilly roads on its way to their bivouac area, they were held up by a truck that was stuck on the road. Eager to get to their destination, driver Adolph Hoppi pulled out to pass the truck. "Hot Box" slowed, lost traction on the same ice that had stalled the truck, slowed more, and came to a halt, also unable to advance. But then came a small lurch backward, another, and then "Hot Box" was sliding backwards obliquely toward the edge of the road. "Hot Box" paused long enough at the edge of the road for the crew inside to take an exploratory breath, and then it tipped to the side. Thirty tons of steel started rolling down the hillside away from the road. The crew and all their belongings rattled inside like peas in a can. On the first 360 degrees, the gas caps became dislodged and started streaming gas. The engine coughed to a halt. There was a second heart-wrenching roll as gasoline was strewn around and basted the vehicle. A third roll, and then the interior went pitch black. A final half roll and the tank came to rest on its turret in the deep snow, with 175 gallons of gasoline pouring out of the four fuel tanks via leaking gas caps located on the rear deck to the left and right rear of the turret.

The crew was thoroughly rattled, and one member was screaming "We're all going to die!" in the total darkness. Homer calmed his crew and became aware that someone was outside, knocking on the upside down hull. Homer yelled to the outside to get all the smokers away, as the gasoline was everywhere, looking for an excuse to ignite. The crew then oriented themselves in the darkness. The turret hatches were shut with the tank resting on them. The forward hull hatches were shut and wouldn't open against all the snow. Worse, the bottom escape hatch on the belly of the tank between the tracks was securely wired shut! (The hatches would occasionally loosen and drop out onto the ground during road marches. As the crew could not stop and retrieve it and the hatch was not a normal item that could be replaced at a repair depot, it meant a long-term loss. So crews commonly wired it shut.) The men outside carefully dug through the snow and ice to allow the driver's hatch to open enough to allow them all to squeeze through and escape, shaken but not seriously injured. The last to leave, Turner was standing outside the tank and saw that his spare pair of combat boots was still tied to the turret. The way they were resting, it looked like the tank was resting on someone. Lieutenant Simpson approached and inquired: "Sergeant, is that one of your men?" Homer had to sit down.

In this phase of Nordwind, the Germans kept sidestepping American resistance and moving to the southeast until they found the hole they were looking for. About a mile and a half north of Wingen-sur-Moder, the front line was manned by the 276th Infantry of the 45th Infantry Division. Wingen itself had some very unlikely defenders, as it was mostly occupied by the Command Post of the 179th Infantry Regiment – the headquarters clerks, the service unit, and the cooks of the 45th Division. They felt confident, however, because they understood that they were comfortably behind the lines. Reinforcing their confidence, some troops of the 70th Division from Task Force Herren had just arrived in town.

The German 6th SS Mountain Division, which was fresh from its prior post in Norway on the Finnish front, found that hole they were looking for and infiltrated behind the U.S. front lines at midnight on the 3rd. They advanced on the town of Wingen-sur-Moder, and kept a large reserve and armor support to the North in position to exploit a breakthrough if they were successful. The 6th SS Mountain Division had a tough reputation; having fought the Russians on the Eastern front from 1941 to 1944, they were used to winter fighting, and they were good at it. Being one of the best German units in the West, they slipped through the front in several places and made advances that weren't discovered right away.

The townspeople of Wingen were correct in taking cover. They reported seeing many men of Hungarian and Romanian descent infiltrating from the west, who were building obstacles and fortifying strongpoints just outside town. At 0700 in the morning on the 4th, the 6th SS Mountain Infantry Regiment 12 attacked the town, and after two hours of house-to-house fighting they captured the entire Allied Command Post, which included more than 250 members of Task Force Herren, placing them under guard in the nave of the Wingen-sur-Moder Catholic Church.

However, there were reports that these German troops appeared to be intoxicated during the initial attacks. Normally pretty savvy on the attack and carefully using terrain to their advantage, this time they just formed ranks and ran over open ground to attack trenches while making gestures and shouting rude remarks and slogans. Unorthodox perhaps, but it worked.

The Germans captured all of Wingen and then tried to break out to the south, but they were stopped by the 781st's tanks. Then "Lady Luck" intervened on behalf of the Americans. When the Germans tried to call their reserves forward to exploit the breach in the line and deal with the Shermans, they found that their radio batteries were dead! The German reserves finally learned that Wingen had been taken by eavesdropping on American radio transmissions, but by then the opportunity had passed. The breach of the American front lines at Wingen was the only place that looked promising so far from the Nordwind assaults, so the German command then decided to make their major push in that area, as they could possibly isolate and destroy a significant chunk of the U.S. 7th Army.

The American command, stunned by the ferocity of the German attack, ordered an immediate counterattack, but Patch's lines were stretched so thin by Patton's departure that there just wasn't much available to do the counterattacking. The 45th Division's 276th Regiment was battered, shattered, and split apart on both the north and south sides of Wingen. The only part of the 276th that was still in decent shape was its 3rd Battalion, which was now supported by second platoon of "B" Company of the 781st under Lt. Francis Coolican. Task Force Herren held the Western and southern approaches to the town and territory to the south. When the defending Americans learned that the Germans now held prisoners, their rescue became top priority on everyone's mind.

"B" Company's Tank Retriever being used to evacuate wounded in Wingen.
(U.S. Army Signal Corps, NARA)

To enter the town from the West, "B" Company had to go through a railroad underpass and head east onto the main road. The underpass was a great natural choke point and the German defenders took every advantage of it. After leading the counterattack through the underpass, the infantry was pinned down by small arms fire. The tanks passed through to lend support, but they were under orders not to shoot their main guns! By order of higher headquarters, the tanks were restricted in the firing of 75mm and 76mm guns during this operation due to insufficient information as to which houses in the town were occupied by the enemy or held friendly troops/prisoners. Then the inevitable happened. Antitank guns and *Panzerfaust* teams hidden in the buildings on the high ground on the north side of the road knocked out the lead tank. The rest of the tanks were forced into a single file and they couldn't squeeze by the KO'd tank. To make a bad situation worse, the third tank was at the underpass exit and the fourth tank was at the entrance with the infantry sandwiched, useless, in between the tanks. A second attempt to advance lost another tank knocked out by shellfire.

"A" Company tanks enter Wingen, day two. (U.S. Army Signal Corps, NARA)

Recognizing a losing situation, they backed off to the west, and in the ensuing debacle lost a *third* Sherman as it slid off the icy road. Of the ten men in the first two tanks, Sgt. Lynwood Spencer, Cpl. Joseph Wecfinski, Cpl. Robert Kennedy, and Pfc. Eli Rawlins were killed and three others were wounded. The Germans captured three crewmen from the first two tanks and added them to the group being held in the church. A third attack was tried just before dark with a provisional platoon composed of HQ personnel at 1630, but it too was blocked by the same two dead tanks and also had to withdraw. The infantry troops kept a toehold in the west end of the town during the night, but the cost was high: the infantry sent over 100 men into that fight and only 38 came back.

The 781st Battalion's After Action Report for this day's fighting didn't pull any punches: "These losses demonstrated results of committing tanks without coordination with infantry, poor recon, and lack of orientation for the tank personnel." Lt. Col Kinne was not a happy guy. As a result of losing the two tanks to the *Panzerfauste*, the 781st tank crews got serious and started adding layers of sandbags to their tanks to counter the *Panzerfaust* warheads.

Brig. General Herren issued a memorandum to the Task Force warning that the Germans had captured American vehicles, and would undoubtedly try to infiltrate using them with captured uniforms. He also ordered that all Antitank and Anti-Aircraft weapons be manned 24/7 with a full load of ammo. Finally, and most significantly, he ordered that all vehicles be placed so that they did not have to turn around in the event of a withdrawal – in essence, face the rear and be ready to move.

A "B" Company tank (B3) in Wingen. Note the destroyed vehicles in the background from the previous days' fighting. (U.S. Army Signal Corps, NARA)

January 5, 1945, was cold and cloudy, with only fair visibility. The Wingen assault continued, and the toehold in the east end of town that was bought so dearly by the 276th enabled the tanks to advance, this time beyond the underpass chokepoint. Command had lifted the restriction on main gun use, and the tanks fired 440 rounds of 75mm and 76mmm at the German defenders. Sgt. Donald Deming of "B" Company saw the U.S. infantry being held up in their attack, and he led his section "up close and personal" and poured direct fire on to the enemy. The infantry was able to re-form and capture the village, taking 60 prisoners. For this and his conduct later on April 7th, Sgt. Deming won a Bronze Star. Another Bronze Star was awarded to Staff Sergeant Earl Brownell, Co "B," for his similar service in the attack that day.

Even better, the Allied prisoners were set free, including the three 781st men who had been captured the day before. The number of Allied prisoners who were liberated by that time was 250. They had been kept in the church without food or water for four days. But the tanks were shooting off a *lot* of ammo and needed to refuel and re-arm to comply with General Herren's "always be fully loaded" directive. The tanks went back to their bivouac area behind the main line to dismount, refuel, resupply, and perform quick maintenance. But the German troops heard the tanks departing, and they launched a savage counter-attack; as night fell things were right back to where they started that morning! The 276th Infantry held the west end of Wingen and the Germans held the east end of Wingen. The benefits of a coordinated tank-infantry team were being learned the hard way. They had to go in side-by-side in order for this to succeed.

In a horrible *déjà vu*, the battle for Wingen restarted the morning of the 6th, with more troops entering the fray. The Infantry commander wanted the B/781st tanks to once again drive in from the west. The 781st Platoon leader demanded that a specific infantry group be attached to the tanks to protect them from *Panzerfaust* teams before he would begin his advance! That was done, but the tank advance was delayed again because of a minefield found in their path of advance. The Engineers cleared the minefield and then things got rolling. All this demanding and delaying was escalating tensions between the tankers and the infantry. Making matters worse, General Herren watched from the sidelines, and he was not satisfied with the speed of advance.

The final fight for Wingen reached an intensity that was more suited to the Eastern Front. The fight for Wingen turned into a savage house-to-house struggle, with fire coming from all directions, and it became impossible to distinguish friends from foes. Tank-infantry coordination was awful, and everyone paid for it. A house would be cleared, only to be reoccupied, and it would have to be cleared again. U.S. tanks shelled U.S. GIs, and GIs cleared a building, only to find wounded friendlies inside. The civilians that were still hiding in their cellars were decimated.

The American forces used their superior numbers of machine guns, tanks, grenades, and bazookas to level the town and drive any defenders out once and for all. Anything that moved was blown away, and there was no retreat. This was close combat at its worst, from room-to-room and house-to-house, block by block, surrounded by burning buildings. The ammo expenditure was enormous: on this day the tanks fired 35,000 machine gun rounds and 740 rounds of 75mm and 76mm. Late afternoon, Lt. Coolican, the tank platoon leader, requested permission to disengage and reload/refuel before his tanks were left stranded without gas or ammunition. At this point, the simmering tensions between the infantry and the tankers erupted, as Colonel Cheves of the 276th detailed the 781st Platoon Leader's genealogical background and general lack of upbringing in searing detail and volume.

Unfazed, Lt. Coolican then went over the Colonel's head and made his request directly to General Herren, and this time it was allowed. Needless to say, the infantry and the tankers were mutually dismayed with the other. When the Germans heard the tanks moving off they launched a counterattack and reoccupied the east end of Wingen *again*. But by this time, the Germans were feeling the effects of their tortuous supply lines and the intense cold; one source estimated that 30% of the German forces were incapacitated by this time. Food was about gone and so was ammunition. During the night they decided to withdraw.

Going back in to Wingen on the 7th. (U.S. Army Signal Corps, NARA)

On the 7th, a coordinated attack was launched on Wingen at 0900, with a detachment of infantry attached directly to the tank platoon leader to provide anti-bazooka coverage. The tactics had literally been developed over the past couple of days. The Infantry preceded the tanks by 25 yards to flush out and clear away any enemy anti-tank teams and look for mines. The tanks would provide direct fire support and they would shoot High Explosive rounds into upcoming buildings. The Infantry attached to tanks was instructed to enter the houses after they had been shot by the tanks and carefully clear the structure from cellar to attic, paying special attention to the cellar holes where most of the remaining enemy was hidden. A few well-placed grenades tossed through the cellar windows worked wonders to change enemy minds about resisting. The infantry would then post a guard at street level to prevent reoccupation of the rubble. While this house was being searched, the next house was being shot by the tanks. The tanks themselves learned to increase the distance between vehicles, stagger their lines, and vary their speed of advance to throw off any anti-tank gunners missed by the search.

Most of the Germans had slipped away, leaving pockets of isolated resistance that had to be mopped up. By 1600, the town was cleared with minimal losses. In the entire town, there was only one building that wasn't damaged, and bodies were everywhere. Lt. Augustus "Gus" Sitton played a decisive role in planning and coordinating the final decisive assault on Wingen by both the infantry and tanks under his command. This resulted in the capture of Wingen and 46 POWs with minimum casualties. For his efforts, Lt. Sitton won an Oak Leaf Cluster to his Bronze Star. Captain John Simpkins also played a leading role in the capture of Wingen. He was responsible for maintaining communication and coordination between his company and the infantry regiment. The forward observation post that he was using became very "hot" – and was under fire by automatic weapons and small arms fire. Captain Simpkins remained at his post while under heavy fire and maintained effective coordination between the infantry and his tanks, which was a deciding factor in taking Wingen. For his conspicuous bravery he was awarded the Bronze Star.

Wingen was a tremendous, costly learning experience. Uncoordinated assaults were fruitless. Restricting tank fire was absurd. Having the tanks exhaust their ammo from the rear was fruitless. The 781st learned that coordination of the tank/infantry

On the 7th, the 70th Division opens mail while a 781st tank driver watches in the background. (U.S. Army Signal Corps, NARA)

team was vital to allow maximum tank fire power with proper close-in security against *Panzerfauste*. Most importantly, the battle of Wingen-sur-Moder blunted the Nordwind offensive and held the line, foiling the first German attempt at cutting the 7th Army in two.

First Armored Group's January Report (which was a weekly high-level report of Armored activity and status for the area) for the Battalion showed 534 out of 664 effective for the Battalion ("A" Co was elsewhere). A directive was issued that used crankcase and transmission oil had to be returned for recycling unless it was used for heating. Also included was a notice that Signal Equipment was in very short supply: antennae, batteries, wire, flashlights, radios, radio tubes, etc. Conservation, recycling, and use of captured supplies were encouraged.

15. THE WESTERN ONSLAUGHT

While the fight raged at Wingen, Nordwind kept applying pressure by sliding to the southeast and turned the corner of the American lines, now attacking from east to west. This second pincer was supposed to meet the one heading through Wingen. The final German push was launched northeast of Strasbourg, right where Task Force Linden and "A" Company were stationed. Named "Winter Solstice," this attack comprised the last of the hoarded reserves of the German Army, with the general aim of smashing the Allied armies around Strasbourg and relieving the German troops encircled in the Colmar Pocket. Adolph Hitler selected his trusted right-hand man Heinrich Himmler, leader of the vaunted and feared SS, to personally lead the attack. Perhaps Hitler wouldn't have been so trusting if he had known that at that *very moment* Himmler was extending peace feelers to the Americans and British in the hopes that they would unite with a "reformed, Hitlerless Germany," and together attack the Russians! One really must wonder if his heart was in the fight…

During the night of January 5th, "Winter Solstice" began as Himmler's troops crossed the Rhine and attacked westward toward Lauterbourg. They succeeded in taking Stattmatten with a battalion consisting of troops from the 553rd Volksgrenadier Division. More enemy troops were also across the river in force further to the south at Gambsheim. As fate would have it, Himmler's troops faced off with the 781st Tank battalion in both locations of his attack. The 781st was now embroiled in repulsing both pincers of Hitler's last large offensive in the West.

The 79th Infantry Division still had part of "D" Company of the 781st attached to them, and they had laid a bunch of mines that stopped the enemy armored advance. Hopeful that they wouldn't encounter enemy armored resistance, "D" Company was ordered to retake Stattmatten on the 6th. Task Force Linden was left by itself to handle the German advance at Gambsheim and Company "A" was sent to counter-attack there.

To retake Stattmatten, 1st Platoon of D/781st passed through Sessenheim early on the 6th to positions south of Stattmatten and waited to attack with their infantry support. Lt. Paul Pais, commanding 1st Platoon, attacked the town using surprise and a technique taken right out of Robert E. Lee's playbook. He split his force into two sections and took his half looping to the left to about 600 yards west of the town. The second section went to a similar position on the east flank. His forces then attacked the defenders from opposite directions, adding to the shock value of a surprise attack. Both groups hit the town at the same time, resulting in complete surprise and mayhem. Infantry of the 42nd Division captured the town and 1st platoon then attacked a pillbox, and finally, Lt. Pais used his platoon to go sniper hunting in the town, quickly clearing it. The attack killed or captured 125, and the POWs included a German battalion command post and its staff. They also freed several U.S. prisoners. Lt. Pais netted a Bronze Star for his outstanding leadership of the attack.

The attack was not without cost, unfortunately. During their defense of Stattmatten, a German rifleman aimed a rifle grenade and pulled off a one-in-a-million shot when his grenade arced down right through an open turret hatch into Staff Sergeant Frederick William's M5 Stuart and exploded, killing him instantly. The other three members of the crew were rendered unconscious by the blast, and when they came to, the tank had started to burn, so they got out quickly. Gunner T/4 Ernest Clemens was the first to evacuate, but he was immediately riddled by machine gun fire; he dropped to the ground, dead, next to his tank. Driver T/5 James McKeown, who was semi-blinded by the blast, escaped next, followed by bow gunner Pvt. Richard Van Winkle, who was also hit by enemy fire. He was helped by McKeown to reach safety on the sheltered side of their tank, and then McKeown then left to get aid. When he reached an aid station, McKeown looked such a frightful mess that the medics grabbed him and gave him first aid for his wounds, which unfortunately delayed the aid reaching his crewmate. The next day, while he was at the 57th Field hospital in Hochfelden, France, Pvt. Richard Van Winkle, twice wounded in the last three weeks, succumbed to the wound he received at Stattmatten.

William's tank was recovered, but the loss of "the Old Man" was sorely felt:

> When Sgt. Williams was killed, "D" Company lost a leader, the Battalion lost one of its best men, the country lost a great patriot, and the Williams family lost a much-loved son, husband, and father. – Capt. Joe Graham

Meanwhile, to the south, Task Force Linden was too thin to hold the advancing Germans back. The "Rainbow Division" (the 42nd Division) were simply overwhelmed as the German attack invaded the area around Gambsheim, in some areas penetrating up to 10 miles into the Allied front. The southern pincer was closing! French General DeLattre's forces kept the Colmar pocket in check to the south, but at this point VI Corp was fighting for its life, as it was being assailed on three sides from the North, South, and East, and had no reserves left. The 781st was helping to keep the northern assault in check, and now was tasked to deal with the southern attack.

Just then a forward field intelligence officer informed "A" Company's CO, Captain Camille Pelletier, that the Germans had attacked and broken through on the right at Gambsheim. Captain Pelletier rushed with his Company to the scene and got a double-dose of bad news when he arrived to support the infantry. He was informed that the infantry commander had not returned from a reconnaissance of the enemy positions, and to make matters much worse, the enemy had just launched an offensive that seemed to be aimed right where they were standing! The infantry, having lost their CO and under attack, had one leg out of their foxhole at this point and were ready to retreat when Captain Pelletier stepped in and organized both his Company and the floundering Infantry unit. He immediately sent Lt. Crane's 2nd Platoon to Hoerdt, right in the path of the attack. Having 2nd Platoon's tanks present reassured and stabilized the Infantry, and the combined Infantry/armor group held their ground and stopped the attack. The tanks had their hands full, as they fired 36 rounds of indirect fire while fighting off strafing runs by enemy aircraft. Most importantly, stopping the attack in the center bought time while the U.S. forces on the flanks got ready to attack. Captain Pelletier had sent Lt. Kaiser's 1st Platoon "A" to Wantzenau to be on the right flank of the incoming attack, and Lt. James Barrickman's 3rd Platoon was sent to Weyersheim to be ready on the left.

At 1445, Lt. Barrickman's 3rd Platoon and their covering infantry struck the Germans from the left. Because of the clear weather with good visibility, Allied air support was active in strafing attacks on the German positions and columns. The Weyersheim counterattack on the left pushed the enemy all the way back to the canal leading to Gambsheim and regained all the lost ground. 3rd Platoon gave another push and crossed over the canal via a local bridge, getting as far as the outskirts of the town, but by then the tanks had outrun their supporting infantry. 3rd Platoon was ordered back to the canal, where the infantry had caught up, and set up a defensive line, as night was falling. They withdrew back across the bridge, but due to the icy roads one tank slipped off the bridge and tumbled into the canal. It could not be retrieved and was destroyed as it sat.

The attack on Gambsheim resumed at dawn, and the combined forces crossed the bridge and entered the outskirts of the town. Suddenly, Lt. Barrickman's 75mm M4A3 tank was knocked out upon entering the town by a heavy hit on the turret and immediately burst into flames. Lt. James Barrickman, Corporal Armand Fana, and Sgt. Edward Brannigan were killed in this action. The loss of leadership and ensuing confusion led to a general withdrawal; the force fell back and resumed their defense at the canal, but this time they lost three tanks to mines. These three tanks were retrieved during the night under cover of darkness. Three men were wounded and three more were listed as Missing in Action. (A sad side note is when tanks were hit and burned with the crews inside, they incinerated the contents so thoroughly that the crewmen were commonly listed as "MIA," because there was nothing left of the crewmen to retrieve as proof they were dead.) With Lt. Barrickman's loss, 2nd Lt. Art Sloggatt was transferred from the Assault Gun Platoon to take Lt. Barrickman's place.

Lt. Barrickman's successful counterattack had pushed the enemy back to the outskirts of Gambsheim and eliminated the threat of attack up the center at Hoerdt.

With that threat gone, 2nd Platoon was freed for use elsewhere. Captain Pelletier sent 2nd platoon to Wantzenau to reinforce the 1st platoon, with orders that Lieutenants Kaiser and Crane combine forces and attack Gambsheim from the south with more infantry. Lt. Crane's 2nd Platoon began supporting the attack in open country between Kilstett and Gambsheim. The supporting infantry (Company "L" of the 232nd Infantry Regiment) were getting badly mauled, and after advancing 1,500 yards were pared down to only one officer and six infantrymen, and they had lost contact with Lt. Crane's tanks. Lt. Crane regrouped the force, and they decided to continue the attack (!) with the remaining seven infantrymen, despite the heavy enemy artillery and anti-tank and machine gun fire. This depleted force knocked out an enemy pillbox, captured 24 POWs, and killed a number of enemy troops. They also reached another pillbox, relieving 11 American Infantrymen who had been holding out against the Germans for two days, rescuing them and bringing them back to Allied lines. Lt. Donald Crane won a Bronze Oak Leaf Cluster for his existing Silver Star for this action.

These two American counterattacks nipped Himmler's German offensive at Gambsheim in the bud. The second assault netted a total of about 60 prisoners, but failed to retake Gambsheim itself. The success of this attack blunted the enemy push at Gambsheim, and for his initiative and leadership, Captain Camille Pelletier was awarded the Silver Star. On January 9th, tanks of the French 3rd Army passed through the U.S. lines and attacked Gambsheim in another attempt to reclaim the town. They also found it to be a tough nut to crack, and were likewise forced to withdraw after losing five of their seven tanks that started the day.

The following day, Company "A" moved to Camp Oberhoffen in the rear, so they could do some much-needed maintenance and repair. The last three tanks that had been in position at Weyersheim were also withdrawn, but disaster struck again when they moved. One tank, a 75mm M4A3, tried to cross the frozen surface of a canal. The tank was too heavy and broke through the ice, and did an incredibly accurate submarine imitation. By this point, Company "A" had been whittled down to five 76mm M4A3 tanks (from the six they left with) and seven 75mm M4A3 tanks (they left with 11), representing an almost 30% loss. Before they could rest, Lt. Crane's 2nd Platoon was sent to Soufflenheim to form a mobile reserve.

Back with Task Force Herren near Wingen, neither side was in *any* shape to launch another offensive, having pummeled each other senseless. After the Wingen battle, the remaining tanks of "B" Company were reorganized into two platoons, as there weren't enough left to populate three platoons. The reorganized "B" Company, "C" Company, and the Assault Gun Platoon were then assigned to support the 158th Field Artillery and spent two weeks firing indirect fire missions. During that time they delivered over 2,500 "get well never" rounds to the enemy.

Two-thirds of "D" Company were assigned in their familiar role as Command Post guard for Task Force Herren. The single platoon still supporting the 79th participated in several more snatch and grab raids. The Stuarts were well suited to this role, and the piratical nature of these raids well-suited the men of "D" Company. The M5s had a small profile, and carried a squad of infantry on their back deck on these raids. Their quiet Cadillac engines let them creep up unheard on an enemy outpost. When they reached their objective, the tanks hosed the area while the troops jumped off like pirates boarding a ship. They grabbed the nearest POW nominees and remounted while the tanks kept the opposition pinned down. Those of the enemy who declined the POW invitation were obligingly dispatched. The buccaneers then sped off and vanished into the night with their prisoners. One such raid through Stattmatten netted five prisoners and left three enemy dead. A second patrol from Soufflenheim through Leutenheim didn't take any prisoners, but killed eight more of the enemy for their efforts. A third raid came up with an empty net. One final patrol north of Leutenheim killed five enemy soldiers and captured one wounded officer. The Platoon was placed in reserve at Schwabwiller, but even in reserve, the Platoon was the subject of a historic event. On the 13th, the Platoon was bombed and strafed by jet-propelled planes, which was odd enough to merit mention in their report. This was one of the very first attacks on Allied forces by the German Me-262 jet. These were mostly nuisance runs, and there was no effort to disrupt communications or supply lines – the attacks were very half-hearted.

In the East, from the 10th to the 16th, the fight degraded to a general catfight and the Army commanders gradually lost control of the fight. The front quieted down for a few days from the 16th to the 20th, only broken by incessant strafing runs from the Luftwaffe. The battle turned into a series of local struggles between small units, companies, platoons, and individuals. After the repulse at Gambsheim, Himmler massed his remaining armor and the last of the German reserves and attacked in a line from Gambsheim on the south to Sessenheim on the north, along the Aschbach/Stundwiller/Buhl road. They were immediately successful, penetrating the thin U.S. line and advancing to the Hatten/Rittershoffen line. The Hatten/Rittershoffen battle was of incredible ferocity, equaled only on the Russian front or akin to Iwo Jima.

Calcimine paint was finally getting to the units, and U.S. tanks and personnel were finally being camouflaged in white. The whole camo concept was not embraced by the U.S. troops as whole-heartedly as it was by the Germans. It was not until late in January that all helmets worn by personnel riding in tanks, half-tracks, and jeeps were directed to be painted white, as it was realized that a disembodied dark helmet both gave away the camouflaged vehicle and also made a splendid sniper target. U.S. troops were always getting surprised and playing catch-up in this regard.

However, winter clothing and cold weather items were in very short supply. Some items were simply not available: sleeping bags, jackets, pants, and overcoats. Other items were so scarce as to be near rationing: gloves, sweaters, socks, web equipment, and blankets. Even worse, medium tanks were in short supply and recovery of disabled units was stressed. This was particularly bad news for the 781st, as many of their tanks had already been recovered, patched up, and recycled, and were basically worn out and needed to be replaced. The Germans introduced flame throwing tanks into the fight, appearing just before the U.S. was able to equip their units with similar equipment. These were small chassis, like those used for the Hetzer SP gun, with the gun removed and a flame thrower in its place.

On the 14th, Lt. Colonel Kinne made recommendation to the Infantry Division commanders that the 781st be relieved from going into indirect fire missions and be held in a fluid position as a mobile reserve. But only Task Force Linden heeded the recommendation, and "A" Company was moved to Soufflenheim and Oberhoffen and assigned as mobile reserves. Companies "B" and "C" and the Assault Gun Platoon were still assigned to fire hundreds of rounds in support of the Field Artillery. Second Platoon of "D" Company was now in the Rittershoffen area with the 79th Infantry Division Recon Troop. The next day, the Battalion's S-1 section was destroyed by a fire caused when a gasoline cooking stove got out of control. These gasoline stoves were not good to the 781st, as we shall see.

On January 16, 1945, Task Force Herren was relieved and the 103rd Infantry Division took its place. Unfortunately, rather than following Task Force Herren for some rest and refitting, the 781st suffered the fate of most independent tank battalions and was detached from Task Force Herren, then immediately attached to the 103rd at 1800. Companies "B" and "C" were placed in reserve, but the Assault Gun Platoon was still wearing out its gun barrels firing hundreds of rounds supporting the Field Artillery. The 781st consolidated their position to support the 103rd Infantry Division, moving to a new MLR along the line Rothbach – Muhlhausen Pfaffenhoffen. The roads were very icy, and the move was made safely. It was interesting to note that the 103rd was commanded by General Anthony McAuliffe of Bastogne "Nuts!" fame. One of the General's personal foibles for his division was forbidding helmet camouflage, so the 781st dutifully stripped the camo off their helmets.

Ten days earlier, on the night of January 6, 1945, Private Fred Burton and his friend decided that they were bored with life behind the lines at a 7th Army Replacement Depot. Tired of watching others go off to fight at the front, they really wanted to see some real action and get up close and personal with the Krauts, so the two men left their posts to find it – they went AWOL. They headed toward the sound of gunfire, determined to make a more immediate contribution in the war effort.

Ron O'Donnell, 1945.
(Courtesy of O'Donnell family)

They bumped into Lt. Donald Crane of the 781st. Fred asked for a job in a tank for his pal and him, and Lt. Crane responded with "Hell, why not?" Under normal circumstances they should have been arrested and charged with desertion, but "A" Company needed men pretty badly and two volunteers were hard to pass up. Fred had no training in tanks, so he was assigned to a tank as an Assistant Driver and his pal was made a Driver, and they were immediately adopted into the group.

As an Assistant Driver, Fred sat on the other side of the transmission hump from the Driver in a similar seat. There weren't any driving controls over there, so there really wasn't anything "assistant driving" about the job. In reality, the AD was a spare crewmember and usually the junior crewman. Immediately to his front were the hull-mounted .30 cal machine gun and a tray for an ammo box. He also had a main periscope in the hatch through which he

125

looked and indirectly aimed his fire, and had a second, limited vision back up directly in front. The machine gun didn't have a sight, so it was aimed by tracers. "Tracer" was a bit of burning material on the bottom of the "bullet" that left a streak showing where the bullet went. About every seventh round on the ammunition belt had the tracer material. In battle, it was easy to tell who was shooting the bullets, because the Germans used white tracers and Americans used red. So Fred was basically a machine gunner and a spare hand for his new crew. Fred and his buddy would soon get their wish to be part of the action – and then some.

Just as the AWOL volunteers were welcomed, replacements in the 781st were not ostracized or given the cold shoulder treatment by the original members, as was done in other units. Ron O'Donnell, who joined up with the 781st right around New Year's Day, recalled that was not the case. He was assigned as a Gunner in a "B" Company tank commanded by Earl Brownell, the Platoon leader. Ron remembers that "Earl took me under his wing" and he was "made to feel a part of the team."

16. SESSENHEIM

Way up in the northeast corner of the Allied lines, 1st Platoon of "A" Company supported the 232nd Infantry Regiment in an attack on Dingolsheim. After the town was taken, the tanks withdrew and covered the demolition of a bridge across the Moder River in woods west of Dingolsheim to prevent an enemy advance across the river. After this attack, 1st Platoon joined up with 2nd Platoon at Soufflenheim. Ominously, a few miles to the south, the Germans entered the town of Herrlisheim and surprised the resident American infantry and armored battalion, and in the ensuing fight the 43rd Tank Battalion was vaporized, losing 14 of 29 tanks in half an hour.

That night, T/4 Robert Shepherd of "C" Company was on guard duty near the company command post when an incoming enemy artillery round landed right next to the company kitchen truck, which was a Deuce-and-a-half with a small kitchen on the tailgate. The blast wounded two men, missing Sgt Shepherd, but the force of the blast overturned the cooking stoves, setting fire to the truck. Normally this would be no great deal, other than the loss of a hot meal, except the other half of the truck was carrying a load of small arms ammunition and – the icing on the cake – rocket launcher ammo! As the rear of the truck was becoming enveloped in flames, Shepherd realized what would happen if all that ammo cooked off in the middle of town, so he jumped into the truck's cab and started it up. Flooring the truck's gas pedal, he then drove it, flaming, shedding pieces of burned kitchenware, down the street away from the troops and buildings. Careening and bumping around corners, he finally reached the edge of town. Shepherd then opened the cab door and jumped out, rolling to cover in a ditch just in time as the ammunition exploded and demolished the vehicle. Robert Shepherd was duly awarded a Bronze Star for his wild ride.

In a scenario that was horribly reminiscent of what happened in Wingen, Company "B" of the 232nd Infantry was occupying Sessenheim and was cut off by the German patrols that had infiltrated the lines and surrounded them. The 781st once again went to relieve the infantry. At 1130 hours on the 17th, 1st Platoon of "A" Company's tanks supported an attack to relieve the surrounded 232nd Infantry in Sessenheim and knocked out two Mark IV German tanks of the 10th SS Panzer. 2nd Platoon of "A" moved into a firing position in the woods and fired on enemy infantry, killing an unknown number. All this helped the main force of the 232nd break through to rescue their surrounded comrades and reoccupy the town. Two 1st Platoon tanks were stationed at an intersection to prevent another infiltration, and they were going to be left in town for the night to provide local muscle. But a full-fledged counter-attack at 0630 the next morning by German infantry pushed both tanks and infan-try all the way back out of Sessenheim. At 1300 in the afternoon, the 232nd again tried to take the town, but the right flank of the force was overrun by an enemy flanking assault, exposing the American right flank, and the attack was called off. 3rd Platoon, commanded by Sgt. Kelly, supported this attack and fired off their complete load of ammo before being forced to withdraw. The abortive counterattack stopped at 1400, with the Germans occupying Sessenheim and the U.S. troops pushed into the woods on the outskirts of town.

The tanks of "A" Company, 781st, were by this time also out of ammo, and they withdrew that night to reload near Shirrhoffen. Back at HQ, plans were made and an attack order was given for the next morning. "A" Company was now attached to the 411th Infantry Regiment for another attack on Sessenheim. But those orders had to be delivered to the Platoon leaders, and nobody quite knew exactly where they were! Cpl. James Arsenault of Company "A" was tasked with locating the tank platoon leaders, who were known to be somewhere in the woods south of Shirhof-fen. He had to run the gauntlet of continuous enemy artillery fire, dodged enemy patrols, and kept driving his jeep until he located each of the men and gave them their orders. For his courageous action and determination in the face of grave danger, Cpl. Arsenault was awarded a Bronze Star.

Now that their location was known, the tanks could be resupplied. Pfc. John Hartonchik, a radioman with Company "A," was directed to take two truckloads of ammunition to the tanks. Also detailed on this resupply were Pfc. Amedio Gazzigli and T/5 Donald Harr to drive the two trucks, while Pfc. Hartonchik navigated through total darkness over an exposed road, all the while being treated to the same artillery, mortars, and small arms fire that corporal Arsenault had so thoroughly enjoyed. Remember that they weren't in a maneuverable jeep, but in two lumbering trucks chock full of tank ammo! The trio made it to the woods south of Schirhof-fen, and while still under fire first located each tank and then delivered the ammuni-tion to each. Still dodging enemy fire, they then helped unload the ammunition and stow it on board each tank just in the nick of time. For this "Midnight Ride" these three men each won a Bronze Star.

As Company "A" worked at stowing their ammunition and performing needed maintenance, they hoped to catch a couple minutes of shuteye before morning arrived. They fully expected to pick up where they left off, attacking the next day and pushing the enemy infantry back in a now-familiar house-to-house scrap, and that everything would turn out fine. Little did they suspect that three out of four of them would be a casualty in less than twenty-four hours.

The assault stepped off at 0630, when the infantry jumped off from the edge of the nearby woods through the foot of snow on the ground. The murky day dawned mild and rainy, and the rain hurt visibility by raising a snow fog over the ground. There had been no artillery prelude, so the GIs might surprise the enemy and get inside their mortar fire perimeter before their mortar crews had time to react. At 0645, the artillery started for ten minutes to keep the enemy's heads down, and at that time the two platoons of four tanks each started off so that the tanks and infantry would reach the edge of the town at the same time. Tank/infantry coordination was excellent. Company "A"'s eight tanks advanced in line abreast formation, and they met light resistance. Lt. Donald Crane's platoon took the left hand side, while Lt. Kelly's platoon took the right hand side. But things were going too easily. Gunner Gerald Mercier noted that there was a distinct lack of infantry opposition, whereas the day before they had been persistently obvious: "The town had been packed!" At that moment they reached the edge of the town, which was eerily lit by flickering flames here and there where artillery had set a building or rubble on fire. The firelight danced but revealed no enemy. The crews were beginning to hope that the Germans had bugged out during the night.

They hadn't evacuated at all. Instead, the Germans had brought up four to six Mark VI tanks, hidden them from view behind houses and barns, and had them covered by a number of Self-Propelled guns to thwart flank attacks. "Tiger doesn't hunt alone." The German tank destroyers waited until the last moment and then they pounced. Just as the Shermans reached the edge of town, the hidden German tanks rumbled into view. These were new and entirely different opponents for the 781st. These were not a standard Mark V Panther, which itself was a tough customer for the Shermans, to be sure. These weren't Mark VI Tigers, which with their covering *Sturmgeschutz* guns would be nigh on impossible to defeat. The tanks encountered by Company "A" at Sessenheim were actually Mark VI *Jagtigers* (Hunting Tigers) of the 653rd Heavy Tank Destroyer Battalion, mounting 128 mm main guns and protected by almost 10 inches of frontal armor, which could not be penetrated by a Sherman's main gun at point blank range. In contrast, the *Jagtiger's* main round would often and easily pass completely through a Sherman. The ambush was perfect, and Company "A" was, as Gerald Mercier put it, "annihilated."

When the *Jagtigers* waddled into view, shock and chills ran through each crewman, prompting Sergeant Sexton to exclaim: "Migawd, it's as big as a house!" just before he was wounded. That broke the ice; both sides opened fire and an uneven firefight ensued, as more and more German guns unmasked and spit death. To make matters much worse, German half tracks packed with the "missing" infantry were charging out from behind cover, unloading, and unleashing a firestorm on the accompanying GIs. The *Jagtigers* sent round after round toward and through the Shermans, but Company "A" fought back as they died, first registering hits on the armored front glacis plates of the Mark VIs, which "bounced off like tennis balls." The *Jagtigers'* huge guns required two steps to load: one for the projectile and one for the propellant, and as a result were very slow to reload, but still German rounds flew everywhere; T/5 Huya saw one shell hit to the right of Sgt. Johnson's tank, then one to the left, then one left a trail of sparks as it scraped harmlessly along the belly of the tank. To try and save their infantry, the rapidly-thinning ranks of Company "A" then tried to shift target to the half tracks, but by that point there just weren't very many Shermans still functioning. Ex-AWOL Pvt. Fred Burton stayed at his machine gun and kept the lead flying until his tank was hit and he bailed out with his crew. Fred's ex-AWOL pal wasn't so lucky; his tank was hit several times and it burned.

Gerald Mercier was a gunner in Crane's platoon, and after watching a couple of his rounds bounce off his first target "like ping-pong balls" he was shifting target when his tank was hit. The entering round passed through the transmission on the front left hand side of the tank and travelled down the left side inside the tank and out the rear, immediately killing the driver, T/5 Donie Blea, and the loader behind him, Pfc. James Grantland. Their tank lurched to a halt as the punctured engine died, and the surviving crew needed to get out now. Mercier, the assistant driver T/4 Ruben Parrish, who sat in front of him, and the tank commander behind him needed to escape just as soon as possible before the tank was hit again or caught fire. The intense anti-tank and machine gun fire they would have to endure outside the tank was daunting, but it sure beat cooking! Mercier climbed halfway out of his hatch and stopped when he saw that his buddy Parrish was having trouble getting out. He reached down to lift Parrish out of his hatch and over the side to exit the vehicle, and then he dove off the side of the tank turret, which was still under heavy machine gun, small arms, and mortar fire. (The German infantry had by this time decisively repulsed the 411th.) Unfortunately, his nine-foot dive off the top of the turret to escape the small arms fire caused him to break his arm at the elbow when he landed. Mercier helped Parrish to his feet and then to a nearby embankment, where they both took cover from the heavy fire and watched their tank commander join the rout with the infantry as they escaped to the rear. While they hunkered in the ditch, they watched as their tank "Gee" burned and exploded. German artillery was chasing the retreating U.S. Infantry, and U.S. artillery was firing on the same area to slow up the chasing German infantry. So much shrapnel was flying and so many German infantry were patrolling that Mercier and Parrish decided not to attempt to limp to the rear.

During the attack, after the three near-misses noted by T/5 Huya, the "A" Company tank in which T/5 Berger Johnson was driver and Corporal John Black was gunner was hit in the turret by a shell from a *Jagtiger*. The force of the hit ejected their tank commander up and out of the turret and onto the ground, wounding him seriously enough that he couldn't remount. Black and Johnson both jumped out of their tank to save their crewmate, ignoring the heavy fire from mortars, machine guns, and small arms. They lifted their wounded commander back onto the front glacis plate of their wounded tank. Cpl. Black stayed exposed and cradled the wounded man while Cpl. Johnson jumped back into the tank, spun it around, and sped back to friendly territory, where their friend got immediate medical attention. Cpl. Black earned a Bronze Star and T/5 Johnson won an oak leaf cluster for his existing Bronze Star for their actions. Amazingly, their dismounting to save their buddy probably saved their lives. The German gunners would have seen them bail out and probably figured that their tank was dead, and so focused their deadly attention on other tanks.

The whole fight was over in six minutes. In Gerald Mercier's words: "It was over before we knew it." In that blink of an eye, six Shermans were left shattered and burning in melting snow on the field and they were surrounded by advancing German infantry. Only two Shermans made it back to their lines. Black/Johnson's Sherman was the only tank to make it back in salvageable condition, even though it had suffered a heavy hit to the turret. The other Sherman that made it back was struck in the final drive, but managed to crawl to safety. The Battalion's Tank Retriever section had to drag it to the rear later, as it was so badly damaged it was a complete write-off.

Mercier and Parrish were surrounded behind their embankment by German infantry and they reluctantly surrendered at gunpoint. They were led to the rear, where a great many U.S. prisoners, both armored and infantry, were being gathered by the Germans. During the walk to the rear, an incoming U.S. artillery round exploded nearby and shrapnel from it hit Mercier in the back, narrowly missing his heart. Cold, wet, and now with a broken arm and seriously wounded by friendly fire, he was marched several miles and joined many other POWs. The prisoners were jammed into already-overcrowded boxcars, and the "stench from festering wounds was horrible." Mercier was sent to a POW camp, where he was told by the camp doctor that there was nothing that could be done for his broken arm or shrapnel wounds. Once a day, the prisoners were served potato-peel soup and a slice of black bread without variation. But even this treatment beat that of imprisoned Russians that were being held in the cellars of the POW buildings. They were totally deprived of food, and Mercier could only watch as they reached out the cellar windows and struggled to pick blades of grass for food. Gerry Mercier would remain a prisoner for 90 days awaiting rescue.

After they regrouped, the shattered remains of Company "A" counted the cost. Seven of the eight tanks sent into Sessenheim were destroyed. More importantly, two men were known to be dead, 10 were missing (either dead or captured), and 18 were wounded. That meant thirty of the original forty men that went into battle, or seventy-five percent of the 781st "A" Company crewmen, were casualties. From a mechanical standpoint, they left the battalion for duty with Task Force Herren with six 76mm M4A3s, eleven 75mm M4A3s, and one Tank Recovery Vehicle. After this day, they had one 76mm M4A3, three 75mm M4A3s, and the TRV operational. They had lost 72% of their starting force. "A" Company was almost gone; only 1st Platoon was left. To put this in perspective, Tennyson's famous poem "Charge of the Light Brigade" was written when a British cavalry charge lost 30% of its force.

The after action report stated "this is further proof of inability of present medium tanks to successfully fight the German Mark VI tank." The lack of success for the mission was blamed on bad intelligence information, in that the presence of the enemy armor was not known. Fixing the blame wasn't important to the remnants of "A" Company as they returned to Oberhoffen to rebuild and reorganize. Sessenheim had unfortunately just surpassed Wingen as the "most costly town" for the 781st.

After Sessenheim, the Hunting Tigers of the 653rd Heavy Tank Destroyer Battalion continued to dog the 7th Army, laying ambushes and traps while they slowly fell back as the 7th advanced. The Tiger tanks eventually fell victim to their complexity and weak drivelines, and the 653rd grew progressively weaker, as they lost tank after tank to breakdowns. When the war ended, they had been pushed far to the northeast and were but a shadow of their peak strength.

17. END OF THE SOLSTICE

On the 20th-21st, Alexander Patch took stock of his army and didn't like what he saw: one-third of his force (the 36th and 103rd) were fine, one-third (45th and 79th) were satisfactory, and one-third (12th Armored and task forces Linden and Herren) were unsatisfactory. His forces had suffered an average of 15% casualties. Task Force Herren had suffered 58%. He reached the conclusion that his forces could not fend off another hard German push, and after conferring with General Devers, he pulled his line back to behind the Moder River. The weather was snowy and cold, which masked the noise, and the poor visibility helped cover the withdrawal. The Assault Gun Platoon was again used to cover the withdrawal of the 79th to their new main line of resistance, and fired 200 rounds of 105mm HE as covering fire before their departure, which this time was uneventful. Amazingly, the Germans took four days to realize that they were facing empty positions, reinforce their attacking forces, and bring them up to the new jump-off point to continue their attack! This small respite gave the beleaguered VI Corps its first rest in weeks, and they were able to reform and regroup. The 781st Tank Battalion was gathering at Imbsheim for their next fight. Most of "D" Company was en route to Imbsheim, but they lost one tank that became disabled during the trip. When they arrived, the Battalion made defensive plans with the Division and scouted the region for possible attack and counterattack routes.

Second Platoon of "D" Company was still with 79th Recon Troop, and moved with them to Waltenheim. They were attached to 3rd Battalion of 313th Infantry, and given the mission of defending Hagenau.

On the 21st, the remnants of Co "A" were relieved from Task Force Linden at 0100 and given back to 781st Battalion control. The weather had by now gone back to bitter cold with clear visibility, and a coating of ice from the moist weather covered everything. While returning to their Battalion, the last surviving 76mm M4A3 in 1st Platoon was damaged and rendered out of action because it slid on the ice and smacked into a building on the icy road at Ringendorf. The depressingly small group halted so the Tank Recovery Vehicle could set up to tow the disabled vehicle. At this point "A" Company was reduced to three 75mm M4A3s, with the lone TRV towing the disabled M4 76mm. The procession started at daybreak with the TRV towing the damaged tank, but they only made it as far as Saverne when both vehicles slipped off a railroad bridge they were trying to cross! The two vehicles, joined by the tow cables, slipped off the bridge and fell thirty feet, destroying both vehicles. T/4 Frederich Lowell was killed and six other crewmembers were injured in the accident. T/4 Herschel Rogers, Co "A," died two days later of the wounds he received in the fall.

Any armored resources were in such short supply that on the same day, the 79th Division Command changed the order and "A" Company (now down to a mere three 75mm tanks) was attached to the 813th Tank Destroyer Battalion and placed

One of the Assault Guns of "Y" Battery getting ready to move out. (Up from Marseille)

in a defensive position at Ringendorf, so at least they didn't have to travel anymore. The 781st Reinforced Assault Gun Platoon was now assigned to independent operations. It was called "Y Battery" after its commander, Lt. Arthur Yonkers. Almost immediately after receipt of their new orders, "Y Battery"'s Command Post was destroyed by a fire caused by another out-of-control gasoline stove. For the near term, "Y Battery" performed the indirect fire missions for the Battalion and saved the tank companies the wear and tear.

During the last two weeks of January 1945, the 781st Tank Battalion was allotted just four replacement men from the "Repple Depple" to cover their losses. 2nd Lt. Arnie Simpson joined up with the 781st in January as a replacement for one of the two platoon leaders that "B" Company lost at Bitche. Lt. Simpson graduated from University of Georgia, and immediately went into Officer Candidate School because of his ROTC work while in college. He made the rounds of Fort Benning, Fort Knox, and Fort Campbell, and was finally assigned to the 781st. Upon arrival, he felt he had received excellent training, especially in his ability to quickly take a target under fire and make a hit. He would get to prove it.

The Radio squad of half tracks had by this time figured out that the Germans were using radio direction finders to zero in on their location when they started broadcasting. Once the enemy RDF had them spotted, the artillery was soon to follow. To counter this, one of the crew rigged a remote operating cable so the radio set in the half track could be operated from a foxhole at a safe distance from the vehicle. First Armored Group's intelligence report of the 23rd urged an emphasis on radio security, as it was found out from a German POW that the Germans were monitoring U.S. radio nets continuously, and that they were actually learning quite a bit. This prompted a wave of retraining for U.S. personnel in radio security procedures.

Lt. Col Kinne issued a directive that drivers and assistant drivers be under closed hatches at all times when operating under artillery or small arms fire. Commanders could button up at their discretion, but it was recommended that they, too, be buttoned up when in towns, in woods, or under artillery. Lt. Col. Kinne took this action because "This Battalion has taken considerable unnecessary loss in personnel due to un-buttoned tanks." The Battalion had already been ordered to button up when under artillery or when stationary, but it wasn't being heeded, despite grenades flying into hatches and personnel being blasted out of hatches. On one hand, when the hatches were open in wintertime, lots of snow fell off branches into the interior of the vehicle and that caused problems. Open hatches defeat the armored integrity of the vehicle, as had been proven, and heads sticking out open hatches made wonderful targets for snipers. On the other hand, the periscopes in the hatches that were supposed to provide visibility when the hatch was closed would frost over from the bitter cold and moisture from breathing, and were most often useless. So common sense and direct orders were again overridden by shortcomings of the equipment, and hatches remained open so crews could see where they were going or what they were shooting at.

Enemy pressure had been increasing along the Moder line, and the Battalion was in reserve and prepared to plug any holes punched in the line. On the 23rd, covered by falling snow and reduced visibility, the Germans attacked and followed their familiar script: they infiltrated around the left flank to the northeast of Hagenau, which forced the 410th Infantry Regiment to fall back, taking "B" Company along with it. German tanks were noted as being well-camouflaged with white cloth covers that made them very hard to see – they were virtually invisible, even as close as 125 yards. Enemy tanks were even being camouflaged as wood piles! In one report, enemy tanks were heard and an investigation in the morning found three wood piles. That night the tanks were heard again, and the following morning there were only two wood piles. This news was disseminated, and tankers were apprised of a new and disturbing trend – camouflaged enemy tanks were knocking out our tanks, but they were remaining under wraps and waiting for the tank retriever to show up and then knocking it out for good measure.

The 103rd decided to counterattack at Rothbach in an attempt to push the enemy back. "B" Company supported the infantry attack on Rothbach and occupied high ground nearby that overlooked the town. They prepared to fire directly into the town, but they couldn't see the target due to poor visibility and withdrew back to Ingwiller.

Meanwhile, back in the Ardennes region, the "Battle of the Bulge" was declared completed, and Ike and his generals were congratulating each other on a job well done. The neglected Seventh Army was fighting for its life while the handshakes and toasts were occurring! The final German attacks of "Winter Solstice" took place on the night of January 24th-25th in the midst of a blinding snowstorm, but they were stopped by the 103rd on the Moder River banks. The Germans managed to penetrate the lines in three places but were repulsed by swift counterattacks.

"A" Company had managed to obtain a couple of tanks from Ordnance for their tankless crews. One M4 tank was sent to Neuberg with a mission of guarding a bridge across the river there. They were joined by "D" Company's 2nd platoon, as they too took up a defensive position as part of the new Task Force Wall. Two other tanks – all that remained of Staff Sgt. Robert Kelly's section "A" – were posted as a lonely roadblock on a bridge across the Moder connecting Schweighouse and Hagenau. The enemy soon attacked that bridge, and in the face of the infantry assault and without infantry to cover them, the tanks were forced to withdraw south to Ohlugen. Here they then met some friendly infantry that was headed north, and everyone turned around for a counterattack on Schweighouse. Again, it was a familiar story – during the attack, the Infantry support lagged behind the attacking tanks. That provided an opening which allowed an enemy bazooka team to strike the lead tank. It was abandoned in enemy territory with the crew still inside and their fate unknown. As the second tank tried to pass the disabled leader, it became stuck in a ditch, and soon it, too, was hit, and Pfc. Frederick Sensel and S/Sgt. Robert Kelly were killed. All but two of both crews were KIA or captured. The attack sputtered to a halt – this was the first penetration of the U.S. lines as "Winter Solstice" waned.

S/Sgt Russell Coyle, Co "A," commanded the lone tank guarding the bridge at Neuburg, and it was also attacked. Coyle was also wounded (hit in the leg by enemy shrapnel) before withdrawing. This was the second of three penetrations by the Germans. Altogether, it was another very bad day for "A" Company, as twelve of the remaining members, including their Commanding Officer, Camille Pelletier, were casualties. Cpl. Vinton Blanchard died on the 29th from wounds he received on the 25th. "A" Company was edging toward total extinction.

The "Battling Bastards of Bastogne" – the 101st Airborne – arrived in the area as reinforcements, and the last remains of "A" Company were attached to the 101st Airborne and acted as their outpost security. One Platoon of "D" Company was also assigned to the 101st in their familiar role as the "Palace Guard." "D" Company took this sterling opportunity to purloin a really nice deuce-and-a-half from the

The "RAC" poses for a picture (Erksel Rhodes in block). (Courtesy of Rhodes family)

101st Airborne. The truck came complete with a trailer, both of which were whisked off to "D" Company's Maintenance officer, Lieutenant Art Best, who quickly re-painted them to bear the D/781st identification markings. This truck/trailer combination was then used to store and haul all the confiscated contraband that "D" Company found, most of which was alcoholic in nature. "D" Company was especially fond of schnapps now. By the time the 101st was in position and ready to fight on the front lines; the attacks had stopped and the situation had stabilized, but the 101st Airborne did manage to counterattack and repulse the first enemy incursion at Schweighouse. In doing so, they were able to recapture one of "A" Company's tanks that had been abandoned at Schweighouse with only slight damage. They weren't able to retrieve the vehicle for another couple of weeks, however.

The third enemy breakthrough occurred when a strong enemy force supported by Self-Propelled guns attacked Mulhousen to the northwest, and an estimated 200 enemy troops had overrun part of the 410th Infantry Regiment and advanced to Schillersdorf. The main portion of the 410th regrouped outside Schillersdorf, and at 0900 on the 25th, the 410th launched a counterattack supported by 1st Platoon of "B" Company 781st with the mission of clearing the town.

First Platoon's tanks advanced out of some woods on the outskirts of town and began crossing a field with S/Sgt. Elmer Shepherd's tank in the lead. Cpl. Vince Sutphin was Gunner, assisted by Pvt. Nick Mincoff. Their first target was the church's steeple, to eliminate any possible snipers. Gunner Sutphin's first shot put a 76mm round right on target and rang the bell. After the church absorbed several rounds to dislodge snipers, the target shifted to a barn next door to the right, and then back to an abandoned U.S. 3-inch AT gun in the church's yard to the left.

The rest of the Platoon echeloned to the right and shot up all the houses that could support the enemy, but in a now-familiar story, the tanks didn't get tight infantry support. The infantry were crossing the field, and drew ahead of the tanks when the tanks had to stop short of a fence that divided the field from the town. The tanks continued to fire over the heads of the infantry, but the rapid fire of the tank guns overhead was causing problems with their concussive reports and the infantry hit the dirt to take cover. As a result, an enemy *Panzerfaust* team on the right, firing from the basement of a house whose top floors had been utterly destroyed, hit one of the leading tanks of the platoon, killing Pvt. Clarence Kelly and wounding two other crewmen. At the end of January, a Tank Corps memorandum was circulated cautioning crews when approaching a hostile town to keep an eye out for *Panzerfaust* teams in the cellars of the second or third house in from the edge of town. "A round of shot followed by HE should be the prescribed dose." It was good advice that came a little late.

S/Sgt Elmer Shepherd's crew was then given the location of a pinned-down platoon from the 410th that had been overrun the previous day and could not make it back to U.S. lines. He immediately ordered his driver, T/4 M. Parent, to reverse and shift left, taking his tank across a stream bed, and they reached the GIs. Shepherd had them group up in back of his tank for protection, and then slowly led them back to safety. He stood in the open hatch of the turret, exposed to enemy observation and fire, directing both the GIs and his gunner, Vince Sutphin, to fire rounds into suspected enemy positions as they made it back to safety. For this rescue action S/Sgt. Shepherd was awarded a Bronze Star.

Despite the snow, poor visibility, and cold, both platoons of B/781st and the infantry succeeded and the town was cleared out by 1100. That afternoon, at 1430, 2nd platoon supported the 410th in a surprise attack on Muhlhousen and Urwiller. The tanks surprised a large enemy column advancing down the road from the north, and upon opening fire killed a large number of infantry and caused the German formation to become an unorganized rout. 2nd platoon of C/781st moved to some high ground west of town to prevent the escape of encircled enemy troops. 2nd Platoon of "B" Company then followed the 410th into Mulhousen and fired 30 rounds of 76mm High Explosive, 70 rounds of 75mm High Explosive, and 20 rounds of White Phosphorous into the town to cover patrol activities of the 410th. One "B" Company tank was in turn knocked out by a self-propelled gun and two crewmen were wounded. "B" Company again supported the 410th the next day, as they pushed on with a successful raid on Nieffern, firing another 90 rounds into that town. The enemy was cleared from the area and the tank lost at Mulhousen was recovered, completely reversing the German gains. This left the last penetration at Neubourg to be cleaned up.

Second Platoon of "D" Company, under Lieutenant Paul Shartel, was assigned a mission to counterattack east of Neubourg with the 3rd Battalion of the 314th Infantry and push the enemy back to their starting point. Things started off badly, as when the tanks joined up they found that the Infantry was taking heavy mortar and small arms fire and they were pinned down by machine gun fire. The M5 Stuarts of "D" Company pounced on the enemy and knocked out the machine gun nest, taking an officer and six enlisted men captive in the bargain. By then it was too late in the day to start the mission, so the tanks dug in with the infantry for the night. The next morning, at 0730, the tanks took off to scout for the enemy near Neubourg. They were headed to an objective on the map that was "indicated by the now-familiar 'Big Finger' method." (This jokingly makes the point that a fingertip pointing to a spot on a map covers a bunch of area.) Second Platoon headed to the designated area, and on the way they passed hundreds of men in white camouflage suits who were busily digging in the woods northeast of Uhlwiller. The tanks reached their destination and the place was clean – there was no enemy activity – so they turned about and went back to report their findings to the Infantry commander, again passing the white-suited men who were still busily shoveling.

During the ensuing debriefing there was a predictable period of stupid silence when everyone came to the realization that those busy shovelers in white suits were Krauts! Second Platoon immediately loaded a company of the 314th on their tanks, just like they learned at Camp Wainwright, and headed out. Lt. Shartel's Platoon crept out of a wooded area and crossed a large open field on their approach. This would normally be suicidal, but the deep snow hid the clank-clank-clank from the M5's tracks and they were able to close to 50 yards before being noticed! Their guns had been loaded with canister, and at such a close range the giant 37mm shotguns had deadly effect. The enemy broke and ran and Lt. Shartel's group achieved total victory. They killed over 300 enemy troops and captured approximately 60 POWs without loss of men or tanks, but there were three tank crew casualties who had frozen feet. This closed the last chapter of "Winter Solstice."

While this was happening, "Y" Battery was scooting from site to site and firing hundreds if not thousands of rounds at the enemy. The targets were enemy in foxholes, columns of enemy trucks, mortar emplacements, enemy infantry, harassing fire, covering fire, and any other fire mission imaginable.

By the end of January 1945, both sides had pummeled each other senseless into immobility. After "Winter Solstice" met the same fate as "Nordwind" and the Ardennes, the German high command called off the attacks, and once again, the Germans went back on the defensive, with their forces still facing the same VI Corps opponents. They had gained precious little real estate for their efforts, and the German forces were now considerably weaker than when they started. While 7th Army lost 14,000 men, the Germans lost somewhere around 90,000 men in the same time period, with the critical difference being that the U.S. losses could be replaced, while the Germans had no replacements left.

The failed German attacks in the Ardennes and Alsace marked the beginning of the end. The German losses – not just in troops, but the loss of equipment and the drain on fuel, food, and ammunition – certainly hastened the end of the fighting on the European continent. The Alsace campaign has taken a back seat to the Ardennes in the history textbooks, but it was no less desperate a fight and no less significant in reducing the Third Reich's ability to continue to wage war.

Duty Before Self

Looking back on January, the 781st fought well and the "new" kids were now fully-tested and considered "veterans." At the tactical level, the men of the 781st had been superb, moving and fighting cohesively while being jerked back and forth across the battlefield, and performed well in the face of conflicting or missing directions from command. Officers stayed awake through the use of Benzedrine, and NCOs administered hot coffee and hot fires to offset the bitter cold and keep morale up. Troops clung to every town and crossroads with great tenacity and greatly outdid the Germans with their aggressiveness and willingness to take the fight to the next level.

18. REBUILDING

Finally, at the end of January 1945, the 781st was *almost* reunited, taken off line, and placed in reserve. "Almost," as D/781st was still doing "palace guard" duties and their 3rd Platoon was still attached to the 101st Airborne. Also, "Y Battery" was still flinging rounds down range in support of the field artillery. The Battalion was down to 611 effective combatants, having lost over 15% of their manpower in the past month, most of them being tank crewmen.

As the remnants met up for the first time in weeks, the extent of the losses became known. In the 781st, the individual tank crews were very tight-knit, as living in confined quarters for extended periods with a small group would naturally force that on a crew. These crew/families were quite friendly with other crew/families in their section, and the platoon was a sort of "neighborhood," and familiar with other crews in their Company, like neighbors who lived across town. They had friends in other Companies, but life in the 781st was very partitioned and governed by "need-to-know." So for the most part they really had no idea what another Company was doing, where it was, or what happened to it; as it was akin to a being a different "town." But this time, as each Company gathered in their reserve bivouac, it didn't take much power of observation to notice that "B" Company was missing a lot of crews – they were awfully thin. But it took no intelligence whatsoever to see that "A" Company was almost *gone*. The weather had gone cold again, matching the chill in people's hearts when they got the news about buddies now gone. The falling snow quieted the scene, and the poor visibility hid the hurt and tears on the faces of the survivors as they remembered their friends among the dead and the missing.

Naturally, one of the top orders of business for the 781st Tank Battalion was to rebuild "A" Company. Because of how few tanks they had available, three 76mm M4s were received from Ordnance, two 75mm tanks were transferred from Company "C" to "A," and the last two 75mm tanks were transferred from Headquarters to "A." All the armor that HQ now possessed (six 105mm M4s) was away on assignment with Battery "Y." An interesting note is that, while other tank battalions commonly used their "D" Company as a training school that fed trained men to the medium Companies, the 781ˢᵗ didn't do that. This was a perfect and justifiable opportunity to strip "D" of all its men to get "A" back on its feet quicker, but Col. Kinne resisted the temptation. (The commanders of "A" Company may also have resisted, as they remembered how "D" was originally staffed and didn't want them back.) Company "A" moved to Steinbourg for reorganization and resupply and received 20 replacements: seven from HQ Company, seven from "C" Company, and six from Service Company. The 781ˢᵗ Battalion was hurt, but it had a quiet sense of purpose. They knew that "There were new men to be trained, battle lessons to be passed on, and new tanks to be processed. We all knew what we were getting ready for. The Germans had thrown their Sunday punch, now we were going to throw ours."

The Company "D" Chow truck with Cpl. E.W. Rhodes, bottom left. (Courtesy of Rhodes family)

But while it's true that the 781ˢᵗ had to be taken off the front lines to recreate one-third of its organization, it also used the time well by participating in development of new techniques for fighting, and they corrected faults that were brought out in past battles. As a result, several new infantry-tank tactical methods were developed and actually field tested with infantry to make sure they worked. Easing the job was the weather; as winter was retreating in lock step with the German enemy. A meteorological light switch had been thrown, and almost the entire month of February was mild, with occasional rain, and the snowpack rapidly dissolved, bringing about memories of Camp Shelby and their old nemesis, mud. Lots and lots of mud.

The men of the 781ˢᵗ lived mostly in buildings while they rebuilt the Battalion, and they had hot food when the nearby infantry had hot food. Otherwise, rations were heated on the engines and the surrounding countryside was scavenged for anything that might supplement the rations. To conquer boredom, the men might write home, play cards, shoot craps, listen to a radio, or resort to some of the liberated Schnapps, champagne, or cognac that was available. To combat the cold, the tankers' coveralls were of some use, but again, the heat from the vehicle engines was used – standing in the wash of the tank engine radiator fans helped quite a bit.

Besides the mud, another old friend started to appear in late January 1945 – the M4A3 E8, which became known as the "Easy Eight" version of the Sherman. The larger armored divisions had claimed all of the first arrivals, but at last, the Independent tank battalions had finally reached the front of the line to receive the new

76mm-equipped tank. The 781st received twelve E8s in exchange for clapped-out 75mm M4s early in February. This was the sweet fruit of the 781st's Fort Knox labors, as the E8 featured a 76mm gun with muzzle brake, revised suspension, better ammunition storage, wider tracks, and a host of improvements over the old models. The E8 didn't have a full turret basket floor, which enabled the loader to reach the ammunition, which was now stored in wet-storage bins under the floor. The lack of a floor was fine until a loader tripped or the traverse mechanism jammed on a casing that was rolling around on the floor.

The 781st certainly recognized the Easy Eight, having played a big role in its development. But other U.S. Army groups didn't recognize it. Some of those groups equated anything with a muzzle brake on a long gun tube as being a Panther, and they shot first while asking questions later. The Easy Eight, with both a long barrel and a muzzle brake, would certainly be subjected to friendly fire if something wasn't done. To help break that bad habit, the 781st provided training by actual display of an Easy Eight and classroom discussion to both the 100th and 103rd Divisions on how to recognize the newest U.S. tank and tell it apart from a Tiger or Panther. The big white American stars painted on the flanks or turrets of the tanks were not a factor for recognition. Recognition works two ways, and that star made a wonderful aiming point, especially on the earlier M4 Shermans. On those vehicles, the flank star was painted precisely over the ammunition storage lockers in the flanks, inviting a round through the spot that was most likely to flambé the vehicle. Needless to say, the stars were often obscured by crews soon after they took the vehicle from Ordnance.

Every day, "A" Company conducted intensive training connected with reorganization of the company. Each day they did something different. One day's training was devoted to safe destruction of ordnance material, followed the next day by taking their tanks to the firing range and learning to shoot the main gun and machine guns. "A" Company essentially "started over," and even had to devote training time to learning how to drive while buttoned up. They were so short of operational tanks that when one of their vehicles went down for repairs or maintenance they had to borrow or trade a tank from the other companies just so they could keep up the training program. The new officers and enlisted men had to compress basic training and quickly learn tactical problems, forming new teams and trusting one another. The training was repeated as more tanks and more replacements arrived. The Battalion received 58 replacements and several new tanks in early February, and the new men were quickly assimilated and training continued to get them up to speed. "D" Company chipped in and helped "A" Company with some of their tactical training by playing "bad guys" while "A" figured out how to deal with them. It was a role that "D" Company enjoyed.

"B" and "C" Companies planned and executed harassing operations while "A" Company was fully recuperating. "B" Company supported the 410th Infantry in a raid on Bischholtz the first week in February, and they fired twelve rounds on targets assumed to be enemy troops. "C" Company also supported a successful raid of 1st Battalion 411th on Rothbach. The Companies moved to ready positions at Ingwiller, prepared to support the raid. Both armored Companies were there "just in case" the infantry raid was not a surprise, or if they hit unexpected resistance. In both cases, the infantry pulled it off without calling on the tanks and it was pretty uneventful. The medium tanks did not go in with the infantry because the objective of the raids was to grab prisoners, not hold ground. If there was a mechanical failure, the tanks would have to be abandoned. Also, the ground wasn't very solid at this time and the tanks might have bogged, which again would have meant that precious tanks would have been abandoned. "B" Company ran a few test-runs to see if cross-country movement was possible, but it was still too muddy. "C" Company 2nd platoon took up camouflage firing positions on the MLR for a couple of days to fire direct at targets of opportunity for their range firing training. "B" and "C" Companies also participated in a practice alert with the 410th Infantry Regiment in a rehearsal of Division counterattack plan "B-2."

"B" Company participated in an experiment with the Division Engineers, who were testing different methods of digging tanks in. (Think of providing a foxhole for a tank.) The digging-in experiment was conducted to find out if a tank could be dug in faster by using a bulldozer to dig a hole, or via using TNT to create a crater. The winner of the methods was a hybrid of the two methods. The fastest method was blowing the crater first with TNT and then using the bulldozer to smooth and clear the hole of loose debris. Ironically, GIs in the Normandy bocage reached a similar conclusion for the fastest method of creating a foxhole – they made a crater with a grenade and used their shovel to put the finishing touches on it.

Toward the middle of February, the whole Battalion, with the exception of "Y" Battery (who were still raining death and destruction over the area), was caught up in the retraining web and performing some much-needed maintenance and cleaning of their equipment. "A" Company was continuing tactical training, driving and firing their equipment, which due to its hand-me-down nature was now starting to break down. Replacement vehicles were coming in, and by the end of February, the 781st was handsomely outfitted with about 50% 76mm M4s. Everyone got the communications training with emphasis on security, and "A" let the new enlisted men fire machine guns. Everyone got an intensive refresher on what was called "Crew Drill." "Crew Drill" consisted of learning a carefully choreographed method of bailing out of your tank, taking your sidearm with you, and landing in the proper spot and in the proper prone/crouched position to provide local fire control when you hit the ground. All of this was total hogwash, since when a bailout really occurred it was a flat-out race with a sure-to-be-after-me fireball, and devil take the hindmost.

Per the advance notice given in December, flame throwers were beginning to make an appearance, and the 781st was scheduled to receive three tanks so equipped. The E4-5 flamethrower bore an outside resemblance to the 0.30 cal machine gun, and it was swapped in for the bow gun in the M4. It spewed a stream of flame that was propelled by compressed nitrogen for about fifty yards. It hadn't been decided where the flame thrower tanks would reside, so each company had three crews trained. "A" Company was first to be trained in its use and sent three crews to Detwiller, France, followed by the other Companies with HQ being last. The Flame tanks eventually made their home in HQ as part of their armored support to replace all the tanks they had given to "A" Company.

Flamethrower training for the 781st. (U.S. Army Signal Corps, NARA)

The Battalion's Command Post was residing in a farmhouse near Bouxwiller when *another* gasoline stove in the attic of the house they occupied got out of control shortly before midnight on the 17th and burned the place to the ground. Just before the CP was toasted, the Battalion learned that intercepted German communications indicated that German armor was so short of fuel and spare parts they could "not permit one meter of unnecessary travel." And if they ran out of fuel or parts they "under no circumstances be retained in line merely to utilize their weapons." In comparison, Sixth Army had established six drive-in "Emergency Aid Stations" in the local area, but these aid stations weren't for people, they were for vehicles. Vehicles could drive in and have the tires checked, flats fixed, and batteries, water, plugs, wipers, and anti-freeze checked and replaced as required!

The Battalion stood in the cool, intermittent rain on the day after their Command Post burned down and held a Bronze Star Ceremony, at which 26 men were awarded the Bronze Star. The next day, they got notice to move under radio silence on the 23rd to a new position, and they were happy to find out that they are to be reunited with the 100th Infantry Division. Lt. Col Kinne summed up for the "Century Sentinel" (the newspaper for the 100th Division) at the time why the 781st liked fighting alongside the 100th: "The 100th puts us into their plans, and then the plan is followed." He said: "The 100th infantrymen have never failed to give us the support we'd been promised. That's superb teamwork."

The Battalion made preparations to join up with the 100th Infantry Division near Montbronn and scouted routes and established communication. While the troops waited for the move they were shown a film titled "Your Job in Germany." "Your Job in Germany" was a propaganda film made by a U.S. Army film unit which was commanded by the famous movie director Frank Capra (after the war he directed "It's a Wonderful Life"), and the script was written by none other than Theodore Geisel (after the war he became famous as "Dr. Seuss"). The film's main message was against fraternization with the German populace, who were portrayed in the film as untrustworthy and having a history of sneaking aggression. It warns especially against the children, who "have been trained to win by cheating" and who have been "brought up on straight propaganda." "Everything you believe in they were trained to hate and destroy." "Be aloof, watchful and suspicious – every German is a potential source of trouble – there will be no fraternization with the German people. Fraternization means making friends. The German people are NOT our friends." "Just one mistake may cost you your life – trust none of them." The message was lost on the troops. According to Joe DeGorter, a member of the Mortar Platoon: "We fraternized anyway! One time a buddy and I were fraternizing with a German girl and we heard a jeep getting closer. Getting caught was serious trouble, and my buddy and I jumped out a back window as the jeep pulled up to the door." This was seconded by Joe Graham, who said, "There was fraternization all over the place!"

The 781st convoy to join the 100th followed Route 17 and left early on the 23rd with Company "B" leading, then "C," "D," and "A" mixed in with the HQ section. Again, it was a slow trip at 15mph, with 88 yards between vehicles and 15 meters between sections. Upon arrival, the companies performed recon and coordination for future operations, then set up bivouac and started to plan attacks. Enemy artillery fell in the vicinity of Co "C's" Petit Rederching bivouac and three "C" Company men were wounded by artillery fire.

On the day after their arrival, the Battalion got a copy of a secret order from Commanding General XV Corps (Gen. Wade Haislip), directing that the 781st "not repeat not be employed without permission of CG XV Corps, except on artillery missions. Tanks and assault guns may be used in artillery role…" There was no explanation given for the odd order given from such a high level. The general shortage in munitions after the recent battle had forced General Devers to drastically curtail almost all expenditures of large-caliber weapons. "Y Battery" had of course been doing this for weeks, and they kept on trying to "reach out and touch someone." "D" Company was back in the "snatch and grab" raiding mode. The rest of the Battalion cooled its heels in artillery mode for the next two weeks, until they got another odd mission.

By this time, the tank flamethrowers had been in service long enough for some Darwinian dropout to think up a stellar way to misuse them. The "Einstein" in question was searching for a way to increase the effectiveness of the flamethrower, so he connected an *oxygen* cylinder in place of the nitrogen cylinder that was the propellant for the flame. He achieved his goal – the resultant flame was greater than he had hoped. As a matter of fact, the resultant flame was way, way greater, and he once again proved that Natural Selection was a viable process. Once the fire was

"And this is what happens when you pull the trigger!" (U.S. Army Signal Corps, NARA)

extinguished, all Battalions having tank-mounted or portable flamethrowers received an urgent bulletin that cautioned about using only compressed nitrogen and not oxygen, hydrogen, or acetylene, or "loss of life and damage to equipment" would occur.

On the other side of the front lines, after the Nordwind and Solstice offensives had burned out, the Germans were quietly shifting their forces back to the Eastern front, where the Russians were massing for a spring offensive. The encircled German forces in the Colmar Pocket were kept *in situ* due to Hitler's obstinacy about relinquishing the Alsace territory. Ike was really worried by its existence, but Devers, Patch, and DeLattre weren't, but Ike used it as an excuse to fret, so Dever's French forces eliminated the Colmar pocket, taking it off the table. Once that was done, Devers gave Patch the go-ahead and he responded by tidying up the lines and getting ready to push on into Germany.

The Seventh Army had used up their "pool" of replacement officer candidates by this time. No new officers from Officer Candidate School were expected before March, and there was a push to spot and promote people who showed potential, and for existing officers to be evaluated for promotion. At General Marshall's request, General Eisenhower turned in evaluations for all his senior generals. Showing his dislike for Jacob Devers, Ike took advantage of Marshall's request and roasted Devers. Devers was rated twenty-fourth of thirty-eight, which was far below Ike's other principal Army commanders, and even below a couple of junior officers. Eisenhower described Devers "loyal and energetic" and "enthusiastic, but often inaccurate in statements and evaluations." Eisenhower couldn't hide the fact that Devers had produced great results, saying that Devers' results were "generally good, sometimes outstanding," but he watered down any faint praise with statements like, "he has not, so far, produced among the seniors of the American organization here that feeling of trust and confidence that is so necessary to continued success." This was an oblique jab at Devers for siding with the French Command and not abandoning Strasbourg when Ike wanted to do so. In return, the French Command was a highly vocal supporter of Devers. Marshall, to his credit, kept Devers in place.

On March 1st, a new Training program kicked off, mandated by Division Command. If not otherwise used for tactical duty, crews were to spend four hours a day, every day, on a set training regimen. Subjects:
• Radio Comm. – maintenance checks and practicing signals while being monitored for security breaches.
• First Aid – basic training and how to remove wounded from tanks.
• Crew Drill – crews practiced dismounting quickly while carrying their individual weapon, then establishing local security around vehicle.
• Conduct of the individual soldier while dismounted – acting as a foot soldier doing patrols and scouting.
• Physical training – marching, calisthenics, close order drill, and organized athletics.
• Guard Duty – how to be a guard.
• And map reading, range firing, tank driving, camouflaging techniques, tactical training, tank gunnery, and practicing alerts.

And because the 781st was still under General Haislip's special order that restricted them from tactical duty, they had plenty of time to take those subjects that they had just spent the last two weeks reviewing in detail and go over them all again. With the warmer weather, the tanks, helmets, and vehicles were painted or scrubbed back to Olive Drab, and the improvised weather protection on vehicles was dismantled. The 781st was locked in a routine of lobbing shells at the enemy near Montbronn and Reyersswiller, retaking training classes for the second or third time, and developing their liking for liberated schnapps. The Luftwaffe made rare appearances, but the 781st was no different from other Allied Armor in suffering the indignity of being incorrectly identified and mistakenly strafed by U.S. planes. They showed their displeasure with some sarcasm – one period report from the Battalion states: "The Luftwaffe came over now and then (often as not in U.S.-made P47s)."

Early in March, the Battalion Executive Officer, Major Morris Tindall, departed for hospital treatment due to heart trouble. Major George Farris was promoted as the new XO and Captain John Simkins was taken from "A" Company and appointed Battalion S-3 to take his place. Major Tindall recovered, and he was posted as commander of a recreation facility/hotel in Paris, France (the Grand Hotel). On those rare occasions when officers of the 781st got a leave to Paris, Major Tindall could be counted on to roll out the red carpet for them.

The HQ Tank section conducted a demonstration with the Division Chemical Officer on the operation and maintenance of their newest Flame Thrower Mechanized E4-5, and then they were subjected to special training with emphasis on the use of their azimuth indicators. "D" Company got a break from palace guard detail and was posted at all important intersections in the Division's rear to check for stolen vehicles. Between the vehicles that had been abandoned by U.S. forces, those that were captured by the Germans and recovered but had not been returned to their proper owners, and vehicles that had been "midnight requisitioned," the vehicle ownership situation was nearly out of control. Division somehow chose "D" Company (the fox guarding the chicken coop, etc., etc.!) to stop all vehicles at checkpoints and check papers to determine if they were lost or stolen, return them to their proper owners if required, check them for contraband, and present the drivers to the MPs. "D" Company took this golden opportunity to stuff their booty truck with so much seized contraband that the springs sagged.

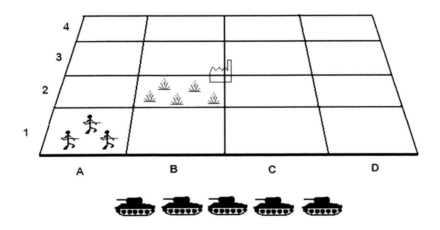

Zone Firing: A detailed map of the area with coordinates is not required. The tank/infantry team uses a grid of set size, orienting the center on a landmark. The attacking infantry in "A1" can then request fire support in "B2" without waiting for maps! Simple and fast!" (author)

General Haislip's secret orders finally were made clear on March 11th. The 781st had been selected to deliver a training demonstration that presented a new technique for tank-infantry teams to attack a defended town. The training was to showcase a technique called "Zone Firing" that the 781st had developed in past battles when taking a defended town. It involved placing a platoon of tanks in direct fire mode and splitting the town into sectors around a prominent landmark in the town – a steeple, smokestack, etc. This created a grid. By doing this, the tanks could direct fire into 100-yard sectors that could be called out by sector number, and they did not have to rely on a description of a building ("fire on sector A-4" vs. "fire on the red house next to the green one – no, the other red house."). The tanks did not rely on visual references and the target could be smoked without loss of fire control. The fire could be accurately controlled by each zone and walked backward at a rate that matched the infantry advance. It was a great technique and would come in handy in the near future. The Battalion prepared and delivered a demonstration of this tactic to attack a defended town using the town of Ratzwiller as the demonstration site.

"A" and "B" Companies provided the Armored support for the demonstration. HQ demonstrated their new Flame Thrower Section as part of the demonstration, and "D" Company's 1st platoon participated in the training demonstration of taking the town of Ratzwiller by towing a section of 3-inch rifles into position, covering the town and providing flank protection. Experiments were desired on the practicality of having medium or light tanks tow 57mm anti-tank guns or 3-inch rifles into close-support positions, and this training demonstration was a great opportunity. The 781st provided the motive power for the anti-tank company of the 410th Infantry Regiment and the 614th TD Battalion. The experiments showed that the M5 was better suited to being a mule than the M4 due to being quieter and more maneuverable, but the M5's automatic transmissions didn't like the job. Ammunition for the towed guns was hauled behind another tank in an armored trailer, and this instantly became a "you want me to do what?!" job. The Gun Commander would ride in the bow gunner's seat of the lead tank so he could direct gun positioning via the SCR 500 radio. While all this was happening, other light tanks were supposed to be furnishing flank protection. Overall the idea worked, and but for the strain on the M5s' transmissions, it might have been fully adopted. This tactic was implemented as a fall back procedure to be used when the normal prime movers for the guns were not available.

The Ratzwiller Demonstration was finished on the 12th. While the rest of the battalion was putting on the show, "C" Company spent half a day firing 184 rounds in support of Field Artillery, dueling with the enemy artillery, and the other half was consumed, as they were "given four hour lecture on mines and booby traps by XV Corps Officer." It was, oddly enough, not well-received.

First Armored Group issued a request for units to report if battlefield experience with liquid ammunition storage in the M4s indicated any advantage over the old dry storage units. While tests in the U.S. indicated it would prove advantageous, no reports had been received to support or refute the theory under battlefield conditions. There was an unsettling indication that crews were installing home-made ready racks or were still carrying loose ammo, and that any advantage of the liquid storage was being negated by this practice. By this time, the Sherman crews were getting demoralized about the quality of their tank versus the German tanks. They felt they were the "best tanks in the world, after the Germans."

19. OPERATION UNDERTONE

Operation UNDERTONE was conceived by General Patch, and was a pincer operation to trap and destroy the German 7th Army west of the Rhine. He presented his plan to Ike and General Patton March 5th. Ike made one small change; instead of letting the Seventh Army do the lion's share of the work while Patton's Army held the net, Ike reversed their roles. Ike's mistrust of Devers extended to the Seventh Army. The U.S. 7th Army was to focus mainly on reduction and crossing of the Maginot and Seigfried lines. Patton would grab the headlines and wield the hammer while Patch played the anvil and used up his army battering against fortifications. Because these were the same fortresses that had proven to be so tough back in December, 3rd Army would lend a hand by flanking the Germans on the left and hopefully dislodging the defenders. 3rd Army would then push the German Army along the west bank of the Rhine until they hit their backs up against the 7th Army, surrounding them. The Germans had made good use of the time that had elapsed since the last Allied push in the sector and their pillboxes and mine fields were awesome and extracted a heavy toll.

On March 14, 1945, after the Ratzwiller demonstration was over, the 781st was taken out of "artillery quarantine" and was returned to the Bitche sector, where they had unfinished business. On arrival, they split up and attached to their old friends in the Century Division: A/781 was attached to 399th Infantry Regiment; B/781 was attached to 398th Infantry Regiment; and C/781 was attached to 397th Infantry Regiment, and they made plans for immediate attacks. 2nd Platoon of "D" Company was attached to 925th Field Artillery to provide a guard for their 155mm M12 Self Propelled guns. "Y Battery" was dissolved, and the mortar platoons and assault gun section reverted to HQ Control. One assault gun each reverted to control of A, B, and C Companies to give them some 105mm capability, and HQ kept three. It is really notable that, while the rest of the Battalion rebuilt itself and retrained, "Y Battery" had stayed on-line and fired 1,800 rounds on an "on call" basis as a portable field artillery unit. Lieutenant Yonkers earned and received a Bronze Star for his leadership of "Y Battery" during this time.

The 781st cruises into Bitche. (U.S. Army Signal Corps, NARA)

UNDERTONE kicked off on March 15th, when the Seventh Army growled as a unit. Thousands of guns started volleys at 0100, and they didn't stop until dawn. The 100th Division and the 781st were once again assigned to knock out the Maginot fortress of Bitche. The day dawned mild and clear with good visibility, and the 781st supported the 100th in its attack on Bitche. 2nd Platoon of "A" Company captured four POWs at Reyerswiller, but two tanks from 3rd Platoon were disabled by mines at Glassemberg and had to be retrieved by the maintenance section while under fire. The second mission of the day was to clear some woods, as the infantry were pinned down by heavy mortar and small arms fire, but the tanks were unable to help due to wooded terrain and went back to mopping up the previous sector.

"B" Company was similarly plagued by mines. They prepared to move to support the attack on Fort Schiesseck, but found they couldn't take the preferred route due to mined roads and the railroad bed secondary route was blocked by tank barriers west of the Freudenburg barracks. They then moved to support the attack on Freudenburg Farm, but 1st Lt. Francis Coolican's lead tank was knocked out by a mine (Again! His tank hit a mine in December as well), this time killing Pfc. Rosendo Garcia and wounding the Lieutenant and two crewmen. 2nd Lt. John Sandroni and another crewman were also wounded in the assault, and the lieutenant died of his

The 781st goes cross country, but the woods near Bitche are not good tank country. (U.S. Army Signal Corps, NARA)

wounds two days later. At that point, they withdrew to the barracks. They were then given a mission to assault a pill box on a nearby hill, but again were held up by a minefield; but this time it was a friendly minefield which was still being cleared!

"C" Company supported their infantry and seized a hill north of Scherbach, but they, too, were held up by mines. Two tanks were disabled by these mines and one was recovered by maintenance. "D" Company was in division reserve, preparing to provide covering fire for two M12, 155mm self-propelled guns that were going to repeat their December performance and use 155mm rounds to knock on the fortress doors.

100 days on the line, and the 781st lines the streets of Bitche March 16th. (U.S. Army Signal Corps, NARA)

When the tanks were knocked out by mines, Sgt Robert Brown and his maintenance crew (T/4 William Turner, T/5 John Bradish, and T/5 Lucien Carey) immediately proceeded to the crippled vehicles and repaired one tank while under fire from small arms and mortar fire and got it back into the fight. They then repaired a second tank while under fire and sent it back to safety under its own power. The third tank they towed to the rear with their recovery vehicle. For their courage and resourcefulness while under hostile fire all four men were awarded Bronze Stars.

On the 16th, the 781st Tank battalion completed 100 continuous days of operations in the line by supporting the 100th Infantry Division in the occupation of Bitche. By the morning of the 16th, the mines had been cleared and the Medium

Sturmgeschutz knocked out at Campe de Bitche with dead crew nearby.
(U.S. Army Signal Corps, NARA)

Companies could really begin the attack. "A" Company entered Camp de Bitche with the 399th and so thoroughly decimated two pillboxes that the German commander surrendered 74 POWs. "B" was held in reserve and "C" was placed in ready position at Scherbach, prepared to resist any attack from enemy armor, which was reportedly spotted northeast of Campe de Bitche. They engaged six tanks in a sort of shooting standoff long enough for one of the infantry to creep up and knock out one German tank with a bazooka, at which point the others withdrew. Also on the 16th, "D" Company and their mastodon-like charges entered the fray.

M12 in the falling snow. (U.S. Army Signal Corps, NARA)

"Avon Calling" with a 155! The 100th/781st team retried what worked last December and detailed the M12 Gun Motor Carriage with 155mm guns of the Division's 925th Field Artillery to concentrate direct fire on the front door. The light tanks of "D" Company were tasked with providing suppressing fire and general cover for the M12s with their 155mm guns while the behemoths waddled up to knock on the front door. Once again, it worked! A ferocious artillery barrage masked the noise of the M12s' approach as they lumbered up to pre-scouted positions that offered the best chance of success. The German defenders were caught by surprise and had their doors literally blown off, and while the M12s retired, the infantry climbed on the light tanks of "D" Company in a familiar role and exploited the gaps. With large holes in the defenses the fortress became untenable for the defenders, who withdrew, and after two days of fighting the Maginot Line Fortress city of Bitche was taken by the 781st attached to the three regiments of the Century Division. It was an easier prize than anyone had thought it would be.

The 781st didn't stop at Bitche, leaving occupation to the 71st Infantry Division while they continued the attack to the north. 1st Platoon of "A" Company attacked to the northeast with an eye toward capturing Hilst, but they didn't make it that far; 2nd Platoon attacked north toward Bouseviller, but they were held up by a missing bridge that had been destroyed by the retreating Germans. "B" Company moved to Freudenburg Barracks, but lost one 75mm M4 which happened to cross the sights of an enemy Self-Propelled 75mm gun near Campe de Bitche, wounding three of the crew. "C" Company supported an attack to clear a wooded area, then moved to Waldhausen and prepared to move north through Rolbing upon repair of bridges demolished by retreating enemy. "D" Company escorted the elephant parade back to their home and then moved to Freudenburg Barracks to hook up with Division Recon troops.

On the 19th, all movement was complete, and the 781st was in position with the rest of 7th Army, ready to provide the anvil against which Patton's 3rd Army would hammer the German 7th Army. By this time, the German armies had fallen back behind the Rhine from Cologne to Arnhem, and the bridgehead at Remagen had been secured. The German 7th Army could see the trap that was being sprung and was trying to avoid the noose. It was making an orderly withdrawal across the Rhine as quickly as each opportunity presented, but Patton's Third Army was close behind and was devouring any units it caught.

While they waited for the blow to fall, the 781st attended an orientation on the situation confronting the 100th Div, VI Corps, the Seventh Army, and the Western Front in general, and reviewed the Bitche operation and movements to the present position. Battalion staff discussed plans of attack for fortified areas and anticipated the forcing of river crossings. The next day (the 20th), Patch's Seventh Army met Patton's troops, encircling the German Seventh Army and destroying it, netting 100,000 prisoners. The 3rd Division sector was where the fighting occurred, so the 781st missed that operation.

Twenty-four thousand German prisoners ranging in age from 14 to 62 are penned up in Worms. This is about one-fourth of the total bag captured by the Seventh Army during the offensive east of the Rhine. (U.S. Army Signal Corps, NARA)

20. RACE
TO THE RHINE

With the defeat of Nordwind and Solstice, the German Army's withdrawal became more akin to an implosion. The Century Division mounted up with the 781st and began charging due East through the gaping void in the Siegfried Line that used to be the German city of Zweibruken. Two things stuck the men of the 781st: the total devastation and the streams of refugees that were headed west to safety. "Zweibruken was a pile of smoldering ruins."

From the 781st Diary:

> But one of the most impressive things we saw were the streams of men and women moving down the road toward France. They were French, Dutch, Belgian, Polish, and Russian. They had been brought from all over Europe to work as slaves of the mighty war machine. Like slaves, they wore little tags to show which was a Pole, Russian, or a Belgian. They seemed never to grow tired of telling of the three, four, or five years of being pushed around by German soldiers and civilians; of not being able to go to church or the movies, or buy new clothes, or have a vacation, of four or five years wondering where their families were; of remembering how their homes had been burned and their children murdered by the conquering Wehrmacht.

The 100th Division and the 781st had come up with a system to transport the Infantry on board the tanks in the event of rapid pursuit. One platoon of "D" Company's light tanks was attached to each medium tank company to provide flank protection while in this mode. Here the Stuarts and "D" Company were in their element, being used as the tip of the spear point during this rapid pursuit. The Stuarts raced ahead, like redbone hounds ranging back in forth in front of the hunters during a coon hunt, hoping for a whiff or a sighting so they could bring the troop-laden Shermans onto their prey. The Stuarts were assigned a daily drive that was right at the far limit of their gas tanks' range. To keep the tanks rolling, a Deuce and a Half filled with five gallon gas cans closely followed the leaders; the driver of this rolling firebomb praying that any *Panzerfaust* teams or Luftwaffe aircraft had already been neutralized.

"Dragon's Teeth" tank obstacles of the Siegfried Line are passed by the 781st. (author's collection)

"Saddle Up!" D/781st gets ready to move out. (Rhodes family collection)

After VE-Day, the rapid pursuit system developed by the 781st and the 100th was compiled and published in "Combat Lessons No. 9" on Tank-Infantry Teamwork to serve as an instruction manual for the rest of the Army. The entire section on transporting infantry on tanks is a lesson written by Lt. Col. Kinne. Among the lessons taught are:

1. Maximum of 10 men per tank.
2. Preserve the unit's tactical integrity so there's no need to reform when the infantry dismounts.
3. You can carry an entire mortar crew on a tank *with* their weapon.
4. The tank looks out for the infantry and the infantry protects the tank in return.
5. Communication using an EE8A telephone was best. The handset inside the turret was wired in parallel to a flashlight so when the infantry riding on the tank called the commander the light lit up to catch his attention.

One day, the 781st and

781st Tanks with 100 Div Infantry on a roll. (U.S. Army Signal Corps, NARA)

the 100th managed to advance 110 miles in a single day, which is very close to being a record for the longest day's advance by any unit in the U.S. Army in WWII. On the 21st, the Battalion's HQ Section moved to Brenschelbach, becoming the first Company-sized unit to have their Command Post located on "Sacred German Soil." A new, harder heart was starting to appear in the crews toward the civilians. As Cpl. Ronald O'Donnell remembered:

> When we were in France, we'd stay in the houses with the French people. They'd give us a room in their house. We'd take our bedrolls and bed down there. When we got into Germany, we'd just take over the house. The first night we were in Germany, we crossed the German line about 9:00 at night. We went in to take over a big house there. The women and kids were crying when we were running them out. I said, 'Well, let's just let them go and we'll go somewhere else.' One of the guys spoke up and said, 'My wife and kids were crying when I left. We're going to stay right here.'

Looting also became common after the German border was crossed.

At this point, the added weight of the sandbags and supplemental "armor" applied to the tanks, combined with carrying a number of combat soldiers and their gear, the warmer weather, and the high-speed driving on roads, were overtaxing the Sherman's suspensions, and the rubber tires on the bogie wheels that supported the tanks were overheating and failing at a considerable rate. It was truly wondrous that the Service and Transport crews could keep up with the advance, supplying fuel, spare parts, and food by driving up and back, day and night, round the clock.

As they tore through the villages, they saw flags of surrender hanging from buildings and windows – anything white was used by the populace to denote submission. By the 24th, "D" Company had the town and Luftwaffe airfield of Ludwigshafen

Wishful thinking. (Up from Marseille)

in sight, and across the Rhine, the spires of Mannheim beckoned. That afternoon, the airfield was cleared by "A" Company and the other companies were clearing the west bank of the Rhine to the south of Ludwigshafen, without enemy interference. "D" Company continued their advance and moved on Mundelhelm, finally meeting some resistance. It was nothing they couldn't handle, and they eliminated three machine gun nests and captured 73 POWs (two captains, four other officers, and 67 enlisted men). The airfield was a bit of a sightseeing magnet, and some crews took an opportunity to visit and have their picture taken among and astride the wreckage of the Luftwaffe aircraft that littered the field.

March 25, 1945, was remembered as a happy day. While the companies were engaged in patrols around the Ludwigshafen area and "D" Company added four more POWs to their bag, news arrived that Cpl. L. T. Beauchamp of Company "A,"

who was captured during the disaster at Sessenheim, was liberated and returned to allied control this day. March 26th was just as happy, as it was noted that for the first time in 110 days, the Battalion was not in immediate contact with the enemy. The tank companies were all being used to patrol for snipers, trading a 76mm round one-for-one for each sniper round fired. There were more than enough snipers to go around, so an HQ Tank Section patrol of two M5s, three half tracks, and a jeep were sent to Ruppertsberg to clean out snipers located in that town. Their report: "Town was thoroughly searched and 4 POWs and considerable weapons taken."

The Battalion spent the last three days of the month on vehicle and weapon maintenance, training, and recreation, waiting for a bridge to be built so they could cross the Rhine. They were part of an Allied force that numbered close to 4.5 million personnel and ninety divisions

Taking your picture on or around the wrecked Luftwaffe planes at Ludwigshafen was the thing to do. (author's collection)

that were preparing for the next operation. The training courses had a serious side, as they trained in use of gas masks because of the unsettling possibility that gas might be used as a weapon by a dying regime. On a lighter note, they were also doing refresher training in Military Courtesy, as that aspect of behavior *might* have started to erode while deployed, especially in *one* of the Companies.

The 1st Armored Report at the end of March was again concerned with the suspected vulnerability of the Sherman tank. This report tells the results of an analysis and subsequent test that the Division had done on a M4 tank that had been hit by a 75mm A/P shell at a range of 250 yards. Analysis showed that, despite having approximately seven inches of reinforced concrete on the sides, and even though the round cracked but failed to penetrate the side armor, the M4's gas tank ruptured and caught fire, and the ammunition stored inside exploded even though it was a wet-storage unit that kept the ammunition in a liquid. After burning out, the same tank was tested to see if a *Panzerfaust* could penetrate the opposite side through the concrete. Depressingly, it did.

The Army Administration was calling for all winter clothing and supplies to be turned in. This turned out to be premature for the 781st, but it was done readily, as the troops needed to make room in their vehicles. As they passed by abandoned houses and through towns, there was a fair amount of looting that was occurring. One guy in Joe DeGorter's half track used to be a tailor before the war, and he found a really nice sewing machine and brought it aboard the track. It was a godsend that the Luftwaffe was out of business, because pretty soon there was "*so much junk* in the half tracks that we couldn't get to the machine guns!" "D" Company waited in Neustadt for the bridge to be completed. Upon their arrival, the local Burgermeister greeted Capt. Graham on behalf of the community and thanked them for liberating his city. (Capt. Graham wondered where he had hidden his Nazi Party card…) As a token of gratitude, the Burgermeister promised to provide two bottles of Neustadt's "good wine" to every officer and one bottle to each enlisted man every day. When "D" Company left Neustadt, their Bootymobile and trailer carried as much of the local wine as the vehicles could hold.

Even though March 31st dawned mild and clear, the 781st moved into a cloud of artificial smoke and fog and crossed the Rhine using an engineer-built pontoon bridge, using the techniques that "D" Company had pioneered at Fort Wainwright. On passing through Mannheim, Ron O'Donnell remarked "I don't believe there was a building left standing in Mannheim." Once across, they fanned out to clear the east bank and then moved south. On April 1st, they got word that the First and Third Armies had encircled and captured the Rurh region and bagged 21 enemy divisions, as well. The Rurh region was the breadbasket and arms factory for the Reich, and it was now denied to the enemy. The general feeling was "It won't be long now."

The trains in Karlsdorf weren't moving. (author's collection)

Long now or not, when "C" Company advanced south from Eppelheim, they met considerable small arms and HE fire. They cleared enemy troops from Wiesloch, killing an undetermined number. The going was not uncontested; each platoon fired approximately 100 rounds of 75mm HE, and they lost three tanks: one to a mine, wounding two crewmen, and two tanks were stuck in the mud. "D" Company 1st platoon was given a mission to contact French forces on the right flank. They sped over and joined up on the 3rd French Army. Other "D" Company tanks assisted in clearing Wiesloch, and they also lost three tanks to the mud. The following day, "C" Company returned to retrieve the two stuck tanks and were successful, but during their next advance to Michelfeld, Lt. Joe Trombetta's lead tank fell prey to a *Panzerfaust* and all four crew were wounded as a result. "D" Company was also successful in yanking their three mired tanks back into service.

The 100th Division and the 781st motored on to the southeast out of Mannheim, past Hiedelburg and Karlsdorf. During the advance, the 781st continued to innovate and experiment. "A" and "B" Companies took part in a tank-to-plane coordination test using the Division Artillery Liaison plane. They were pioneering the use of an airplane to scout for enemy formations and relay the information in a real-time manner to the combined forces on the ground. The use of radio telecommunication gear to enable direct contact between air observers and ground forces is standard, even mundane, on today's battlefield, but on April 2, 1945, it was cutting-edge use of technology, and the 781st was a leader in its use.

At this point, most German civilian support for the fighting was gone and organized resistance had collapsed, and most units were speeding through Germany at will, gobbling up territory, much as the 781st and the 100th Divisions had enjoyed up to this point. But the war was by no means over yet for the 781st.

21. HEILBRONN

The 781st again fought the Germans at Heilbronn, a city that straddles the Neckar River about 35 miles to the southeast of Mannheim. The previous December, the RAF literally leveled the city with a single night's raid of almost 300 Lancaster heavy bombers, each delivering nearly two tons of high explosive with love from Winston. Given the massive overkill size of the raid, the RAF couldn't help but achieve its objective to destroy the railway yards on the west bank of the Neckar, but in doing so, they caused a fire of such size in the adjacent city on the east bank that all containment measures were quickly overwhelmed. The people that took to air raid shelters either burned to death or were asphyxiated, as the immense firestorms consumed all the oxygen. It is estimated that over 6,500 people died in little over half an hour during this raid.

Heilbronn lays smoking from a recent artillery attack. A destroyed bridge can be seen in the foreground with the trainyards immediately behind. (U.S. Army Signal Corps, NARA)

Once the fires burned themselves out, the survivors found that the wounded couldn't get treatment, as the hospitals were gone, and there weren't enough coffins or graveyards to handle the dead. This left a city full of survivors without shelter at the start of a very harsh winter, which in turn resulted in a localized seething pocket of intense hatred for the Allies at Heilbronn. The destruction from the bombing provided a large, ready supply of construction materials and the civilians readily pitched in to help the German Army turn the ruins of the city into a fortress. German Artillery was hidden in nearby hills and had carefully zeroed in on the river and any potential crossing sites. The local militia, the Volksturm, then helped man the town to make a "last stand." But the Volksturm and small number of Artillery troops in Heilbronn needed more manpower, and the Allies gave them an unwitting hand.

As the U.S. Army was sweeping all before them in their rapid advance, the German troops being swept ahead gravitated to Heilbronn, as it was a local transportation hub, and as a result, an astonishing variety of troops were gathered in the city, with more arriving each day. Led by the 17th SS Panzer Grenadiers, the planeless Luftwaffe pilots and ground crews, shipless sailors, engineers, Hitler Youth, Africa Corps, and remnants of many other army groups joined with the Volksturm and were ready to make a stand at the willing, prepared site at Heilbronn. They were angry, desperate, tired of retreating, and they held out for an astonishing 10 days against one of the best U.S. Divisions, while all around them in Germany resistance was caving in.

As the lead unit of the advance, "D" Company ran into the Hielbronn pocket first and stepped aside as planned so the Shermans and infantry could take over. The 781st and Century Division arrived at the Neckar River April 3, 1945. The Neckar, at this point, was a fairly narrow, deep stream that was ideal for barge traffic, with steep banks and a strong current of perhaps 5mph. The U.S. forces surged up and down the west bank, but found to their disappointment that all the bridges had been destroyed in the area. "A," "B," and "C" Companies then began implementing the planning discussion of a week earlier on how to force a river crossing with their infantry counterparts. The patrols on this side of the river found a tough pocket of resistance on the west side of the river, but there was no warning of what lay in store in the city on the east side. Major General Withers Burress of the 100th concentrated his forces across from Heilbronn city and left the west bank pretty lightly defended. In case the Germans were thinking to counterattack, the 781st Headquarters and "D" Companies were detailed to patrol a stretch of the river north of town.

Nicknamed "Task Force Graham," from the 3rd to the 13th, this group had about thirty vehicles to cover ten miles of riverbank north from Ober Eisenheim and Unter Eisenheim, with the mission to prevent any enemy penetration from across the river. If they could attract attention and keep some enemy troops occupied that would be a plus. So to make their numbers seem larger, Captain Graham had the tanks and half tracks run up and down the roads that were visible to enemy observers and shift positions often so the enemy observers would be fooled. The Assault, Rocket, and Mortar Platoons would periodically pause in their travels and bring fire on enemy emplacements, then move on. Without Infantry support the lines were so thin that, according to Homer Turner, "the Germans could have come over anytime they wanted."

Homer remembers that the routine became "Hide during the day and shoot at night." During the day, when they weren't playing decoy, the tanks and tracks would hide behind a building or in some luckless farmer's barn, hoping to remain out of sight of the German Artillery spotters on the opposite hills. They would observe during the day and lob some harassing fire over the river during the night. During one stop, Homer became enchanted with the idea of sleeping in a real bed in a real bedroom instead of on the ground in damp, smelly basements or barns. The watch schedule the crew of Hot Box was using rotated so that every fifth night a crewman got to sleep undisturbed all night. Since Homer had this night off guard duty he made his way to the adjacent evacuated farmhouse and went upstairs to realize his dream – sleeping in a real bed. Wouldn't you know it, the Germans picked that night to send in some counterbattery fire, one round of which blew off an entire corner of the farmhouse in which Homer was peacefully sleeping in his nice cozy bed. Homer was shaken but uninjured by the blast and evacuated his sheets and ran downstairs. His thoughts: "To hell with this; I'm going back to the basement!"

Adolph Hoppi in Hot Box while in Bivouac with the Assault Gun Platoon. (Courtesy of Hoppi Family)

The German troops across the river had also taken to hiding during the day and moving at night, both to avoid observation and to escape Allied aircraft. Captain Graham was with one of the mortar half tracks one night and they could hear noises of horse-drawn carts clip-clopping on the streets across the river. The next day, of course, there was nothing to be seen, but the roads the enemy had used were identified. After a couple of nights the pattern emerged, and the captain had the mortar squad zero in on an intersection during the day and they then waited for nightfall. Sure enough, under cover of darkness, the movement and the noise began again.

When the noise was coming from the right spot the mortar team sprang into action and rained HE on their target, firing for effect. There were several large explosions as the wagon train's ammunition wagons exploded. The field telephone rang and Captain Graham's boss, having heard the ruckus, wanted to know what he was doing. "What the hell is going on over there?" "Just doing my job, sir," Graham replied. Morning revealed the considerable destruction they had wrought.

The long nights in foxholes peering into the inky blackness frayed everyone's nerves, and it just wasn't safe to venture too far if at all from one's own foxhole for fear of being shot on your return by your own tired and jumpy friends. Fear of being shot on return didn't stop Sgt. William Hooper of "D" Company and one of his buddies from leaving camp. They borrowed a Browning automatic rifle from the Infantry and, taking a rowboat they'd found, the two rowed across the river one night, right into enemy lines! They were "looking for some Germans to kill," and fortunately for both sides, they came up empty handed and returned. They weren't shot on their return, but the two men were on the receiving end of a "constructive chat" from their commanding officer.

The 781st takes a break while waiting for the engineers to construct a bridge over the Neckar. (U.S. Army Signal Corps, NARA)

Downstream, the 100th Division was discovering that they had a larger problem. When the Div CO learned the bridges at Heilbronn were gone, he proposed to cross at Bad Wimpfen (about eight miles away) and attack the city from the rear, but he was overruled. So attack plans were made in which the 398th Infantry regiment would lead the attack with the 397th in reserve, supported by both "B" and "C" Companies of the 781st. The 399th and "A" Company were to guard the right flank and stay in touch with the French Army.

The 398th crossed the Neckar using rubber boats and advanced into Heilbronn with surprising ease; they started to fan out, meeting sporadic resistance, hoping that it might go easy. That thought was shattered as Heilbronn's defenders surged into the open and launched a furious counterattack. They poured out of buildings, ruins, and cellars, and the 398th found itself being attacked from all directions and viciously cut up. They fell back to the river, losing many casualties and being captured in wholesale lots on the way. Once again, the Germans had dug a network of interconnecting tunnels in the debris that allowed troops to appear, disappear, move, and reappear on the flank or rear. The 398th managed to keep a toehold on the east bank north of the city, but they needed close armor support and quickly.

781st HQ Company rocket tank. (U.S. Army Signal Corps, NARA)

But the Neckar could not be crossed by armor! The Engineers constructed several pontoon bridges, and the German artillery deployed in the hills east of the city would patiently wait for the bridge to near completion and then atomize it with their artillery. "C" Company watched helplessly as their bridge was destroyed. The strong current and steep banks exacerbated matters, making it hard to launch pontoon bridges and tough to control them in the current once launched. Making matters even worse, hundreds of escaped slaves who had worked in the factories in Heilbronn were crossing the river in boats or with floats, or just swimming for freedom, often under German small arms fire. The 781st started to refer to the bridge as the "Yehudi" bridge, in deference to the running gag that comedian Jerry Colonna had on the Bob Hope Show which referred to "Yehudi," the invisible man.

Arriving with perfect timing, three modified Sherman tanks were received by Headquarters Company. They were equipped with the "T34," a 60-tube rocket launcher that was nicknamed the "Calliope" because of its resemblance to a steam pipe organ. The powerful rockets were 4.5" in diameter, and each rocket packed the punch of a 105mm artillery shell when it exploded. Mounted on two legs above the turret top, the launcher consisted of a rack of 36 tubes laid horizontally with two smaller sets of 12 tubes each hung under the larger rack. The rack was hinged and had an arm that hooked to the gun barrel – raising the gun raised the rack, and vice versa. The gunner had a small electrical panel with a button, and he could press the button to shoot individual rockets or hold it down and fire them all. One full salvo took 60 seconds to fire from start to finish. The tank commander could traverse the turret while the gunner fired and sweep the target area. The single Calliope launcher, with its 60 rockets, had the same impact as an artillery battalion firing 60 guns.

HQ Rocket tank launches a salvo. (author's collection)

The orgasmic ferocity of the launch, the long flaming tails of the rockets, the enormous, choking smoke cloud they generated, and the noise – such a roaring, unending cacophony! – engendered awe in everyone who witnessed a launch. German POWs related that they considered the Calliope more demoralizing than artillery. Homer Turner managed to retain Hot Box and didn't get the rockets, and he wasn't disappointed, as the one downside to having the rocket tubes was enormous – it was not possible to fire the gun with the rack arm attached due to the recoil of the gun. Lots of crews took to firing one salvo and then jettisoning the tubes, which got expensive, so later versions allowed use of the gun without disconnecting the launcher.

The Calliopes got a workout at Heilbronn with the 781st and were immediately positioned in hull-defilade right across the Neckar River from Heilbronn, where the rocket squad started to execute the "Zone Firing" technique in support of the infantry, firing 96 rockets on the first day they were there. The Division Engineers tried moving the bridge sites to escape the rain of artillery, but the Germans kept destroying them, thus preventing the tanks from joining the infantry. The infantry had to rely on air support and remote firing to take care of the German armor. SP guns were lying in wait, hidden in the fortress/town, and the defenders also made liberal use of *Nebelwerfers*, their counterpart to the Calliope rocket launcher. The *Nebelwerfers* emitted a shrill shriek when fired and earned the nickname "Screaming Meemies" from allied troops. The T34s attached to HQ company tanks helped support the now house-to-house advance through the town. Most allied troops saw this as payment in kind to the Germans for their *Nebelwerfer* rocket attacks.

The 397th crossed the Neckar two miles below the city, covered by a smoke screen (Fort Wainwright techniques again) and a mortar barrage to aid the 398th. But they were set upon by a strong counterattack that included tanks. The Germans tried a push with their limited armor, which included four Tigers, and the 781st, firing from across the river, managed to blunt the blow. Tanks were desperately needed across the Neckar to turn the tide. But like moths to a flame, German defenders were coming from the surrounding towns and outskirts to lend their weight to the defense. At least 10 SPs and five tanks were active in the area, from the German 667th Assault Gun Battalion and 17th SS Panzer Grenadier Division, with SPs being used as roving artillery.

"D" Company lost a tank to a mine, and one crewman was wounded in the blast. S/Sgt Ameede Burrell's tank from Company "B" was surprised and outdrawn by a German self-propelled gun, and the Sergeant and two crewmen were wounded in the exchange. Sgt. Donald Deming took command of the platoon after his platoon leader was wounded and enabled the platoon to continue their support of the action. This second meritorious exhibit, in conjunction with his prior efforts in January, earned Sgt. Deming a Bronze Star. The pesky pocket of defense on the west side of the river forced the Battalion to split their efforts between supporting the engineers as they tried to construct some way of conveying tanks over the river and clearing towns on the west bank. Company "B" was engaged with the 398th in reducing that pocket of German infantry that was on the west bank of the Neckar.

During the attack, a squad of infantry was pinned down close to the river, and this time Sgt. Earl Brownell of Company "B" was asked by the Infantry CO to go rescue the men. The 398th's CO honestly described the job as "a suicide mission." Sgt. Brownell turned and asked his driver, Pvt. Ron O'Donnell, what he thought. O'Donnell replied: "Well, if I was down there, I'd want somebody to come after me." The Sergeant said "Well, let's go!," and took his tank to the rescue. Pvt. Ronald O'Donnell, driving the tank, maneuvered across an open field per Sgt. Brownell's directions and used his tank to block the intense MG fire that was pinning the GIs down. The GIs took cover behind the tank, and Pvt. O'Donnell drove using the periscope, because to show anything else would have been suicidal. The squad was rescued safely, and for this action Brownell and O'Donnell were each awarded the Bronze Star.

During this fight a truly unusual event occurred. One of the German troops was wounded and the German Army medics couldn't treat him. Vince Sutphin recalls that right after Sgt. Brownell's tank rescued the trapped GIs, the Germans then radioed the 398th, asking if they could take their wounded soldier and treat him! A truce was called, and during the discussions, it was agreed that the Americans would take the soldier, treat him, and not imprison the soldier as a POW, instead delivering him to Switzerland to be interned after he was well enough to travel! After reaching this agreement and during the ensuing ceasefire, a U.S. ambulance was dispatched into the German lines to collect the soldier, who was then sent to an American hospital for treatment. All this took about two hours, and after the ambulance departed the field the truce was lifted and the fighting resumed, but it had lost much

The 781st gets DD driving lessons on the Neckar 4/6/45. (U.S. Army Signal Corps, NARA)

of its prior intensity. As Vince recalls, "I have never been so proud of my country as I was when this happened."

On April 6th, the engineers tried to get vehicles across the river using a four-pontoon ferry while the Rocket Platoon fired 106 rockets into Heilbronn to keep the defenders' heads down. First Platoon of "B" was with them, lending their weight to the barrage aimed at one of the factories in Heilbronn. First Platoon of "C" Company covered the ferry as it sent a load of infantry over and 2nd Platoon lined up to cross. The ferry worked fine, but the tank couldn't climb the steep opposite bank. Then the tank tried to claw its way up the bank, which caused the ferry to break apart, and the tank toppled into the Neckar! Adding to the general failure of the assault, up on the hilltop overlooking the scene, the HQ rocket tanks and "B" company were driven from their position by a furious blast of direct fire from across the river and they "Got the hell out of there!," according to Vince Sutphin. In the meantime, other paths across the river were feverishly sought. First and Third Platoons of "A" Company went to Neckarbischofensheim to get intensive training on the use of nine Sherman DD tanks received from VI Corps to try to cross the river.

The Sherman DD was a tank that could float and maneuver, albeit clumsily, in water. It used a canvas "hull" that was attached to the basic Sherman. The canvas coverings were attached to the lower hull of the tank and raised mechanically. They also had 36 inflatable tubes that supported the screen, but were especially vulnerable to puncture by floating debris and small arms fire. They used two propellers attached to a standard truck differential that was connected to the tank's drive sprockets. When afloat, the tank was entirely below the waterline and all one could see was the canvas.

The tank commander stood on top of the hull and steered by means of a tiller, which tilted the propellers to give some measure of directional control, roughly what one might expect when steering a floating anvil. The tank commander could fire the turret MG, but the main gun could not be fired while the canvas was raised. DD tank crews were usually given training in the use of the Momson Lung, which was a submarine escape device that was on board. Besides the obvious use for the breather, if/when the canvas was holed and the tank sank, another reason the Momson Lung was included was that if the DD had to travel more than 4,000 yards, there was a good chance that the driver and other occupants inside the hull would be asphyxiated. That was because the engine's exhaust fumes had nowhere to go and collected inside the canvas. The 781st received one day's quick training in the DD use on the 6th and they attempted to cross the Neckar on the 7th. They failed miserably, and it wasn't the crews' fault.

The problem was that the DD was designed to exit the water on a gently sloped firm beach, helped by the tide, and was not intended to climb riverbanks or fight river currents. The top speed of the DD in water was barely sufficient to cope with

The 781st pilots a DD Sherman into the Neckar River during training. The twin props can be seen on the rear of the tank. The top of the brave driver's helmet can just be seen. U.S. Army Signal Corps, (NARA)

the Neckar's swift current, and the bottom of the tank's tracks was about nine and a half feet below the water line. The result was that the tanks successfully entered the river, fought the current, and reached the other bank as planned, but they then ran up against an almost vertical bank on the opposite side. They couldn't climb out, and then struggled to prevent getting swept away while the tank commander was standing, choking on exhaust fumes, exposed behind a canvas tarp that if punctured would send the vehicle to the bottom like – well, a tank! The first attempt at crossing the Neckar in the morning of the 7th was abandoned when the first tank wound up stuck in the river, unable to get back out on *either* bank.

A second attempt at 1730 involved having the Engineers blow up the vertical walls in the soft banking with TNT in an effort to make a ramp that the DD could negotiate. But while the TNT was able to blast the banking, the soft blasted dirt

During training the tank missed the exit ramp, couldn't climb out, and the DD Screen was lowered too soon, almost sinking the tank. (U.S. Army Signal Corps, NARA)

turned into a soupy mess and the tanks couldn't get traction in the muck, so this attempt was also abandoned, leaving two more tanks stuck in the river, unable to get out. The next day's attempt involved construction of a cable and winching system that would pull the DDs up the far banking, but this was dropped because by this time bridges were finally constructed. Lt. Sloggatt happily commented, "I hope that's the last damned time I get into a tank that's got a life preserver on it." This was the penultimate use of the DD Sherman by Allied Forces in World War II.

Again using what the 781st learned at Fort Wainwright, the Division used smoke generators to obscure the river, and on the morning of the 8th, the Engineers managed to get a pontoon bridge up and operating long enough to get "C" Company's tanks across before it, too, was vaporized when the wind picked up and cleared the fog. But the door had been opened. "C" Company's tanks had just hooked up with their infantry when one tank was knocked out by a *Panzerfaust*. Thus began the slow advance over the next five hellish days in some of the toughest urban close combat seen in Europe. "B" Company milled about impatiently and fired 50 rounds over the river while they fumed for another bridge to be erected. The German artillery was now too busy supporting their troops in the city to pay close attention to the bridge building.

The rubble-strewn streets of Heilbronn provided excellent cover for the German defenders. The tanks of the 781st had to be used to blast the defenders out of their concealment one step at a time. German children roamed the streets and would

They raised the screen, backed off, and made it on the second attempt. Note the height of the DD. (U.S. Army Signal Corps, NARA)

happily point out German tanks, pillboxes, and strong points in exchange for a Hershey bar. But that sword cut both ways – other children pointed out U.S. forces to German artillery spotters, who then used the information to call in artillery strikes. Hot spots included a glass factory, a Knorr food facility, and the ruined rail yards, but the fight was finer-grained than that. It wasn't street-to-street or even house-to-house. At times, the 100th Div Infantry was embroiled in combat that was literally room-to-room in the same building. At night, the German infantry would try to infiltrate the U.S. lines by slipping heavy socks over their hobnailed boots to muffle the sound on the cobbles. A two-man *Panzerfaust* team was intercepted and killed on the 8th just before they fired on Sgt. Dunn's tank. This naturally made the folks on guard duty nervous and trigger-happy, and this caused one fatality, as Sgt. Stanley Gorisek of Company "C" was shot and killed by a guard that same night.

The teamwork between the 100th and the 781st was really working. The first tank taken out by the *Panzerfaust* turned out to be the only tank lost by the 781st during the Heilbronn battle. The other Companies weren't faring as well, however. "D"

Once out of the water, the crew had to scramble to drop the screens before the DD could be used as a tank. The 781st in training. (U.S. Army Signal Corps, NARA)

Company supported the 398th Infantry in an attack near Unter-Griesheim and fired 200 rounds of 37mm HE and 5,000 rounds of .30 cal MG ammunition in this assault. They unfortunately lost two tanks during the attack: one tank to bazooka fire and one to a self-propelled gun, killing Corporal Morris Brown, Jr., Pfc. Steven Strutinski, Sgt. Patrick Perry, and Pvt. John Jennings and wounding three others. The following day, "D" Company was again patrolling and fired 450 rounds of 37mm at targets in Kochendorf. The next day, they fired on an enemy patrol at 0130 with no counter fire. The next day they detected the enemy crossing the river southeast of Ober Eisenheim, but 2nd Platoon drove them back.

Rivaling "D" Company for activity were the HQ tanks. The Flame and Rocket section patrolled the river between Biberach and Unter Eisenheim. The Rocket Section fired 54 rounds of 75mm HE at an enemy S/P gun and then fired 60 rockets

A "C" Company tank poses for a quick picture in the factory section of Heilbronn. (U.S. Army Signal Corps, NARA)

at it with unknown results. HQ Company's Flame Section fired 100 rounds of 75mm HE, and the Assault gun section fired 150 rounds of 105mm HE and 10 rounds of smoke at targets. The next day the Flame section fired 85 rounds of 75mm across the Neckar River into some woods. The Assault Gun Platoon fired 150 rounds of 105mm into Kochendorf and the Flame Sec fired 172 rounds of 75mm direct fire into Kochendorf.

Back at Heilbronn, "A" Company's First Platoon crossed the Neckar by barge on the 11th and took up defensive positions in support of 399th Infantry. They engaged three enemy tanks (probably Mark IVs) in woods near Biberach, with two of them driven off and the third taken under fire by Artillery and burned. They then supported an attack on a barracks area southeast of Heilbronn and took approximately 40 POWs with the loss of one tank knocked out by a *Panzerfaust* and one tank knocked out by artillery fire, killing Cpl. Max Ruple. Third platoon crossed Neckar River and took up a defensive position on the south edge of town.

And in a classic case of slamming the barn doors *long* after the horse has departed, second platoon of "A" Company was summoned to Mossbach from the 11th to the 13th for amphibious training under VI Corps control. After the Heilbronn debacle with the DD Tanks, the First Armored Group organized a school for operation of those tanks: one platoon of the 781st and one from the 753rd attended. At the completion of the school, each battalion had one platoon capable of operating the DD tanks.

Dejected German Prisoners from Heilbronn are marched to the rear.
(U.S. Army Signal Corps, NARA)

The First Armored Group's final report of the DD training had a few "notes." It was noted that most navigable streams in the area had steep banks that were revetted with stone, and so were "totally unsuitable for employment of DD tanks." Also noted were the following:
- if the depth of the stream was less than nine feet the DD was no good.
- if the current was more than 3mph the DD was no good unless a guide cable was used.
- a recon of the entrance and exit must be made for underwater obstacles or debris that might puncture the canvas.
- each tank handled differently, and training on one tank might not carry over to the next.

- a guide cable was required for night crossings.
- crossing sites can't be under direct fire, as the DD tanks were extremely vulnerable to even small arms fire.

All those notes were pretty discouraging, but that wasn't all. The last note of the report sums it up: "Unless suitable crossing sites exist, it would appear more feasible to raft conventional tanks across streams rather than to construct an entrance and exit and employ DD tanks." (In mid-1946, the Army totally ignored the DD disaster at Heilbronn, disregarded the First Armored Group's report, and recommended further development of a DD tank by the Armored Ground Force Board at Fort Knox.)

On the 12th, "B" Company crossed via the new bridge and all three Companies were now directly in the fray with their regimental combat teams. By this time, under the constant pounding from the infantry and "C" Company, the defenders had

Heilbronn aftermath. (U.S. Army Signal Corps, NARA)

started to lose their starch; the *Volksturm* and *Hitlerjugend* were at the end of their line and started surrendering *en masse* as they were surrounded and beaten. Their officers were dismayed, and actually opened fire on their own troops as they threw up their arms and moved toward the U.S. lines. It didn't matter; the city was captured on the 13th and the Allied troops surveyed a ghost town of burned-out buildings, piles of brick and rubble, and dead bodies. Heilbronn itself was a moonscape, and according to a witness, "so many people were buried under the ruins that Heilbronn

had a noticeable stench all during the summer of 1945." For their service in wrest-
ing Heilbronn from the very determined enemy, the 397th Regiment of the 100th
Infantry division and Company C of the 781st were recognized with a Presidential
Unit Citation.

One of the 781st vets noted the graffiti on the ruins: "As you walked down the
alleys of rubble that had been streets, you could read the messages written in German
in chalk on the ruins of houses and apartments. The people who had lived there
wrote them for friends or relatives to tell what had happened to them. 'Otto: Little
Albert was killed and I am with the Karlesbergs,' or 'The Schmidt family has moved
to Sontheim. Heil Hitler!'"

The 781st reported at the end of the month that they had been whittled down
to 506 effective personnel after having lost three M4s and two M5s in the past two
weeks. The tank losses were not as big a problem as the lack of personnel to man
them. For the first time the losses were being felt, as it was reported that "three
tanks are unable to operate due to lack of personnel" in Company "C."

What Wingen and Bitche did to "B" Company and Sessenheim did to "A"
Company, Heilbronn did to "C" Company.

The 1st Army Report issued a warning to Battalion that the retreating Germans
were leaving behind extensive booby traps in utility stations. There was also an alert
about the "lavish use" of *Panzerfauste* by the Germans, and that in addition to being
used against armor, they were being used against infantry and in an indirect fire
mode. The 781st already knew all about that.

22. BREAKOUT!

The 781ˢᵗ burst from Heilbronn in all directions with the Century Division. They took Neckarsulm and Jagstfeld to the North, Flein to the South, and Willsbach to the east.

On the way to Willsbach, "B" Company and the 398ᵗʰ ran into light resistance. Corporal Roy Faulconer was gunner in a tank headed toward Willsbach, and he spotted a wounded GI lying in the open, pinned down by enemy fire and trying to

100th Div Troops take cover behind "B" Company tank "Blood and Guts II."
(U.S. Army Signal Corps, NARA)

reach cover and safety. The tank got close to the wounded man, who couldn't climb to safety. Faulconer jumped out of his tank, dodging intense fire, and reached the wounded man, hoisting him up and placing him on the rear deck of his tank. He then stayed with the GI and directed the tank to safety. For this action in the face of fire he was awarded a Bronze Star. "B" company fired 80 rounds in this attack and overran two machine gun nests in the process while suffering three crewmen wounded, two seriously.

The front being pushed by the 100th and 781st was growing like an expanding balloon, and like the wall of that balloon, the troops expanding that front were thinning out. But there weren't enough troops to keep expanding without special measures being taken. The 100th Division formed a "Provision Reconnaissance Squadron" using the 100th Division's Recon troop, HQ and "D" Companies of the 781st, Co "E" of the 399th, one Platoon of the 399th Anti Tank Company, and the Recon Company of the 824th Tank Destroyer Battalion. Commanded by Lt. Col. Kinne, its mission was to establish and maintain contact between the rest of the 399th Infantry and II French Corps. It was in essence an independent "mini-division," having a little armor, a little infantry, and a little artillery compared to a full-sized unit. However, it had good reconnaissance capability, so it could hold a line and go scout things out, but it wasn't designed to slug it out. It was supposed to establish and then hold a north-south front that would normally be held by two full Battalions. This allowed the bulk of the 100th Division to execute a flanking attack on the German 19th Army that would hook around the southern bottom of the Provisional Squadron's line, head back west, and then trap the enemy between the Rhine and the Division. This would destroy the 19th Army, which was the nemesis of the U.S. Seventh Army since last August's landings. They weren't chasing anymore, the Seventh was destroying. The squadron would form the east wall of the sack, the Rhine and the French Army on the other side of the river would form the west wall, and a holding force of the 103rd Infantry Division closed the trap to the north while the 100th crushed the enemy. So, while the PRS held the line and watched for signs of trapped enemy forces, the other Companies swept around with the 100th and looped to the southwest, then turned toward Stuttgart. The city fell and over 1,000 prisoners were bagged.

This surfaced another problem for Devers, as he had been ordered by Ike to invest Stuttgart, but behind the scenes the ever-cooperative Charles DeGaulle had ordered General Leclerc to take and hold the city first. The U.S. really wanted the contents of the local university, which was rumored to contain the German atomic bomb research records and the related scientists. DeGaulle just wanted the prestige. After requests and threats were ignored by the French, the Allies sent a clandestine team to retrieve their records and scientists and let the French have their parades and reprisals.

Good News! T/4 Ruben Parrish, Sgt Wendell Wusterbarth, and Cpl Gerald Mercier of Company "A", who were all captured during the disaster at Sessenheim, were liberated and returned to Allied control today when the 781st's own "B" Company captured their POW camp on the 16th. POWs were generally allowed to recuperate, then flown home and given an honorable discharge. Gerald Mercier was sped to a

Paris hospital to recover, got overdue treatment for his wounds, and then was returned home.

The PRS grouped up at Flein and ran a practice alert to simulate an enemy penetration. After that exercise Lt. Col. Kinne split the PRS into four "Task Forces" to further increase the PRS' reach. The Task Forces were named for their command-

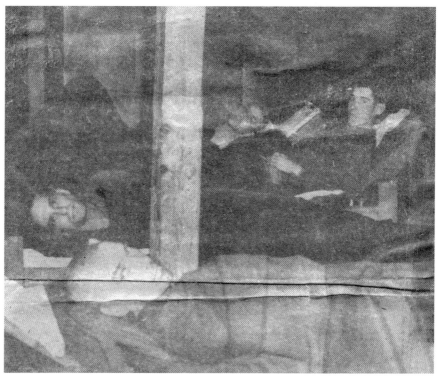

Gerry Mercier (sitting) with other POWs on the day he was liberated. (International Newsclip)

ing Captains: "Task Force Graham," commanded by Captain Joe Graham of 781st / "D" Company; "Task Force Smith," commanded by the CO of "E" Company of the 399th; and "Task Force Gulliver," commanded by the CO of Recon Company, 824th Tank Destroyer Battalion. Each group contained elements of each unit in the squadron and got roughly one-third of the assigned zone to patrol. Squadron HQ and a small reserve force (the HQ flame section and the Assault Gun Platoon) were kept in Flein and named "Task Force Bosch," commanded by the CO of the HQ Assault Gun Platoon. Task Force Graham's and Task Force Smith's mission was to initiate aggressive patrols in strength to contact the enemy and report back. Task Force Gulliver was to hold and prepare to bring mortar fire on call to any point in the zone.

Task Force Smith had a Div Artillery Observation plane, and they tried using it in an air-ground coordination role, which was just beginning to be explored. Task Force Smith patrolled their allotted zone and had air cover for their advance, and it worked perfectly. The plane sighted an A/T gun which had a direct field of fire on the advancing patrol. The plane alerted the patrol, which halted before the A/T gun could draw a bead on them. The plane then called in the position of the A/T gun to the Assault Gun Platoon, which blew it away. The plane next spotted vehicular activity near Schozach and called to both the Assault Gun Platoon and Divisional Artillery, who promptly ruined their day.

The PRS' Assault Gun Platoon was having a busy time, firing 318 rounds harassing fire, and they put 48 rounds into Neckarwestheim, 76 rounds on some enemy dug in on a ridge, eight more rounds on enemy in a woods, 48 rounds at a pill box, and 64 rounds on dug-in enemy as the calls came in for assistance.

Task Force Gulliver patrolled their area and cleared 32 refugees and captured one POW. They sent a patrol to Wustenhausen and contacted the town's burgermeister, who obligingly had all weapons and ammunition turned in and white flags flown from all houses. Civilian info stated there were no German soldiers in Ilsfeld, Auenstein, and Abstatt. They then patrolled and cleared the local autobahn.

The civilian information was proving correct – there weren't any enemy soldiers to sweep up and trap in that area. No direct contact was made with the enemy by the PRS. The Task Groups were instructed to make patrols during the night and try to make contact, but that came up empty as well. On the 20th, the PRS was dissolved as the trap had been successful, and all the groups went back to their normal assignments.

There were still enemy soldiers out there, however; while advancing south to Korb and Hertmansweiler with 399th Infantry, Company "A" had one tank knocked out by A/T fire, killing T/4 John Anderson and Pfc. Harry Mc Bride and wounding Lt. William Kaiser. "C" Company got the jump on an enemy 88mm gun and knocked it out on the 21st before it could get off a shot. Enemy resistance had become centered on *Panzerfauste* and AT guns. Due to the fact that defense was shifting to the *Volksturm*, who were trained with emphasis on *Panzerfauste*, these deadly rockets were found everywhere. Anti-tank guns were situated in the larger cities, as they used to be the anti-aircraft guns and now lowered their muzzles for A/T defense.

During one of these encounters, Homer Turner and "Hot Box" were patrolling down a road into a valley when he saw some German soldiers running into a warehouse building. He directed his gunner to light it up with White Phosphorous to set it on fire, which was done. At that moment Homer spotted a glint in the woods and he "threw one round and saw black smoke." He buttoned up "Hot Box" and was carefully scanning the scene to the right when a German 88mm anti-tank round screamed in and struck the dirt just to the right of his tank. Had he not been looking to the right he could have missed it. Homer yelled "Back up! Back up!," and Adolph Hoppi managed to throw "Hot Box" into reverse and scoot just as a second round hit where they were just moments before. They didn't wait to see where a third round hit.

The Battalion and the 100th kept up the quick advance to the south and east, with "D" Company now leading the advance as part of the Division Recon Group. Their mission was to be the tip of the spear, eliminating any resistance it could handle and reporting any resistance it couldn't handle to the main body. "A" Company was the farthest south, advancing to Stetten, almost on the Swiss border. "B" Company spent time in Stuttgart "mopping up the city," and "C" Company was "batting cleanup," clearing out pockets of enemy that were passed by other battalions – the woods from Schanbach to Archschiess were cleared, meeting slight resistance. One tank broke through the bridge at Baltmannsweiler and turned over. The Mortar Platoon was even getting into the act, scouting woods near Winneden for possible enemy pockets. This showed both how thin the advancing elements were and also how confident the Battalion was, both in the Mortar Platoon's abilities and the low probability of meeting determined resistance. According to a vet, "The main difficulty was due to blown bridges and occasional mine fields." The objective of this expansion was to cover ground to the southeast, and they didn't even stop to make formal prisoners of the groups of German soldiers who were heading toward the American lines trying to surrender. The crews would just wave them off the road and keep moving, allowing them to be mopped up by rear elements. The crews were being pushed hard, driving day and night, and at times they were so tired that, as Ron O'Donnell put it, "they didn't know what day of the week it was."

The wonderful pairing between the Century Division and the 781st once again came to an end, as the 100th Division was placed in reserve. And once again, the Infantry headed for some rest while the 781st stayed on the line. The 781st was taken from the 100th and attached to the 103rd Infantry Division on April 23, 1945. The change in attachment caused a few handshakes and farewells, but it didn't cause any delay in the advance – the next large city in their sights was Munich. "D" Company was just now starting to receive new M24 Hellcats as replacements for their worn-out M5s. Armed with a 75mm rifle and capable of speeds approaching 55mph, the Hellcats were nimble and exceptionally speedy, which suited "D" Company well. Personnel inventory on the 25th shows that Company A had 14 fighting crews, B had 12, C had 13, D had 17, and HQ had six crews.

"B" Company participated in an attack at Munsingen with the 410th Infantry Regiment that netted 200 POWs. "C" Company cleared out the very southwest tip of Germany and then swung to the east to join up with "B" in time for the attack on Munsingen. They knocked out a prime mover, an 88mm gun, and destroyed an ammo dump near Munsingen while supporting the attack.

"D" Company was attached to the 409th Infantry Regiment and was given the mission of clearing the towns of Holzkirch, Weidenstetten, and Neenstetten. They swarmed the countryside like locusts and secured those towns, destroying a 126mm mortar and taking 12 POWs. They then plowed into the suburbs of Ulm and cleared the towns of Beinerstatten, Varder, Jungingen, Orlingen, and Bofingen, taking another 65 POWs, which included three officers. They continued to swap out M5s for M24s. They now had 11 M5s and five M24s.

The next major natural obstacle confronting the Battalion's advance was the Danube River. "D" Company could see the bridges in the city of Ulm had been demolished, so they raced north to check out the Donau Bridge over the Danube near the smaller town of Oberelshingen. Private Benny Naujokes was a bow gunner in the lead tank of the tanks assigned to make the recon of the Donau Bridge. As they neared the objective they saw a log roadblock, and just then, the tanks and

Headquarters 100th Infantry Division
Office of the Commanding General
APO No. 447, Care Postmaster
New York, N. Y.

14 July 1945

Subject: 781st Tank Battalion.

To: Commanding General, United States Forces, European Theater
        (Main), Frankfort, Germany.
        (THRU CHANNELS)

During a large part of the combat activities of this Division, the
781st Tank Battalion was attached to it. I consider this battalion a
superior combat unit. Its conduct was such that it gained the respect
and admiration of the entire Division, and I have it from the Commanding Officer of that unit that it felt the same way towards this
Division. I therefore request, in the interests of the combat efficiency
of this unit, that, if feasible, the 781st Tank Battalion be attached to
the 100th Infantry Division for any combat operations it may be called
on to conduct.

W. A. BURRESS,
Major General, U. S. Army,
Commanding.

General Burress of the Century Division provided this recommendation for the 781st to General
Eisenhower. (U.S. Army)

accompanying infantry came under intense enemy fire. The lead tank was hit by a
Panzerfaust, disabling the tank and wounding Pvt. Naujokes. Rather than be evacuated, Benny stayed by his disabled tank, helped repair it, and then got back behind
his bow gun. When reinforcements arrived, he allowed himself to be evacuated and
treated. For these actions he earned a Bronze Star and a Purple Heart. The *Panzerfaust*
shooter was found lying against the logs with a bullet through his forehead.

PFC Lawrence Trombetta was in one of the other tanks when Benny Naujokes'
tank was struck. Stunned by the blast himself, Private Trombetta nevertheless opened
fire on the enemy and suppressed their fire so the supporting infantry could secure

the position and rout the enemy. For his service PFC Trombetta was awarded a Bronze Star. Sergeant Harold DuBois was also on this mission, and when the lead tank was disabled he dismounted, ignoring the small arms fire and the direct and indirect artillery fire, and worked on the lead tank for 15 minutes out in the open. He fixed the disabled tank's track, enabling the tank to proceed with the attack. For his efforts under fire Sgt DuBois earned a Bronze Star. This show of resistance bought the German defense enough time to accomplish their mission. "D" Company neared the bridge just in time to see it drop into the Danube with a roar, demolished by prepared charges. ("D" Company checked out the river and was rather dismayed to find out that this stretch of the Danube wasn't blue after all!)

The Division Engineers then had to construct pontoon bridges, and while everyone waited "D" Company was assigned to patrol a 50-mile stretch of road between Plochingen, just outside of Stuttgart, to Winterbach, northeast of Ulm, so the rest

The 781st crosses the Danube. (Up from Marseille)

of the attacking force could come forward and wouldn't be ambushed by small pockets of enemy troops who had been bypassed. The 781st waited a day and a half and performed maintenance on vehicles. These rapid advances were taking their toll on the equipment. At this time, the 781st had seven tanks sidelined for blown bogie wheels (the rubber facing of the bogie wheels would overheat, wear out, tear, or throw the rubber off because of the amount of high speed running in dry conditions.) and one tank was out for a blown transmission. By the time the bridges were ready, the 781st had taught the 103rd how to ride. The 409th and 410th were completely motorized – all the infantry had rides on tanks, tracks, Self-Propelled Tank

Destroyers, and anything else with an engine. With this newfound capability this team could *really* cover ground!

Around this time, the 781st took its most beloved prisoner while passing through the town of Oberelchingen. The HQ Communications Section found a dachshund puppy and "captured" him as a mascot. Named "Shortwave," the "hot dog" soon

captured all the men's hearts in turn, and he took to riding on the hood of Joe De-Gorter's HQ radio half track as it advanced from town to town, a low-slung brown hood ornament with flapping ears. For some reason Shortwave detested Hungarians and would snarl, get pretty rude, and try to bite them whenever he met one! How could he tell who was Hungarian? Shortwave never divulged his secret.

While they waited for the engineers to build the bridges over the Danube River, "D" Company made great use of their time by robbing a bank. Bored, and curious as to whether or not their 37mm rifles could penetrate a bank vault, a couple of crews decided to perform a "test" on a nearby bank. After a few rounds had been fired the vault stood wide open, and inside were bags and bags of Riechmarks. The

Shortwave! (U.S. Army, NARA)

firing of the guns brought the rest of the Company to the bank, where they reasoned that since Germany was beaten, all that money would certainly be worthless, and wouldn't it be fun to rob a bank! So they backed the Booty Truck up to the vault and everyone had great fun passing bags of money to the next guy. Soon the vault was clean, the truck was full, and most of the other "D" vehicles had a bag or two of "funny money" to play with stashed inside.

The bridges were ready on April 27, 1945, and the 781st, with their infantry riders, crossed the Danube. Elsewhere, the U.S. First Army linked up with Russian Marshal Koniev's First Ukranian Army on the Elbe. It was now fervently hoped that the rest of the war might be confined to accepting the surrender of white-flag-waving Germans without any shooting. "C" Company headed toward the next big apple to be captured – Munich. About 40 miles west of Munich they took the town of Landsberg, which was an ancient fortress city and the capital of the local district.

Before the war, Adolf Hitler was imprisoned in castle Landsberg after his arrest for a failed coup. While in prison, he wrote his infamous *Mien Kampf*. After his release and return to power, he felt that Landsberg prison would best be served by imprisoning others, and he directed that the prison cell he occupied be turned into a shrine. What "C" Company uncovered wasn't a shrine, but a horror story when they liberated a German concentration camp.

During the war, the Landsberg area housed 11 Kaufering concentration camps. The Kaufering camps were started in June 1944, when prisoners who were still able to work were transferred from Auschwitz so they could start building underground bunkers and factories in an effort to hide them from the Allied air bombing campaign.

Troops of the 103rd rounded up male citizens from the Landsberg area to care for the suffering prisoners and bury the dead. (U.S. Army Signal Corps, NARA)

The Kaufering camps housed foreign workers, POWs, and the so-called "Judenlagers" (camps for Jews). The camp liberated by the 781st was named Kaufering I, and it was the largest of the 11 Kaufering camps, housing approximately 5,000 male prisoners and 200 women prisoners, mostly Jewish prisoners from the Soviet or Baltic areas. The prisoners worked in factories or in munitions plants, and some worked on secret projects like one that was attempting to build an underground aircraft factory at Landsberg. Earlier in the war, when Kaufering workers could no longer work, they were sent back to Auschwitz or to Dachau to be "processed," but as the volume of sick and debilitated prisoners increased, they were simply pushed into the wet concrete of the bunkers that were being built and entombed, causing the Kaufering Camps to acquire the repugnant nickname "Cold Crematoria." While the world knows of Auschwitz's and Dachau's fearful reputation as factories of death, it is reported that the Kaufering camps killed prisoners at a rate that was *six times worse* than Dachau. As the Nazis retreated before the quick Allied advance, the camp guards left the camps in a rush. At some of the Kaufering camps, the guards attempted to "destroy the evidence" and locked the inmates in their huts, then set the huts on fire before leaving.

The emaciated Kaufering I prisoners liberated by the 781st were so weak that they could not eat or digest solid food, and had to be nursed back to health through intravenous feeding. One 781st vet recalled that "Some, who were able to walk, went to a medic's peep and started to eat packages of three-inch bandages thinking they were food [jeeps were also called "peeps"]."

"C" Company remained in Landsberg for a couple of days, making sure that the prisoners were transferred to proper care before moving out, this time with considerably hardened hearts towards the German soldiers and citizens.

23. CHASING A GHOST

At this point, the Allies were afraid that Hitler and the surviving Nazis might literally "head for the hills" in the Austrian Alps to concentrate their remaining forces and make a last stand in the mountains. The German concept *Alpenfestung* (Alpine Fortress) was well known, and it was suspected that stores of food and ammunition had already been secreted in the area and fortifications had already been prepared to enable the effort. For some reason, earlier in the war Joseph Goebbels, the Nazi propaganda minister, fueled the fire, and he went so far as to set up special propaganda units whose job it was to invent and then spread rumors about the fortifications and preparations for the last stand of the Third Reich. The territory in which the last stand of the Nazi Party would be conducted was given the name "National Redoubt," and Swiss newspapers dutifully reported the rumors. The Allies saw no reason to disbelieve the rumors, and feared that close to a quarter of a million fanatical Nazis might congregate there for a last stand, and so they acted accordingly.

The First Armored Group was watching intently for any sign that German armor was concentrating or entrenching in the Redoubt area. Over the past couple of weeks there had been such a fast advance, coupled with so little enemy armor activity, that it stoked Allied High Command fears that the defensive forces were being withdrawn into the Redoubt Area. Fear of the Redoubt myth becoming operational reality drove SHAEF to prioritize rapid occupation of the area. As a result, Eisenhower ordered Patch to block the escape routes to the Redoubt. General Patch flowed the order down to the VIIth Army to occupy the Austrian area and the passes as fast as possible. The 103rd and 781st did as directed, racing toward the area where the German National Redoubt was rumored to exist, and they prepared to block any serious attempt to implement *Alpenfestung*.

This directive was met with some dismay by the 781st. Nazi propaganda had dwelt on the strength of the Redoubt and the incredible defensive capabilities it possessed. Supposedly manned by rabid Waffen-SS troopers who would fight to the last man and employ every and any weapon imaginable, the Redoubt, if real, was worrisome. Secret doomsday weapons and German use of poison gas were assured. "D" Company found this to be especially worrisome, as most of the men had by this time disposed of their gas masks, and they were using the empty gas mask pouch to carry a ready bottle of hootch!

In case they met Russians, recognition signals for use in identifying advancing Russian troops were disseminated, and the pressure was on to cover ground to the southeast, toward Austria and the Alps. The vehicles had just switched back to their warmer weather setup and the men had turned in all their winter clothing, but orders came to change everything back into winter mode. Requisitions were made to issue winter clothes and lay in a supply of extra anti-freeze, as it was anticipated the troops would be going into snow country again. It was rainy and cold with poor visibility when Co "A" made contact with advance elements of the 10th Armored Div. "A" Company was advancing on the town of Schongau when they hit a pocket of resistance on the 28th.

2nd Lt Arthur Sloggatt was advancing as the lead tank with his combat team when they encountered heavy small-arms fire and fire from an SP gun. Lt. Sloggatt dismounted from his tank and, ignoring the hail of bullets, went forward on foot

The Seventh Army passes over a bridge in Schongau, Germany, after the town was cleared by the 781st. Defending troops destroyed the bridge, which held up the 7th Army's advance for a mere 24 hours. (U.S. Army Signal Corps, NARA)

to recon the situation. Despite being wounded by the small arms fire, from his lead position he directed the fire from his section and succeeded in knocking out the SP gun. He then had his section shift fire and reduce the enemy small arms fire so the infantry could advance and secure the situation. It was a surprise to find that the defenders were trying to protect *two battalions of horse drawn artillery*, which surrendered along with 100 POWs. For his bravery Lt. Sloggatt was awarded the Silver Star, and he also got a Purple Heart. The Germans were running out of gas, and they relied more and more on horse-drawn and stream-powered vehicles for transport. One such formation wasn't lucky enough to be captured by the 781st and was caught by the Air Force out in daylight and was decimated. The roads were so clogged with dead animal carcasses that a bulldozer tank had to clear a path before the Companies could pass through.

Twenty-Five miles to the southeast, "D" Company and their now heavily-laden booty truck arrived at Oberammergau. "D" Company was previously ordered not to shoot in Oberammergau by the Regimental Commander, who had attended the 1930 Oberammergau Passion Play and who considered the town to be a "holy city." The Oberammergau Passion Play was performed every ten years by the citizens of Oberammergau, and the Play depicts the life of Christ. It involves approximately 2,000 actors from the village, and the complete performance takes over seven hours, including a planned meal break. Since its inception in 1634, it has only missed two curtain calls, the second being in 1940 due to WWII. The "no shooting" order didn't sit well, but "D" Company performed exactly as ordered and they invested the town without firing a shot.

"D" Company did not appreciate the town or its occupants, as they noted, "The little village that is associated with the Jew from Nazareth paradoxically had a large poster on the main street complete with cartoon and anti-Semitic message." But "D" Company was under orders and they behaved with decorum. Well, maybe not. The RAC struck again. Unbeknownst to the officers, the mischief makers had arranged a small demonstration. As a gesture of disdain for the town, everyone in the "Best Light Tank Company in the U.S. Army" paused in their work, dismounted, and formed a single-file line along the side of the main street of Oberammergau. Then, and in unison, they unzipped their trousers and "presented (short) arms." Then one hundred and fourteen men simultaneously urinated in the gutter. "D" Company then zipped up, about faced, remounted their tanks, and left town.

Their exit was prompted by a request for 3rd Platoon of "D" Company, under Lieutenant Paul Pais, to move to outside Schwabmiedershofen to assist elements of the Division "in guarding (an) important captured enemy installation." This was a top secret operation – "D" Company had no idea what they were guarding, only that it was really important.

As the war closed, the German V2 rocket program, under General Hans Kammler (who had supervised the construction of several concentration camps prior to turning his talent for forced labor toward rocketry), was scrambling to evade capture by the Russians, who were getting close to Peenemunde. In April, he ordered the intellectual core of the V2 project (the rocket science team) to move with some of their most important equipment and supplies to – you guessed it – Oberammergau.

This included the most important member of the German rocket development program, Werner Von Braun. The team was under the watchful "protection" of the SS, who had orders to *execute the team* if their capture was likely!

By using the rationale that they would be harder to hit by an air raid, Von Braun managed to convince his SS guard/captors to let the rocket science team split up and disperse to the small towns around Oberammergau. On May 2nd Von Braun, the man who was Number One on the Allies' "Most Wanted to Interrogate" List, walked into American lines and surrendered. The "important enemy installation" being guarded by the group from the 781st was most likely part of the V2 Rocket science team and their truckloads of rocket parts and equipment that was scattered about the area. Once secured, the equipment was whisked off to a safe location and the Allies got their wish to interrogate Dr. Von Braun, who later became the leading rocket scientist in the United States' space exploration program. General Kammler, who was also sorely wanted by the Allies so he could stand trial for his war crimes, had absconded into the nearby town of Garmisch-Partenkirchen.

The Germans had almost 10,000 wounded soldiers in the Garmisch-Partenkirchen area, and sent a notice to the Allied troops at Obergammerau that the town was an "open city" and contained many hospitals. Garmish was the site of the 1936 Winter Olympics, and as a result of being declared an "open city" was spared the destruction wrought on other cities. The 781st went to the city and were snowbound

Prisoners being marched to the rear near Oberammergau. (U.S. Army Signal Corps, NARA)

for five days there, stopped by a five-day blizzard that dumped eight inches of snow on the area – in May. The 411th Infantry Regiment and "C" Company captured the troops in the town, which included an entire regiment of Hungarians. When that occurred, Shortwave was just beside himself and had to be restrained. Despite the thorough searching, General Kammler had made good his escape and was never seen again. While at Garmish, one "A" Company tank slid on the snow and ice and tipped off a bridge into the river. By this time, the 781st had recuperated to having enough crews to man almost all their tanks: Company "A" had 10 crews available; Companies "B," "C," and "D" all had 16 crews; and HQ had eight crews ready to fight. While "A" was still short of crewmen, their tanks were falling out at a high rate with blown bogies, so the number of tanks they had to crew was also less.

As soon as the roads were passable, the 103rd moved out with the 781st, advancing south into Austria. Pockets of resistance were still being met in every direction. While the bulk of the Division moved south, "D" Company and HQ's Assault Gun

In the drink at Garmische. (Up from Marseille)

Platoon were given a mission of taking the small towns of Krun and Wallgau to the northeast to protect the left flank of the 103rd. Once these towns were secure, "D"

Company and the Assault Gun Platoon were to establish roadblocks on the roads exiting Wallgau to the North and East.

The first town "D" Company approached was Krun, which was entered and taken without fuss, but as they continued on the road north to Wallgau, they encountered small arms fire from the village and surrounding hills. The Commandant and his staff from the German Infantry School at Mittenwald (which trained mountain troops for the Wehrmacht) had directed the construction of a strong position on the other side of the town, but they sprung their trap too soon and the lead tanks were narrowly missed by *Panzerfauste*. The strongpoint was destroyed by the combined fire of the Mortar platoon, the Assault Gun Platoon, and the light tanks of "D" Company. The town was then searched house-to-house and many prisoners were taken.

The Commandant, a "full bird" colonel, came into town in his full dress uniform, complete with sword, and he wanted to surrender. He requested that the ranking American officer be brought to see him. He was impertinently told by "D" Company

781st Tanks assault Auland, Austria. (U.S. Army Signal Corps, NARA)

men that if he wanted to see the ranking American officer then *he* could *go to see him*! He was brought under guard to Captain Graham, who was wearing his fatigues and filthy boots, with no insignia showing. The German Colonel wanted to surrender his sword in a formal ceremony to an officer of equal or higher rank and was dismayed to find out that he might have to surrender to this filthy pup who was many years his junior, as well as lesser rank. Meanwhile, his 200 accompanying troops had quietly surrendered and were being loaded into trucks. The Colonel wanted Captain Graham to send for a superior officer, then he started to protest when that request was declined. When he started to argue, one of the Raggedy Assed Cadets lost his patience and stuck his Tommy gun in the Colonel's side. The soldier told the Officer, "I'm a Colonel, you get in the damned truck!" With this pronouncement the pompous bastard was taken bodily by his RAC guards and physically *thrown* in a heap in the back of one of the trucks. Amazingly, the German prisoners already in the truck started cheering!

Once resistance was eliminated, the 781st group established their own roadblocks to cover the roads as directed, and Company "D" was headquartered in Wallgau until they were relieved by the 107th Cavalry. While stationed at Wallgau, another

GIs take cover as tanks advance toward machine gun fire coming from the hills near Scharnitz. (U.S. Army Signal Corps, NARA)

German officer came into town under flag of truce to speak with Captain Graham. The officer wanted to notify the advancing Allied troops that there was a hospital about five miles away, and he asked for assurance that it would not be leveled, because his orders were to stay in place with the sick and injured. Captain Graham confidently assured him of the hospital's safety and the officer thanked him. But as the German medical officer turned to leave, he hesitated and made a final request to Captain Graham. It seemed that his wristwatch had been stolen by one of the RAC when he crossed the lines to speak with Captain Graham, and he asked if it could please be returned. It was.

During the brief stay, Pfc. Frank Bucks and Sgt. Clarence Barber, both of Company "D," were now awarded Bronze Stars for heroic achievement in battle. Whenever foot patrols were required for flank or reconnaissance missions, regardless of the danger or scope of the mission, these two soldiers always volunteered for the missions.

"A" Company advanced with the 409th Infantry to the South through the violin-making center of Mittenwald toward Innsbruck, but ran into a pocket of resistance at Scharnitz. Captain Camille Pelletier of "A" Company was wounded again in this fight, earning an oak leaf cluster for his Purple Heart, and 2nd Lt. Arthur Sloggattt was wounded. But in exchange, "A" Company knocked out two A/T guns. During the battle, a 409th infantryman was wounded on the opposite side of the Glessen River, which divides Scharnitz, Austria, and it was not possible to evacuate him because the bridge across the river had been destroyed. Pfc. Robert Worden of "A" Company and Pvt. Robert Jones of Service Company leapt to the wounded GI's rescue and swam through the swift, icy current to the other side, dodging small arms and sniper fire to give first aid to the downed soldier. Their actions in saving the life of their comrade earned them both Silver Stars. The 409th kept encountering strong, heavily armed strongpoints and a rocket tank from HQ Company was assigned to help those strongpoints see the error of their ways. At the end of the Scharnitz fight "A" Company had six tanks sidelined with blown bogies.

And as April closed, so also closed the fears of *Alpenfestung*. The National Redoubt was nothing more than a propaganda myth – they had been chasing a ghost. While not having to deal with a bunch of dug-in last-stand mentality Nazis was a good thing, the whole campaign diverted a huge number of Allied forces that could and would have been used to occupy more German territory up to and perhaps including Berlin itself. The "what if" possibilities that this would have had on postwar Europe and the ensuing Cold War are staggering. And if the German propaganda ministry had known early-on that by propagating the National Redoubt rumor they would directly cause more of their country to be occupied by the Russians, would they have done it?

The month of May dawned with more snow and cold weather, but the news that reached the 781st was heartwarming. The Battalion learned that T/4 Antonia Lenzi, captured by the enemy during the Gambsheim counter-attack, was liberated today. They heard the news that Mussolini was shot in front of a firing squad on April 28th, and Hitler was reported to have died on April 30th at his own hand. More good news was happening each day. On May 2nd, 900,000 Nazi soldiers in Italy and Western Austria surrendered and Berlin fell. But the 103rd and the 781st still fought on; it seemed their opponent hadn't gotten the news that the war was lost and nobody was throwing in the towel yet.

"A" Company captured the town of Reith, to the east of Innsbruck, knocking out more two A/T guns, which turned out to be the last two SP guns knocked out by First Armored Group before the war ended. They also moved to capture Telfs, to the west of Innsbruck, but two tanks bogged down in narrow defile and then threw their tracks, which blocked the way and held up the platoon until they were retrieved. "B" and "C" Companies both moved to Mittenwald, and lost one tank to suspension failure and one to power train failure.

On the evening of May 3rd, the 781st and the 103rd entered Innsbruck. At this point, it was evident that the National Redoubt was a myth and everyone breathed a bit easier. Just to make sure there were no Germans hiding between Innsbruck

Over 1,000 German officers and men surrender peacefully just outside Innsbruck. (U.S. Army Signal Corps, NARA)

and Italy, on the 4th, the first and second platoons of "C" Company, part of the Assault Gun Platoon (Hot Box included), and the 411th Regiment of the 103rd were sent south through the Brenner Pass. The 175-vehicle force linked up at 10:00 on May 5th eight miles inside Italy with members of the 88th Mountain Division of General Truscott's 5th Army and made history in doing so – by going through the Brenner Pass, they entered the record books as the first tanks in history to do so. One vet remembered on the trip:

> We were halted by a soldier with a red lantern at a bridge. It was a Nazi complete with potato masher grenades and a burp gun. He said to Captain Kelly, 'Your 32-ton tanks will be able to get across this bridge but you'll have to drive slowly.' Captain Kelly had them drive slowly. They made it okay.

Later on, the folks who made this side trip were profusely thanked by the rest of the Battalion.

On the 4th, "D" Company moved to Innsbruck, transporting the 410th Infantry Regiment. Right after they arrived they were split up and given two important missions. 2nd Platoon was assigned a mission of picking up some high ranking German

"C" Company's Tanks stand guard with a GI from the 103rd at the Austrian border. (U.S. Army Signal Corps, NARA)

officers who were to be waiting at a position 20 miles south of Innsbruck. 3rd Platoon was given a similar mission to pick up some French political prisoners at a position approximately 45 miles east of Innsbruck. Both details moved out to accomplish their missions.

Second Platoon of "D" Company met and then escorted the top-ranking German officers from the German XIX Army back to Innsbruck. Led by General Brandenberger, they met with General Edward Brooks of the VI Army at the Landhaus in Innsbruck, General Brooks' Headquarters. They discussed surrender terms for all of German Army Group G, of which XIX Army was a part. At the end of the meeting they surrendered at 1530 with a cease fire in effect from 1800. When they returned to their lines they contacted Field Marshall Kesselring of the German Army, and it was arranged that Group G would surrender to General Devers at Haar, Germany. Rather than capturing headlines announcing the surrender to Devers, the Seventh Army awoke to the news that while they were penning their surrender,

Admiral Carl Doenitz surrendered the whole of Germany unconditionally one hour later to Bernard Montgomery. Fate again stole the headlines from the Seventh Army and they would be forgotten.

And in a final act of camaraderie, the French refused to recognize either of the surrenders because they didn't have an emissary at either signing ceremony. General DeLattre went so far as to proclaim that his army would continue hostilities until all the German representatives presented themselves to him and signed a separate surrender! He would not be placated, but after a while the whole matter became moot, as he couldn't find any Germans who were still game enough to fight back.

The Germans surrender to General Devers at Harr. (U.S. Army Signal Corps, NARA)

With that news even the weather smiled and changed to clear and mild with good visibility. Despite the formal surrender of Group G and the cease fire, stubborn elements (mostly SS fanatics) remained who still waged war. 3rd Platoon of "A" Company and two HQ rocket tanks moved to a point six miles east of Innsbruck to fire on an enemy force who would not surrender. This exercise cost one tank due to thrown track, and 1st Lt. Donald Crane and Corporal Donald Devries were wounded in the last firefight of the war for the Battalion.

With the cease fire in effect, the 781st was united under Lt. Col. Kinne's control for the first time since their arrival in France. The U.S. forces now spread out to occupy the immediate area and establish a measure of "Police and Security" for the area. "Police and Security" detail meant:

1. Protection of supply dumps, power plants, pipelines, railroads, and signal stations.
2. Protection and disposition of captured enemy munitions.
3. Disarming the police and civilian populace.
4. Support of military government.
5. Control of allied troops.
6. Maintenance of roadblocks to prevent unauthorized movement of German military or civilian personnel. Also to check for proper use of vehicles and to report equipment or uniform violations.
7. Maintain security of occupied towns and arrest suspicious individuals.

Each Company was assigned an area, and on May 6th they moved out to their assigned towns. "A" went to Obsteig and lost one tank with a thrown track. "B" went to Unter Meiming, "C" moved to Telfs, and "D" moved to Wildermieming. HQ was also assigned to Telfs to help post check points and road blocks. Service Company was moved to Ober Meiming.

The power plants and municipal facilities were frequently booby-trapped, as were enemy munitions sites as a last-minute search by U.S. troops for war trophies ensued. The following day, May 7, 1945, the remaining German armies surrendered and a cessation of hostilities was scheduled for 0001 May 8th. As a 781st vet put it: "It was the end. Free men could breathe again in Europe."

But "D" Company was having trouble breathing – they had a huge problem. As part of the decisions made by the Allied High Command for postwar control, it was decided that the Riechemark would remain as the recognized German currency for the foreseeable future (in fact, it remained until it was replaced in 1948 by the Deutschemark), and "D" Company had a truck full of stolen, now-still-valuable money. Had anyone at the bank identified them? They couldn't just drive back and give it back! They agonized over various solutions, ranging from keeping it to burning it and everything in between as they patrolled their area, keeping their eyes on their mirrors as they waited for the MPs to show up.

Gerald Mercier heard the news of the surrender while he was being outprocessed at Camp Edwards, Massachusetts. After a short drive he was home to celebrate with his family. Three weeks later he was married to "Gee," who no longer needed a code to know where he was.

Arnie Simpson heard the news just as his birthday cake was arriving from the States. Arnie and his entire platoon of 25 men helped celebrate as they all shared and ate it.

24. POSTWAR

On May 7th, the VI Corps issued a Training Memo that required all units to embark on an extensive training program designed to, among other things: "Obtain the highest standard of military courtesy, uniform dress, and discipline." Of course, "D" Company welcomed this program with open arms. Training was to be conducted on every day except Sunday. Subjects: Small arms firing; organized athletics (which was undefined, but everyone was supposed to frequently participate); tactics; and tank gunnery.

Despite the victory in Europe, there was a 500-pound gorilla in the room. The war was still going strong in the Pacific theatre. VE Day meant there were a lot of extra troops in Europe that could now be assigned to the Pacific. Some troops would be kept in Europe as occupation forces, and the less lucky would be whisked off for a quick refit and reassignment to the CBI (China-Burma-India Theatre of war). By this time, however, the CBI was imploding as the Japanese "Co-Prosperity Sphere" rapidly collapsed. A more likely assignment for the 781st would have been redeployment as part of the Japanese homeland invasion force. The initial invasion of the Japanese island of Kyushu (the most southwest island of the home island chain), called

"D" Company in Bivouac in the Alps. (Courtesy of Rhodes family)

Operation Olympic, was scheduled for November 1, 1945, with the invasion of Honshu (the largest island of the mainland) scheduled for March 1, 1946 (called *Operation Coronet*).

But with their current missions in place, the 781st heaved a sigh of relief, as it looked like they were destined for assignment as occupation troops. On May 9th, a provisional tank company consisting of four tanks each from Companies A, B, and C participated in a VE Day parade in Innsbruck at 1600. Over 15,000 men marched down Marienstrasse (the main street) and passed in review. Tanks that were selected to be in the parade had rubber tracks to spare the roads. "D" Company couldn't send tanks to the parade because their tanks had steel tracks that tore up the roads.

And on the subject of "D" Company, they had arrived at a unique solution to their money problem; one that was sublime and yet superbly fit the personality of the Company. In order to get rid of their stolen loot without calling *too* much attention to themselves, they would spend it. Wherever they went, the men of "D" Company slept in the finest beds, ate the finest meals, had the finest company, and drank the finest beers and liquors, and lots of it. They spent money like – well – like they had a truckload of it! Several of the men came home bearing expensive gifts for loved ones – ruby necklaces and the like, all bought and paid for from the local populace. Sergeant Waldron arranged for a local brewery to supply a keg of their best beer, properly chilled of course, to the Company kitchen every morning so the men of "D" Company could fill their canteen cups with cold beer as they ate breakfast.

From May 10th to the 16th, the Battalion enjoyed a spell of clear, mild days and split their time between police and security efforts in their zones and carrying out maintenance of their vehicles, which were breaking down frequently with all the patrols and movement – they were plain wearing out! During the month nine Shermans were inspected and condemned by Ordnance as being too worn out for further service and had to be replaced. In a move toward normal living, blackout restrictions were rescinded on the 11th, so lights once again lit streets and houses, and it was a whole lot easier to drive at night.

On the 17th, the 781st was relieved of their patrol assignments by the 614th Tank Destroyer Battalion. The Battalion congregated at Telfs, performing maintenance of weapons and vehicles and engaging in organized athletics. According to Joe Graham, the favorite "organized athletics" was 12-ounce weight lifting at the local beer halls. At the end of the month, the 781st underwent Table of Organization & Equipment Inspections, then went back to "maintenance and organized athletics." The T/O & E inspections checked that each company had all the vehicles and inventory that they were supposed to have, no more or less. While the war was raging, if an item was reported as "lost" and then showed up or was retrieved at a later date, units would keep the item and use it, as it provided an extra or backup. It was easier to just keep it and throw it away at the next T/O & E Inspection than it was to do the paperwork explaining how the item reappeared. The T/O & E meant that extra stuff had to be stashed or lost. The stolen trucks and equipment definitely had to be ditched. It was actually common for U.S. units to pile all their excess equipment they had that wasn't "on the books" into a vehicle (itself probably also excess) and then drive the vehicles with excess equipment into swamps, lakes, etc., to dispose of them. The Booty Truck and trailer were disposed of.

The Battalion also underwent physical and dental checkups, and physical profiles of all members of the unit were completed. All this activity made people nervous that a move was coming. In the meantime, everyone engaged in small arms firing, maintenance, and more "organized athletics."

"Small Arms Firing" in this context is commonly known elsewhere as "hunting." Lt. Colonel Kinne and his staff dined one night in Telfs at the Gastof Hotel Munde. Lt. Col Kinne let it be known that he wanted his staff to dine that night on venison.

Venison at the Gasthof! Front row, kneeling L-R: Lt Gus Sitton CO "B"; Capt Bob Rich CO HQ; Capt "Doc" Will, MD; Lt. Col Harry Kinne, Jr.; unknown; Maj. George Farris, XO; Capt John Simpkins, S3; Capt Camille Pelletier, CO "A"; Capt Joe Graham, CO "D"; Capt Oren Souders, CO Svc Co. Top row, from left: #1 = Lt Bob McIntyre, XO of "D"; #17 blond smiling in front of bush on RHS of door is Lt Paul Pais "D"; Lt Bill Kaiser "A"; unk; George Blanchard, Batt Supply; Capt Vinnie Donise, Batt Maintenance; and Lt Leber, "C". Others are regrettably unknown. (Up from Marseille)

The Gastof needed some venison to satisfy the Colonel's wishes, so earlier in the day members of the Battalion engaged in "small arms firing" and procured the required deer. The venison served that night at the Gastof Hohe Munde to the officers of the 781st Tank Battalion was the first and only time the deer on the Gastof menu had been shot with a Thompson submachine gun.

May ended on a rainy and cool note and the 781st fought boredom. "D" Company conducted range firing of their new M24s' 75mm guns. Everyone engaged in marking of clothing, gas mask drill and inspection, orientation, and organized athletics. And the final day of May they were given another hint of the future, as the 781st engaged in instruction in malaria control. Right on month's end, the Battalion received the dreaded alert order from 7th Army to ready for indirect redeployment. Battalion personnel read between the lines: "indirect redeployment" meant that their next assignment wasn't nearby – the Battalion would have to travel to get there. And that probably meant that occupation duty was over. General Alexander Patch's duty as head of the Seventh Army was also over. He was rotated back to the States to take command of the U.S. Fourth Army and General Wade Haislip took his place.

The calendar flipped to June, the weather turned sunny and warm, and the 781st was still engaged in occasional inspections, repetitive training classes, caring for vehicles that didn't move, drinking, hunting, and generally relaxing. Once or twice there were medal ceremonies as the paperwork caught up with the Battalion. Numerous Bronze Stars were awarded, some to previous recipients, and a few Silver Stars. Nobody complained, and one 781st veteran likened the time spent as being in a "mountain retreat."

The bureaucratic wheels were heard turning on June 7th, when the 781st was relieved from assignment to the 7th Army and was assigned to the 3rd Army for

The 781st packs up to go to Camp Lucky Strike. (Up From Marseille)

operation, administration, and supply. There was no hint of the future in this, as the Third Army was tasked with the management of occupied Germany. But on the tenth of June moods matched the rainy weather, as the 781st received movement orders to proceed to Camp Lucky Strike (a.k.a. Lehavre). All hopes of closing out the war as part of the European occupation force went away like the rain being washed down the gutters.

They were being shipped out; most likely to CBI, but back to the war, back to the killing. But before they could go, they had to turn in all their heavy vehicles, to which some were quite attached. They turned in their tanks at an ordnance collecting point at Aubing, Germany, and the half-tracks were left at a collection point in Metz, France, and they prepared to move to their next assignment.

On June 12, 1945, Lt. Col Kinne and his staff took an advance detail from each Company and left for Camp Lucky Strike by motor vehicle. The bulk of the Battalion left on the 13th by motor vehicle. They spent the night in Ulm, Germany. The remainder of the Battalions – all of Company "D" and one platoon of Company "C" – departed for Camp Lucky Strike by rail on the 14th, departing at 0900 under command of Capt Simpkins and Capt Joe Graham.

Everyone joined up on the 18th at Camp Lucky Strike and immediately began the processing for redeployment to the Pacific via the U.S. When not engaged in the intensive processing, everyone engaged in "intensive organized athletics." Here they turned in their equipment and got official permission to bring home souvenirs. Cpt. Joe Graham bid farewell to his warm sleeping bag and recalls: "By that time you could just about stand the bag on end and smell it at thirty paces – upwind!"

While the 781st was at Camp Lucky Strike, Lt. Col Kinne made arrangements with Major Tindall, who was still in charge of the Grand Hotel in Paris, to "entertain" one officer and nineteen enlisted men each day for as long as the 781st was in Camp. Since he hadn't had any R&R leave since December, Joe Graham was the first officer to be a guest, and the lavishness and details of the red carpet treatment is *still* "classified." The processing was completed on the 21st, and the 781st received their shipment order June 25th. Four days later, on the 28th, Headquarters, Service, and "B" Companies waded through the surf to board lighters that ferried them to the *USS Alfred Moore*, while "A," "C," and "D" Companies boarded the *USS Leland Stanford*, bound for the U.S. These were plain Jane Liberty ships, nothing like the ex-ocean liner they arrived on. The *Leland Stanford* was named after the tycoon who started Stanford University. The *Alfred Moore* was named after a Supreme Court Justice from South Carolina.

The Liberty ships had tossed boarding nets over the side, and the men were expected to climb up the nets wearing packs weighing close to 50 pounds. Lieutenant McIntyre immediately became seasick on boarding the lighter and remained so for the rest of the return trip. The trip home was uneventful, the seas calm, and the weather nice. On July 4th, each ship held an award ceremony to celebrate those who had won a Silver Star, Bronze Star, or Purple Heart. Lt. Col Kinne awarded the medals on *Moore* while the XO, Major Farris, did that job on *Stanford*.

The *USS Moore* was decorated for the trip.
(Courtesy of O'Donnell family)

Shortwave survived the war in good stead, but he barely survived the long trip home. He became severely seasick – all that time riding on the moving half track hood didn't help him at all. Shortwave was really sick, and his worried companions eased his seasickness by dosing him with morphine from their med packs to ease his suffering! Shortwave survived both the seasickness and their cure.

For some reason, the two ships parted company on arrival in the U.S.: the *Moore* went to New York City and the *Stanford* went to Hampton Roads, Virginia, and both arrived July 11th. The ships were met by bands and celebrities. Homer Turner recalls that they were treated to a concert by Lionel Hampton when they reached New York. Troops on the *Stanford* didn't get as formal a treat; they were welcomed by an Army band, and the locals turned out in force to welcome them home.

Coming Home on the *USS Moore*. (Courtesy of O'Donnell family)

The troops in New York went to Camp Kilmer, NJ, and the Hampton Roads arrivals went to Camp Patrick Henry. Dinner that night at Fort Henry was steak, mashed potatoes, real milk, and ice cream. After their arrival Camp, the troops were shipped to their respective reception stations the very next day on the 12th. At their local reception stations, the troops were turned loose for a 30-day recuperation leave. There were 22 reception stations in use all over the States at the time the 781st returned. To show how diverse a crew the 781st was, troops were sent to 21 of the 22 stations on their way home.

During the 30 days while they were at home, the B-29 bombers *Enola Gay* and *Bock's Car* erased two Japanese cities, and with them they eliminated the need to ship the 781st overseas. But contrary to popular belief, the Army didn't just tell everyone to go home when the Japanese surrendered. Men were discharged in accordance with the Advanced Service Rating Score. Under the system, points were awarded to each individual: one point for each month in service, one more point for each month in service overseas, five points for combat awards (personal medals and service stars that were given to the unit for participation in campaigns), and twelve points for each dependent child under 18. The Armed Forces then established a number as the score to beat in order to go home. The soldiers with the highest scores got to go home first. The system was designed to allow soldiers who had fought the longest and the hardest to leave first. When first put in place, anyone with 85 points or more was sent to separation centers and given their honorable discharges. After VJ Day the bar dropped to 80.

The mission by members of the 781st who went over the Alps into Italy to meet up with the 5th Army came into play here. This excursion by a few crews meant that the 781st got official credit for participation in the Italian campaign, and even though a vast majority of the Battalion never set foot in the country, this earned *all* the members of the Battalion another five points toward their score. Needless to say, the men who made that trip were duly appreciated. But the administration of this new system took time, and to the impatient men of the 781st, it seemed the Army chugged along for a while like nothing had happened.

On August 11th, the advance detachment of three officers and seven enlisted men arrived at the Battalion's reassembly station at Camp Campbell, Kentucky. One week later, one more officer and forty-three enlisted men returned from leave, and at the same time a group of 68 replacements was received from the replacement depot, bringing the 781st up to eight officers and 111 EM. Two days later the Battalion was up to 25 officers and 349 enlisted. By August 25th, more than 80% of the battalion had gathered, and they began training for redeployment to the Pacific.

Vince Sutphin (rt) at Campbell. (Courtesy of O'Donnell family)

Also, by this time the paperwork for more awards had been processed, and on August 29, 1945, the 781st held another ceremony for presentation of Bronze Star medals to officers and enlisted men. On September 8th, the battalion was completely reassembled and began to train in earnest to get the replacements fully incorporated into the companies. This training occupied the Battalion for the next month.

As the Army progressively lowered the bar on the Rating Score, more men became eligible to be processed and sent home, and the training was changed so that soldiers with the lowest scores got the most training, as they weren't going anywhere any time soon, except maybe overseas. Those folks with high scores were busy training their replacements. Homer Turner and a lot of other men were sitting with fewer points and just hoping the bar would continue to drop.

On September 7, 1945, the battalion had 145 men in this "Low Points" category that had to be trained and assimilated into the battalion. But on September 26th, the bar dropped again to 75, more men were eligible to be released, and only 108 low score men were left. Vince Sutphin had a score in the high seventies and just missed the cut point after VJ Day, but he was now discharged. (If one discounts the replacements that came to the unit when they returned from leave, it meant that few if any members of the 781st that had come back from Europe were likely to be redeployed.)

Even while sorting this out, the 781st used its hard-won combat experience and continued to pioneer new equipment and develop new procedures. They helped to test and develop a combat voice communications training unit that consisted of a trailer having communication stations inside for 12 trainees, who were then trained in interphone and voice communication procedures. The trainer also allowed simulated drills to be run without using actual vehicles. Considering the experience that the 781st had with developing the use of the 300 field telephone in tank-infantry communication with the GIs, they were a great choice for testing. The system was a great success and well received. The same concept is still in use today, being used by the Army in its Conduct of Fire Trainers for the M1 Abrams tank.

By the end of September 1945, when the Battalion once again gathered to award medals, the most noteworthy thing was who wasn't there. Captain Will, the Battalion Surgeon, held the honor as being the first person discharged. But other faces were gone: Major Farris; Lt. Sloggatt; Lt. Kaiser; Lt. Crane; Lt. Brown; Lt. Yonkers; Capt. Pelletier; Capt. Graham; Lt. Shepard; Lt. Pais; and more. Captain Simpkins was promoted to Major and others were promoted to backfill the empty slots.

Even Shortwave had departed. The Communications section drew lots to see who could take Shortwave home. Shortwave retired as Official Hood Ornament and Hungarian Biter and lived a great life with Mr. and Mrs. R.J. Sanders in Budd Lake, NJ.

One of the last ceremonies the battalion did was October 19, 1945, when two officers and 30 men departed for Paducah, Kentucky, to be honor guard for the President of the U.S. when Harry S. Truman spoke at a dedication ceremony for the largest dam in the TVA. In October, all the men who were still in the battalion were given a 45-day furlough. Training was seriously impaired, as everyone except essential personnel was away for 45 days. Even the essential personnel were rotated out so that everyone got their 45 days due to them. The ASR Score was lowered again October 1st, and this resulted in the loss of an additional 16 officers and 160 men. Between these losses and the furloughs, at times there were only five men in the training program!

Even more serious, the men who headed home took a lot of expertise with them, and it became increasingly hard to find knowledgeable people to do vehicle maintenance and even basic administrative duties. While all the talent was leaving, only two officers and 14 enlisted men were received as replacements. In November 1945 the pattern continued, as the Battalion outprocessed two officers and 257 men, but only got 19 officers and 85 men in return. As the men returned from furlough, the situation eased until the training classes again had 100 men, and the command and staff again got the administrative end under control. The training was still centered on orientation for the new men, maintenance of motors, weapons, and artillery. The 781st and the Army, in general, were bleeding themselves dry.

To rectify the situation, the Army held a recruiting drive, and some success was had, as in December, the Battalion actually received more personnel than it discharged. Two officers and 120 E.M. were discharged while two officers and 312 E.M. were received. With the influx, it was possible to intensify the training and get into full swing with a target of January 1, 1946, for being back to normal. On December 22nd, the Service Company received a Meritorious Service Unit Plaque for the fine work they had done on maintenance and supply during the war, but few men who actually were there were present to receive the award.

On January 2, 1946, the 781st Tank Battalion celebrated its third birthday in silence. Most of the men were away on furlough or on pass for the holidays, and it wasn't until a couple of weeks went by that it was even noticed.

The 781st Tank Battalion was inactivated February 19, 1946, but it still had life left in it. It was redesignated the 816th Tank Battalion and allotted to the Reserves January 14, 1947. Headquarters was reactivated January 31, 1947, and it was based out of Minneapolis, Minnesota. The now-816th was redesignated as the 816th Heavy Tank Battalion March 22, 1949, and it again changed numbers to the 403rd Heavy Tank Battalion November 25, 1949. At this time, the Army decided that the independent tank battalions would be embedded as organic elements into the Infantry Divisions, and the battalion was assigned to be part of their old friends, the 103rd Infantry Division. It was moved to Fort Snelling, Minnesota, in November 1951. And finally, on April Fool's Day 1951, the 781st was brought back to life as the 403rd and was redesignated the 781st Tank Battalion. The decision to reactivate the 781st over other battalions was made due to the unit's outstanding combat record with the 103rd. During the postwar years it acquired a coat of arms and a motto "Duty Before Self," which was very appropriate.

True to form, the 781st was rated by the Fifth Army as the outstanding reserve Tank Battalion in the Fifth Army in 1953. After a 103rd Infantry Division Review in late August 1953, the 781st was chosen by both reviewing Generals Harrison and Olmsted as the best looking outfit in the line of march. Major General Olmsted, who commanded the 103rd at the time, remarked: "If we ever have to go back into the military business full time, I surely hope we can go together."

The 781st continued to function until it was finally inactivated May 18, 1959.

Lt. Col Kinne went on to serve on General Douglas McArthur's staff during the Korean War, and then returned to the States after the General and President Truman had their historic face-off. He retired from the Army and later passed away from a brain tumor in the early 1970s.

General Alexander Patch didn't live as long; he arrived in the U.S. to take over his new command in August 1945, but was soon suffering lung problems which required hospitalization. They worsened, and he passed away from pneumonia in November 1945.

The Seventh Army continued to exist in obscurity, and was stationed as an occupying force in Germany until 1967, when it was merged into the Overall Euro-

Lt. Col Kinne awards the Bronze Star to Sgt. William Daley while (l-r) Lt. Jason Cohen, Lt. Joe Trombetta, Sgt William Riddle, Sgt. George Doherty, and Sgt Edwin Leinweber look on, September 1945. (Up From Marseille)

pean force structure and sent to fight in the Bosnian conflict and the Gulf Wars. The last trace of the Seventh Army name was quietly dropped in 2010.

The men of the 781st went back to civilian life. Vince Sutphin went back to Virginia and resumed his job as a meter reader, rose through the ranks over the years, and eventually retired from the same company. Homer Turner became a furniture salesman and then owned an automobile service station. Arnie Simpson became a soil conservationist. Joe Graham returned to his interrupted insurance business career and enjoyed considerable success, rising to CEO, and "Tiny" Mitzel started sweeping a floor and thirty years later retired as management. Gerald Mercier and Gee waited patiently for 60 years, and he was finally given his Bronze Star for his contribution at Lemberg. In all, the men of the 781st were just ordinary guys. But these "ordinary" guys stepped up and made a significant contribution to U.S. armored vehicles, armored doctrine, and armored tactics. They played a key role in stopping Hitler's last offensive in Europe, and along the way touched on a surprising number of significant events in the ETO.

During the war, the men of the 781st were awarded the following Combat awards:
Bronze Star: 152
Oak Leaf Cluster to Bronze Star: 11
Recommended for Bronze Star: 14
Silver Star: 9
Oak Leaf Cluster to Silver Star: 1
Presidential Citation: 30
Purple hearts: 81
Oak leaf Cluster to Purple Heart: 6
Recommended for Purple Heart: 17
Killed or Died of Wounds: 32
Recommended for Distinguished Service Cross: 1

Keeping in mind that there were about 650 people in the Battalion, 311 awards is extraordinary.

And the tank the 781st helped develop, the "Super Sherman" or "Easy Eight," after having played a pivotal role in defeating the Axis in WWII, served *far* beyond its expected life. It went on to play a major role in the Korean War for the U.S., and was then gradually phased out of front-line service with the U.S. Army, being relegated to National Guard units and training use. But it also continued as a front-line main battle tank in other countries, and in fact was called into front-line service during the Pakistan-India War, and again in the Arab-Israeli Middle East conflicts. During this quarter century of service, the "Easy Eight" successfully faced off with armored opponents that were much fresher designs. Today, they have earned their place as revered museum pieces.

MAPS

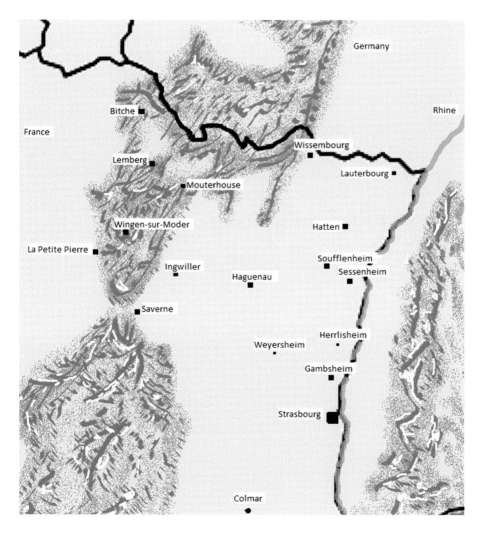

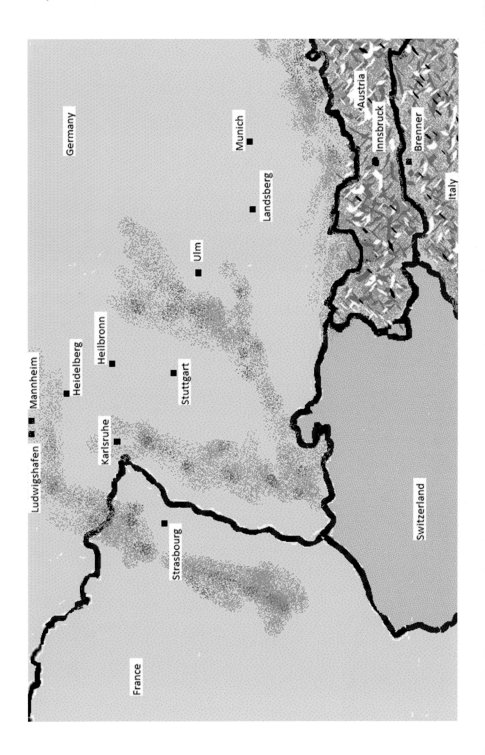

BIBLIOGRAPHY

Books and Periodicals:

Bergmann, Linda, *Wingen-sur-Moder dans la tourmente de l'OPERATION NORDWIND 3-7 Janvier 1945*, (Wingen-Sur-Moder, France, Claude Bovi, 1989)

Cameron, Robert, S. *Mobility, Shock and Firepower, The Emergence of the US Army's Armor Branch, 1917-1945*; (Washington DC, US Army Center of Military History Publications, 2008)

Clark, Jeffrey, J & Robert R. Smith, *Riviera to the Rhine,* (Washington, DC, U.S. Army Center of Military History Publications, 1993)

Cooper, Belton, *Deathtraps*, (New York, NY, Presidio Press, 2003)

Foley, William, A, Jr, *Visions from a Foxhole,* (New York, NY, Presidio Press, 2004)

Gawne, Jonathan, *Finding Your Father's War*, (Havertown, PA, Casemate, 2006)

Green, Michael & James Brown, *M4 Sherman at War,* (Minneapolis, MN, Zenith Books, 2007)

Hargreaves, Richard, *The Germans in Normandy*, (Mechanicsburg, PA, Stackpole Books, 2008)

Hunnicutt, R. P., *Sherman: A History of the American Medium Tank*, (New York, NY, Presidio Press, 1976)

Jackson, Robert, *Tanks and Armored Fighting Vehicles*, (Amber Books, 2009)

Jarymowycz, Roman, J, *Tank Tactics,* (Mechanicsburg, PA, Stackpole Books, 2009)

Longacre, Edward, *Heilbronn, One Last Place to Die,* (Harrisburg, PA, America In WWII Magazine, April 2010)

Macksey, Kenneth, *Tank versus Tank,* (Avenel, NJ, Crescent Books, 1988)

Marshall, George, C. *Report on the Army, July 1st 1939 to June 30 1943*, (Washington, DC, The Infantry Journal, 1943)

McKinney, Leonard, Lt. Col., *Chemical Corps Historical Studies, No 4: Portable Flamethrower Operations in World War II* (Washington, DC, Historical Section, Office of the Chief of the Chemical Corps 1 December 1949)

Mueller-Hillebrand, Burkhart, *Project #47 - Tank Losses,* US 3rd Army Historical Section (Washington DC, U.S. Army, 1950)

Orth, E.C. Lt. Col. *Development of DD Tanks,* (Fort Knox, Kentucky, Headquarters of Army Ground Forces, 6 June 1946)

Pritchard, Paul, *Smoke Generator Operations in the Mediterranean and European Theaters of Operation* (Washington, DC, Historical Section, Office of the Chief of the Chemical Corps, reprinted 1985)

Quinn, William, W, Major, *Dachau,* 649th Engr Topo Battalion, U.S. 7th Army

Ringquist, Capt. John, *US Army Flamethrower Vehicles, pts 1,2,3,* Army Chemical Review(Fort Leonard Wood, MO, US Army Chemical, Biological, Radiological, and Nuclear School and the Directorate of Training, 2007)

Ross, G McLeod, *The Business of Tanks, 1933-1945,* (North Devon, England, Stockwell, 1976)

Salecker, Gene, E, *Rolling Thunder Against the Rising Sun,* (Mechanicsburg, PA, Stackpole Books, 2008)

Stanton, Shelby, L; *World War II Order of Battle,* (New York, NY, Galahad Books, 1984)

Turner, John F, & Robert Jackson; *Destination Berchtesgaden,* (New York, NY, Scribner, 1975)

Whiting, Charles, *America's Forgotten Army,* (New York, NY, St. Martin's Press, 2001)

Yeide, Harry, *Steel Victory,* (New York, NY, Presidio Press, 2003)

Zaloga, Stephen, J, *Operation Nordwind 1945: Hitler's Last Offensive in the West (Campaign),* (Essex, England, Osprey Publishing, 2010)

Zaloga, Stephen, J, *Sherman vs. Panther,* (Essex, England, Osprey Publishing, 2008)

Zaloga, Stephen, J, *US Tank and Tank Destroyer Battalions in the ETO 1944-45 (Battle Orders),* (Essex, England, Osprey Publishing, 2005)

War Department or
Department of the Army Documents

Consumption Rates of US Forces in the Final Advance to the Rhine, Statistics Section, Office of the Chief of Staff, G-4 Division, Supreme Headquarters Allied Expeditionary Forces, 25 April 1945

Weekly Intelligence Summary No 33 for the Week Ending May 8th 1945 Headquarters 6th Army Group, 8 May 1945.

Armored Bulletin, Numbers 1-19, Headquarters, First Armored Group, VI Corp, 7th Army, 8 Jan – 6 May 1945

Operations Memorandum, Numbers 1-48, Headquarters XV Corps, United States Army; 17 June 1944 -20 Dec 1944

Operations Memorandum, Numbers 1-12, Headquarters, VI Corps, United States Army; 10 March 1945-29 May 1945

Operations Memorandum, Numbers 43-71, Headquarters, VI Corps, United States Army; 30 June 1944 -26 December 1944

Operations Memorandum, Numbers 1-38, Headquarters, European Theater of Operations, United States Army; 16 May 1943 -11 May 1945

Armored Force Board Project #AFP-378, *Final Report on Special Test of 40 Medium Tanks, (10 Each M4A1, M4A2, M4A3, M4A4)*, (Fort Knox KY, Armored Force Board 1943

Armored Board Project #P243-4, *Test of Ten (10) Light Tanks, M5A1, Incorporating the Latest Improvements*, (Fort Knox, KY, Armored Board 1944)

Armored Force Board Project #AFP-208, *To Establish a Long-Range Program for Standardization of Engines in the Armored Force*, (Fort Knox KY, Armored Force Board 1942)

Armored Force Board Project # P5-1 *Adequate Headroom in Tanks*, (Fort Knox, KY, Armored Force Board, 27 Nov 1942)

Military Intelligence Service, Informational Bulletin #17, *Removal of Wounded from Tanks*, (Washington, DC, War Department, June 5th 1942)

Truck Loading Reference Data, Pamphlet, Headquarters, ETOUSA, Office of the Chief of Transportation, Motor Transport Division, March 1944)

Department of the Army Pamphlet No. 672-1: *Unit Citation and Campaign Participation Credit Register,* (Washington, DC, Headquarters, Department of the Army, US Government Printing Office, 1961)

G3 Reports, Nos. 10-20, Headquarters, Task Force Herren, 10 January 1945 to 20 January 1945

Operational Instruction, Nos. 1-4, Headquarters, Task Force Herren, 6 January 1945 to 18 January 1945

Operations Instruction, Nos. 15, 16, 17, Headquarters 100th Infantry Division to 781st TB, 21 December 1944

Operations Instruction, Nos. 50-64 & 86-95, Headquarters 103rd Infantry Division to 781st TB, 14 January 1945 – 21 February 1945 and 23 April 1945 – 9 June 1945

Unit Citation, Headquarters, 398th Infantry, 10 April 1945

Battle *Honors – Citation of Unit*, Headquarters, 7th Army, US Army Presidential Unit Citation for B/78, 16 April 1945

781st Tank Battalion Documents

Unit History, Headquarters, 781st Tank Battalion, Monthly from 2 January 1943 – 31 December 1945

Up From Marseille, Headquarters, 781st Tank Battalion, 1945

Brief History of the 781st Tank Battalion, anonymous, probably attributable to Erksel W. Rhodes, October 13th 1944 through October 12th 1945.

Standard Operating Procedures, Headquarters, 781st Tank Battalion, 19 January to 3 December 1944

781st Tank Battalion General Orders 1 through 6 for 11 January – 8 October 1945, Headquarters, 781st Tank Battalion

781st Tank Battalion General Orders 1through 19 for January 1 – December 31 1943, Headquarters, 781st Tank Battalion

Operations Memorandum, Numbers 1-16, Headquarters, 781st Tank Battalion, 14 Dec 1944 – 3 May 1945

Operations Memorandum, Numbers 1-5, Headquarters, 781st Tank Battalion, 14 Dec 1944 – 28 December 1944

After Action Report, Headquarters, 781st Tank Battalion, Monthly from December 1944-June 1945

S-3 Report, Headquarters, 781st Tank Battalion, daily from Dec 8st 1944 - June 1945

U.S. Army Technical Service Documents

FM17-10 *Armored Force Field Manual, Tactics and Technique*, (Washington, DC, U.S. Government Printing Office, 1942)

FM17-12 *Armored Force Field Manual, Tank Gunnery*, (Washington, DC, U.S. Government Printing Office, 1943)

FM17-15 10 *Armored Force Field Manual, Combat Practice Firing Armored Force Units*, (Washington, DC, U.S. Government Printing Office, 1942)

FM17-27 *Armored Force Field Manual, 81mm Mortar Squad and Platoon*, (Washington, DC, U.S. Government Printing Office, 1942)

FM17-33 *Armored Force Field Manual, The Armored Battalion, Light and Medium*, (Washington, DC, U.S. Government Printing Office, 1942)

FM17-71 *War Department Field Manual, Armored Command Crew Drill for Half Track Vehicles*, (Washington, DC, U.S. Government Printing Office, 1943)

TM 9-710 *War Department Technical Manual: Basic Half Track Vehicles (White, Autocar, and Diamond T)* (Washington, DC, U.S. Government Printing Office, 23 Feb 1944)

TM 9-759 *War Department Technical Manual: Tank, Medium, M4-A3*, (Washington, DC, U.S. Government Printing Office, 1943)

TM 9-1725 *War Department Technical Manual: Ordnance Maintenance, Ordnance Engine Model R975-C4 (Continental)* (Washington, DC, U.S. Government Printing Office, 1944)

TM 9-1730E *Department of the Army Technical Manual: Hydraulic Turret Traversing and Gun Elevating System for the 76-mm. Gun Tank T41E1 and 90-mm. Gun Tank M47*; (Washington, DC, U.S. Government Printing Office, 23 Feb 1952)

TM 9-1731B *War Department Technical Manual: Ordnance Maintenance, Ford Tank Engines, (Models GAA, GAF, and GAN)*, (Washington, DC, U.S. Government Printing Office, 1945)

TM 9-1731C *War Department Technical Manual: Ordnance Maintenance, Accessories for Tank Engine Model GAA V8 (Ford)*, (Washington, DC, U.S. Government Printing Office, 1945)

TM 9-1731K *War Department Technical Manual: Ordnance Maintenance, Auxiliary Generator, (Homelite Model HRUH -28) for Medium tanks M4 and Modifications*, (Washington, DC, U.S. Government Printing Office, 1943)

TM 9-1750 *War Department Technical Manual: Ordnance Maintenance, Power Train Unit, Three Piece Differential Case for Medium Tanks, M3, M4 and Modifications*, (Washington, DC, U.S. Government Printing Office, 1942)

TM 9-1751 *War Department Technical Manual: Ordnance Maintenance, 9-Cylinder, Radial, Gasoline Engine (Continental Model R975-C1)* (Washington, DC, U.S. Government Printing Office, 1944)

TM 9-1756A *War Department Technical Manual: Ordnance Maintenance, Ordnance Engine Model RD-1820 (Caterpillar)* (Washington, DC, U.S. Government Printing Office, 1943)

INDEX

M5 Stuart tank, top view. (U.S. Army, NARA)